IMAGES
of America

Jamaica Estates

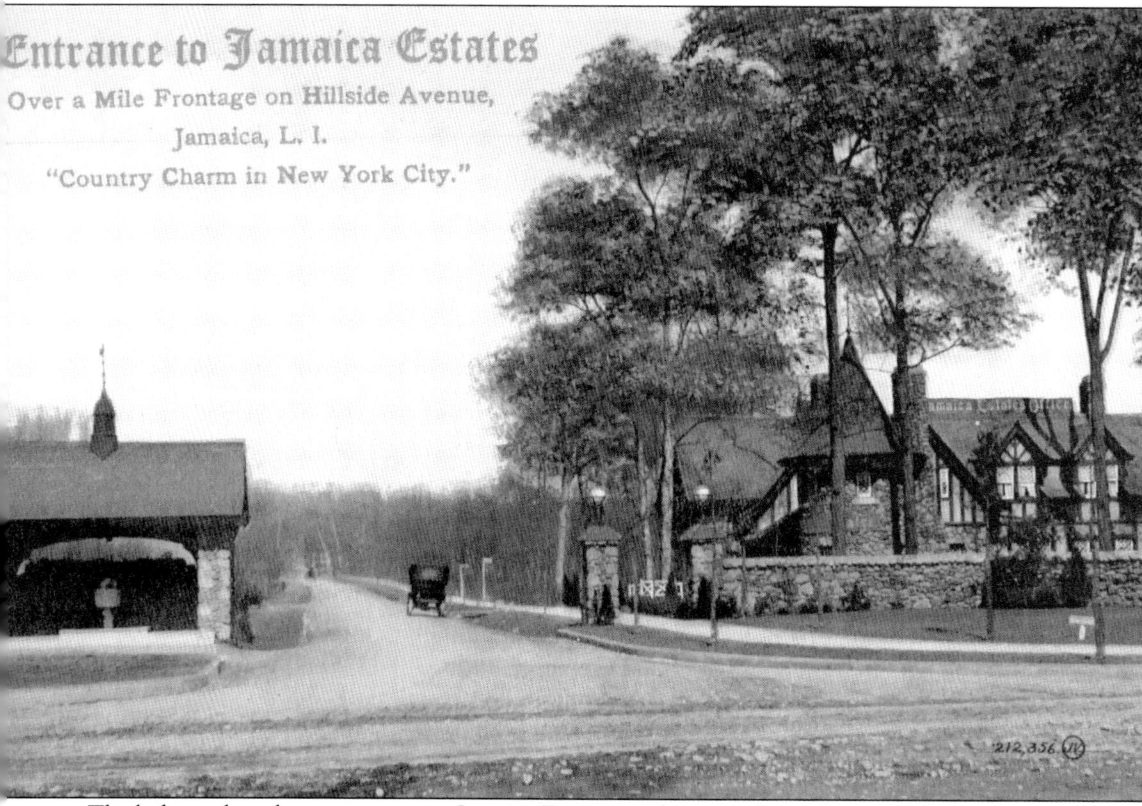

The lodge and gatehouse entrance to Jamaica Estates are shown in this early postcard advertisement titled "Country Charm in New York City."

On the Cover: This photograph dated August 1930 shows Homelawn Street. (Courtesy of Q Gardens Gallery.)

IMAGES of America

JAMAICA ESTATES

Carl Ballenas with
the Aquinas Honor Society of the
Immaculate Conception School

ARCADIA
PUBLISHING

ISBN 978-0-7385-7255-0

Published by Arcadia Publishing
Charleston, South Carolina

Printed in the United States of America

Library of Congress Control Number: 2009936160

For all general information contact Arcadia Publishing at:
Telephone 843-853-2070
Fax 843-853-0044
E-mail sales@arcadiapublishing.com
For customer service and orders:
Toll-Free 1-888-313-2665

Visit us on the Internet at www.arcadiapublishing.com

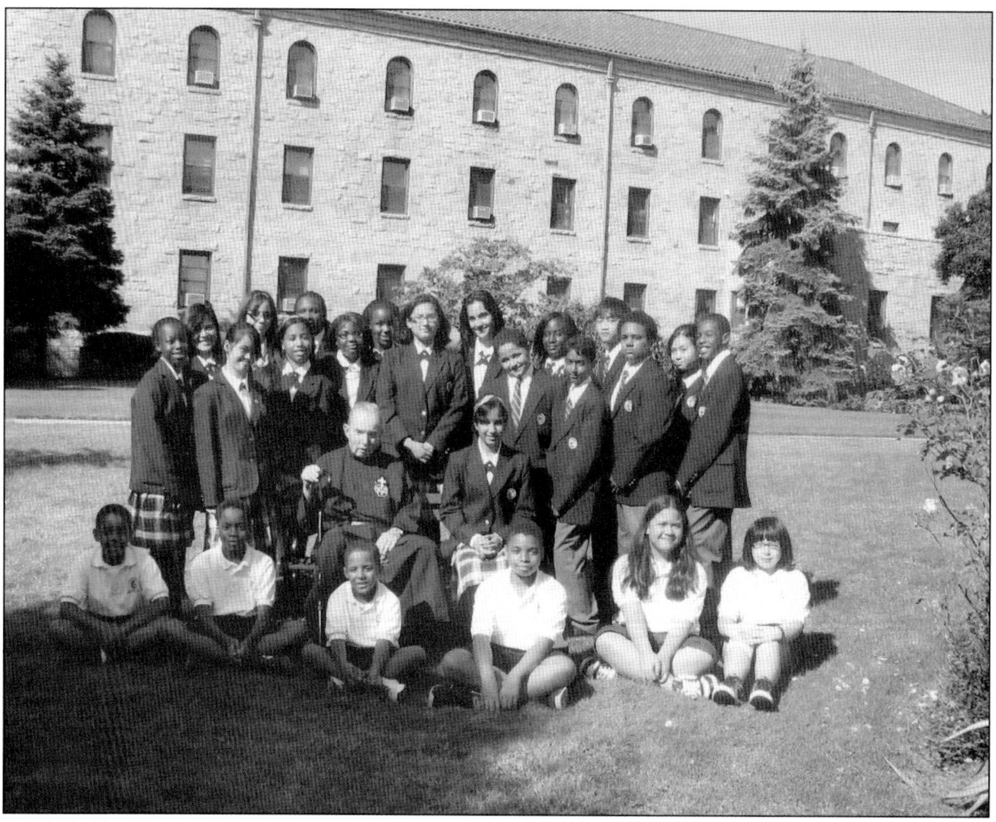

In 1982, Fr. Thomas Joyce, C.P., became the ninth pastor of the Immaculate Conception Parish, serving his flock for 25 years. Generations of students from the parish school have been nurtured under his care. The students dedicate this book in his honor.

Contents

Acknowledgments

In creating this book, we, the authors, have ventured to acknowledge our past and look to the future. The authors are Carl Ballenas, Tashanie Narain, Derek Netto, Jean-Philippe Rancy, Corey Strickland, Nicholas Strickland, Jada Quinlan, Carluto Toussaint, Dominique Leone, Katherine Virgino, Ysabelle Bismonte, Puni Samaroo, Tahina Felisca, Gabriella Ulloa, Julio Ulloa, Brandon Arjun, Nicole Anigbogu, Tarah-Anne Rancy, Cliff Mayard, Jewel Sabordo, Michelle Gan, Michael Gan, Amne Madi, Amarachi Abakporo, Cristina Agudelo, Karla Freire, Krystal Madrinan, Jessica Netto, Arianna Goberdhan, Roseanne Hernandez, Saranya Radhakrishnan, and Zeena Samad. Along the way, we have encountered individuals and institutions that have offered their invaluable services, such as the families of the authors, the Immaculate Conception School faculty and staff, Long Island Room Staff, Judith Todman, Eric Huber and John Hyslop, Philippe Woolley and family, Erin Vosgien and Arcadia staff, William Loftus, Helene and Bob Stonehill, Enyi Lu, Edward and Joyce Morrill, Michael Bookbinder, Susan Zigman, Kem Boatwright, Ron Marzlak, Lucy Ballenas, Dr. Carlos Ballenas Laos, Dr. Edgar Ballenas and family, and Dr. Nancy Baxter Ballenas and family. Photographs in this book belong to the private collection of the author unless otherwise noted.

Introduction

It is somewhat remarkable that in the ever-changing environment of New York City, Jamaica Estates in the Borough of Queens has maintained its character from its founding in 1907.

When real estate speculators and developers Ernestus Gulick and Felix Isman purchased 500 acres of wooded land north of the village of Jamaica, they dreamed to establish an affluent resort with an English flavor. Today Jamaica Estate remains one of the most desirable neighborhoods to reside in New York City.

Gulick and Isman admired the natural beauty of the area and vowed to keep its charm as they developed the land, preserving the forests populated with towering oak, elm, maple, and chestnut trees. It became a residential park, a concept where the development would be laid out with an eye to beauty and exclusiveness rather than to profitable economy of space by preserving the natural beauties of the land. Gulick and Isman named the area Jamaica Estates and opened their Jamaica Estates Corporation office in Manhattan, with Gulick serving as president and Isman as vice president. The boundaries were as they are now: Union Turnpike on the north, 188th Street on the east, Hillside Avenue on the south, and Utopia Parkway/Homelawn Street on the west.

Breaking from the city practice of laying streets in a grid, architect Charles W. Leavitt designed a parklike suburb with all the advantages of city life. He chose Midland Parkway as the centerpiece and continued the English theme by naming the streets Tudor, Aberdeen, Kent, Avon, Wexford, Henley, and the like. Strict building requirements and exclusiveness also were of obvious importance. Only one detached one-family homes that were two-stories high with an attic could be built on a minimum of two lots.

Greeting visitors was a picturesque entrance resembling an English estate in the Elizabethan style. John J. Petit designed the Elizabethan stone lodge with imposing pillars and gates in 1908. The gatehouse, using stones, red clay roof tiles, and stucco still standing today, houses the Jamaica Estates War Memorial, but sadly the lodge was razed years ago.

In 1908, a golf course was part of the vision of the early developers and laid out to the west of the burgeoning Jamaica Estates neighborhood. By 1924, it became known as the Hillcrest Golf Course and was later sold to the Vincentians Order of the Catholic Church who built Saint John's University on the property.

Former New York State lieutenant governor Timothy L. Woodruff became president of the Jamaica Estates Corporation in 1910 and was instrumental in creating a Tennis Club. He also made arrangements with the Long Island Railroad to construct a passenger and express station called "Hillside" for Jamaica Estates.

Michael Degnon, who was responsible for engineering portions of the city's subway system, became as early Jamaica Estates resident, building a sprawling manor on 16 acres. In 1908, his company was contracted to build a system of sewers, macadamized streets, sidewalks, a water supply, and electric and gas lighting systems for Jamaica Estates.

In 1924, Degnon sold his property to the Passionist Order of the Catholic Church, which became the Immaculate Conception Parish with a monastery and retreat house. In 1938, the Sisters of Saint Joseph opened and maintained the Immaculate Conception School. In 1960, a massive Romanesque-style church was built, solidifying its place in the history of Jamaica Estates.

However, with only some of its dreams realized, the Jamaica Estates Company declared bankruptcy in the early 1920s. At the time, there were 275 home in the neighborhood.

Realizing that the restrictive agreements on which Jamaica Estates was founded would expire December 31, 1929, the residents formed the Jamaica Estates Association. The group's first order of business was assuring single-family zoning would remain intact.

When the Grand Central Parkway threatened the serenity of the neighborhood, the Jamaica Estates Association joined with other community groups to form the Grand Central Parkway Assessment Protest Committee and successfully rezoned for both sides of the parkway to make business there impractical.

In the 1940s, the association's community center was converted to house the headquarters of the Air Raid Warden Service. Later an ornate honor roll with 249 names was erected on the grounds of the property. As the war went on, 10 names were given a gold star. A permanent war memorial was placed inside the gatehouse with the names of those 10 individuals. Since 1950, Memorial Day ceremonies are held at the gatehouse to honor the brave men and women from Jamaica Estates who have served and died in the military service.

There are a number of noteworthy people who have resided in Jamaica Estates such as Edmund Breese, silent screen star; Dr. J. Wilbur Chapman, noted evangelist and pastor; Capt. Dod Orsborne, adventurer and author; Sammy Fuchs, owner of Sammy's Bowery Follies; James Kendis, songwriter; and international famed classical composer Bohuslav Martinu.

Today Jamaica Estates is a vibrant multicultural community diverse and inviting. It has great promise for the future with the young people who reside here. There is no better example of this than the fact that this book was researched, developed, and written by young students of the Aquinas Honor Society of the Immaculate Conception School under their moderator, teacher, and historian, Carl Ballenas. They have undertaken a monumental project and have uncovered the rich history of our community. I salute their drive and energy.

—Councilmember James Gennaro
Jamaica Estates
July 2009

One

The Mother Village

Jamaica

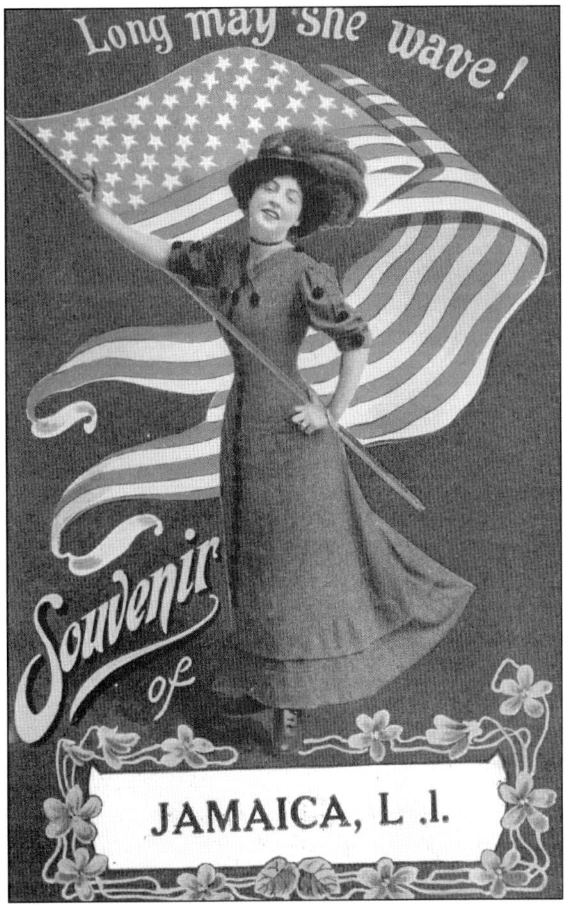

The prevalent opinion concerning the origin of the village name was after a Native American tribe who resided near the head of Jamaica Bay. It was originally spelled "Jameco," "Jemeco," or as it appears in town records, "Yemacah." Another idea is that it was deprived from "Amick," the Native American word for beaver, which abounded on the land.

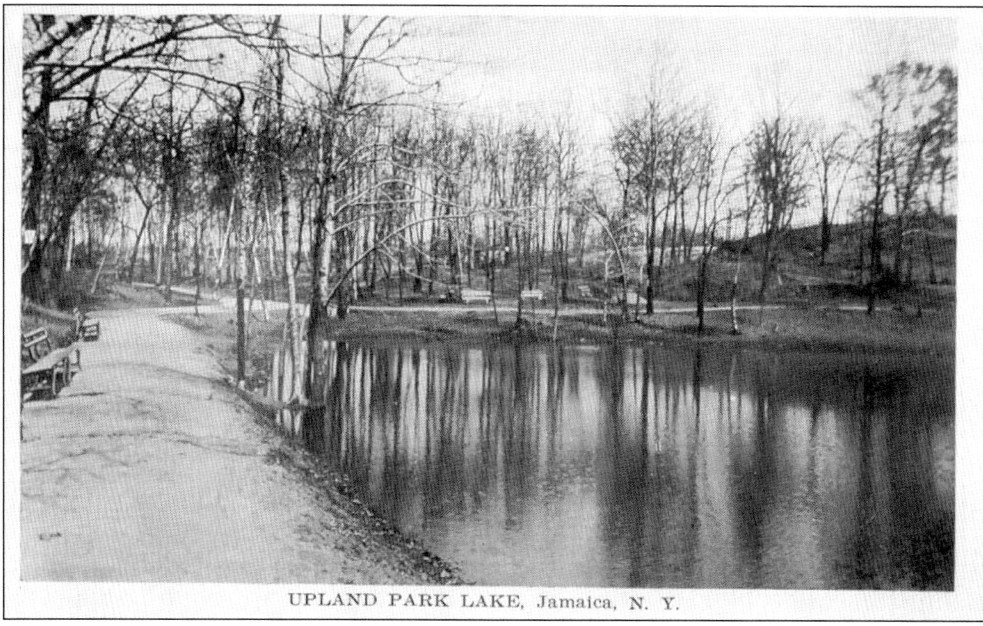

The settlers of Jamaica came from Hempstead, first settled in 1644, so they might subsist decently, a comfortable livelihood. Originally calling their Dutch town Rustdorp, which translates to "quiet village," it changed to Jamaica under the English. The oldest known document is a deed from the Native Americans dated September 13, 1655. In 1662, the town voted to buy more land from the Native Americans for a trooper's coat and a kettle.

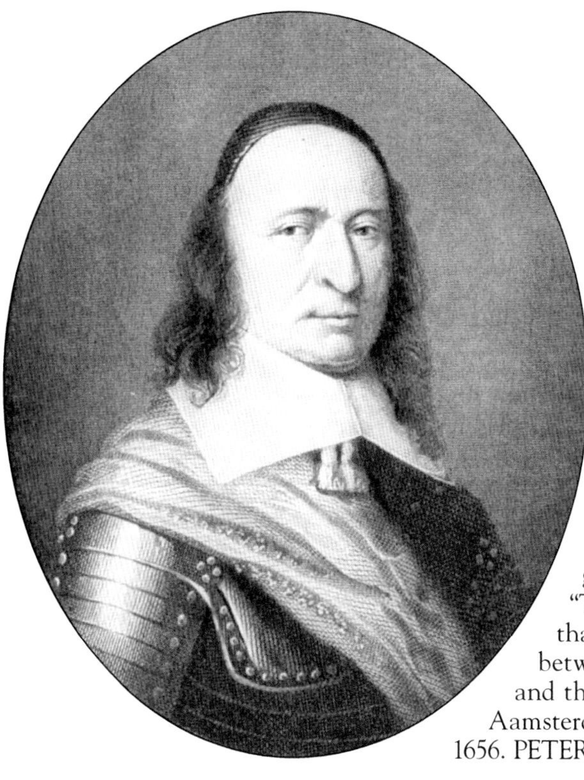

Robert Jackson, Nicholas Tanner, Nathaniel Denton, Richard Everit, Rodger Linns, Daniel Denton, John Lazar, Abraham Smith, Thomas Ireland, Thomas Carle, Edward Sprague, John Roades, Andrew Messenger, and Samuel Matthews petitioned Dutch governor Peter Stuyvesant. He replied, "The Directors and Council . . . do consent that the petitioners may begin a new town between the land called by us Canaresse and the town of Heemsteede. Done at Fort Aamsterdam, in New Netherland, March 21st 1656. PETER STUYVESANT."

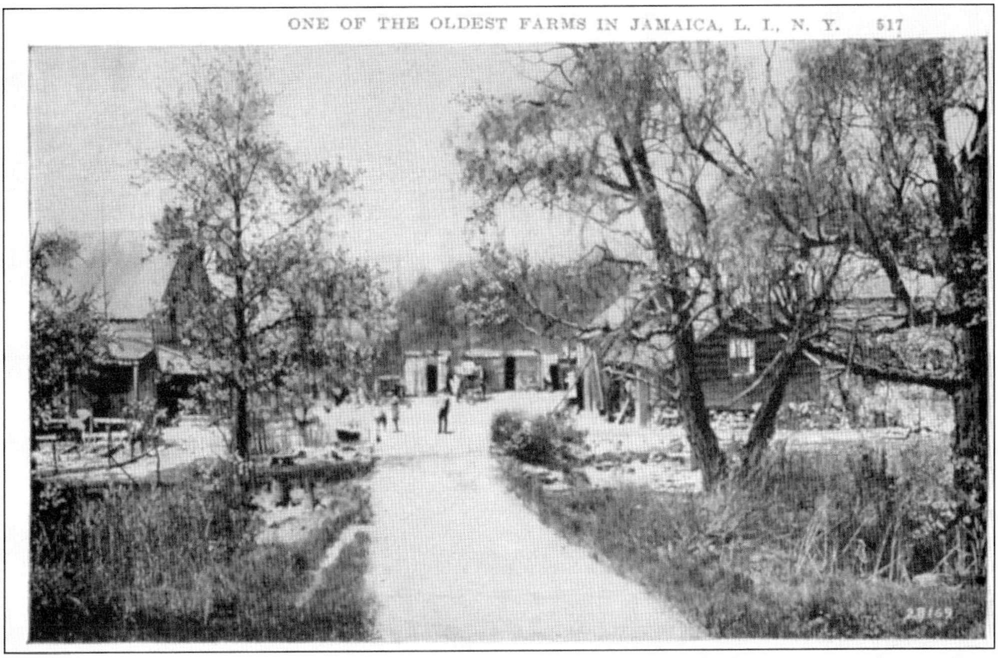

Early Jamaica was a cluster of log houses in the wilderness, roofed with thatches from the marshes. There were two rooms below and lofts above for sleeping and a lean-to kitchen. Food was mostly venison and fish, and dinner was boiled Indian pudding, corn mixed with beans, a slice of salted venison with boiled cabbages, baked or boiled pumpkin, and cider or home-brewed beer.

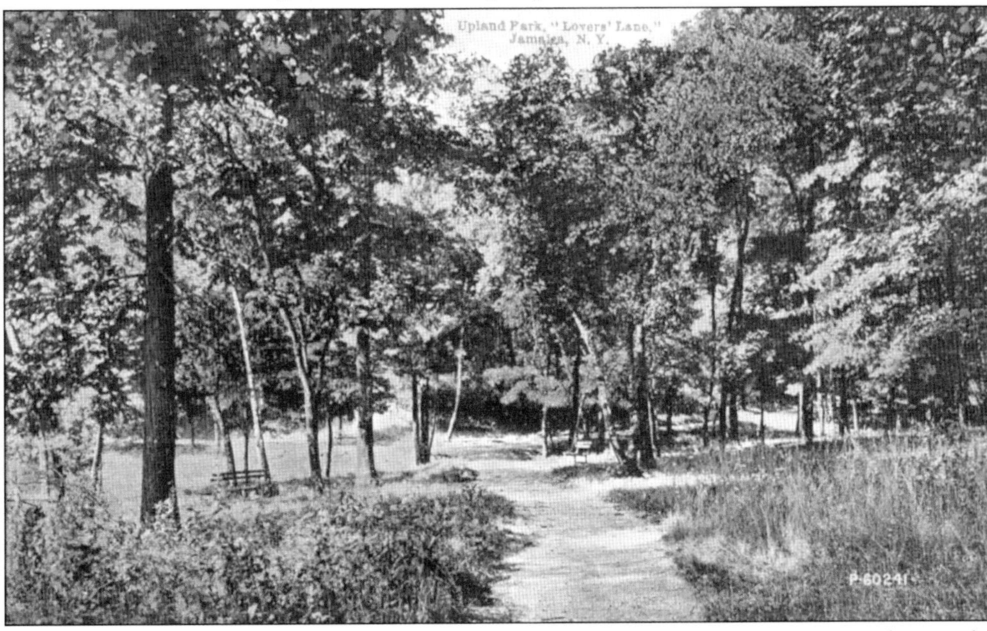

The early pioneers arose before dawn, breakfasted, had family worship, and were early into the fields. Agricultural implements included a musket for use against a possible wolf or bear or in the event of a deer being discovered during their labor. The duties of the women were more demanding. Whether sick or well, the baking, cooking, washing, ironing, clothes making, and mending had to be done.

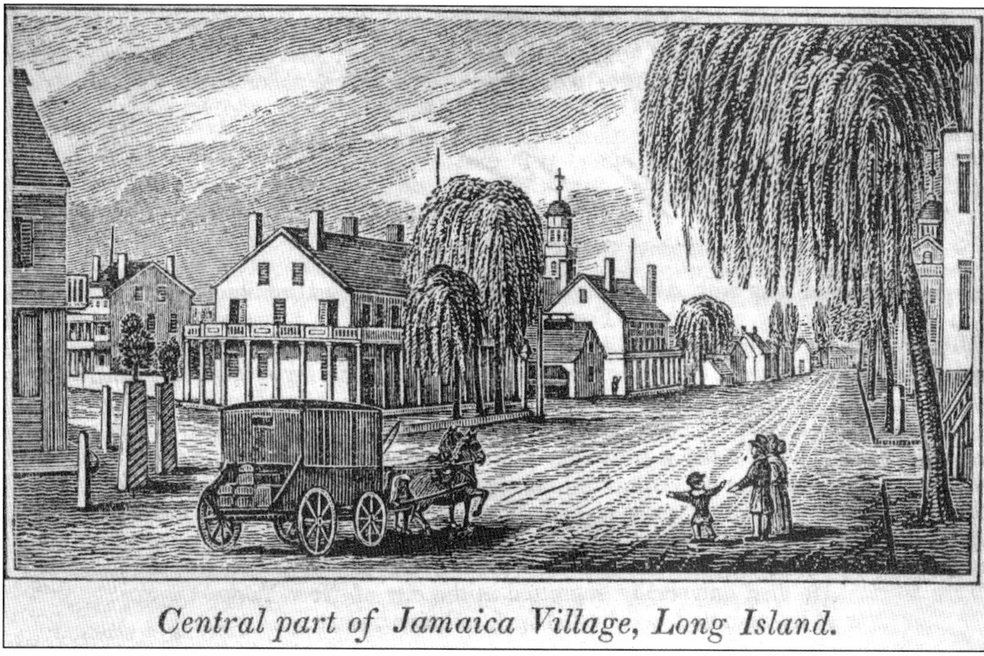

A stagecoach on Jamaica Avenue passes through Jamaica in this 1841 engraving. Originally established as a path by Native Americans, it became the foundation for Jamaica Avenue, the oldest continuously traveled highway on Long Island. George Washington wrote in his diary on April 20, 1790, "Jamaica Road is more sandy and appears to have less strength, but is still good and productive."

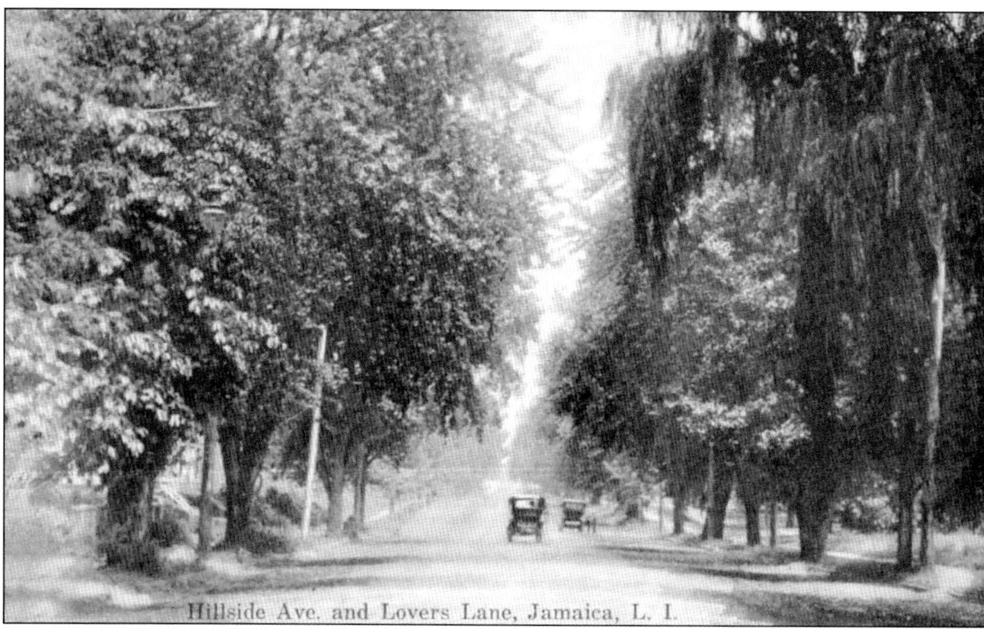

On March 1, 1870, the *Long Island Democrat* wrote, "There is a bill now before the legislature to open an avenue on the north side of Jamaica Village under the hills, 100 feet in width, and lay sidewalks and plant trees. The proposed improvement—is taxed upon the owners of property through which it passes, and those benefitted by the opening, and not upon the town."

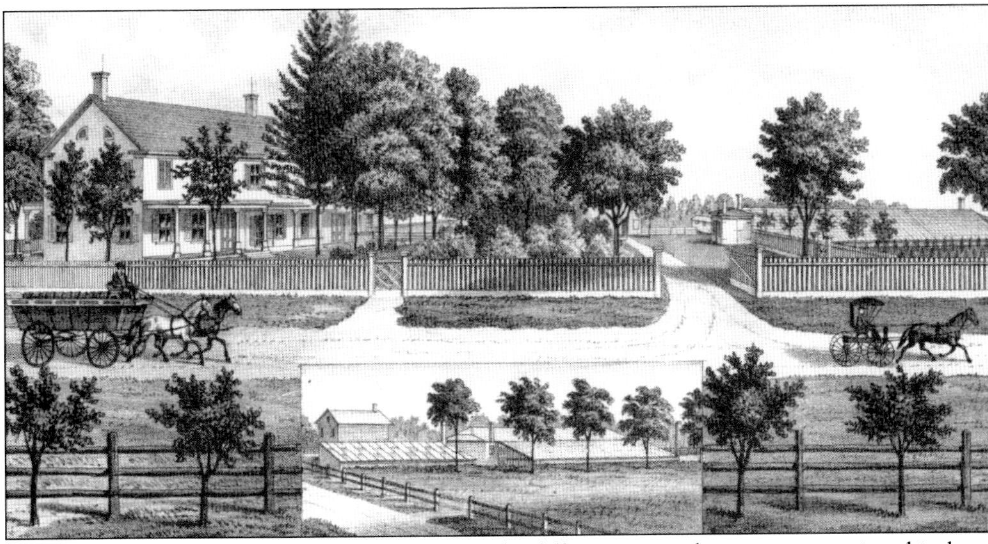

Slavery prevailed in many Long Island towns. The following are advertisements printed in local newspapers: "Andrus, a negro slave of Captain Wm. Lawrence, was whipped 39 stripes, and branded on the forehead with a hot iron, for theft and larceny of some linen etc., at Jamaica." (1672) and "A mulatto fellow, Isaac, aged 24, as having run away from John Betts, of Jamaica." (1749). This engraving depicts a Jamaica farm.

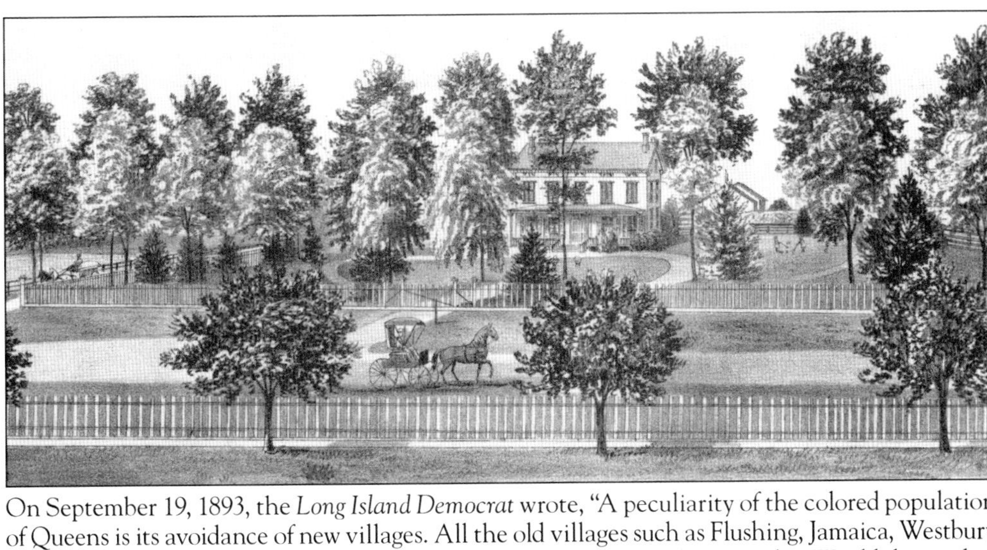

On September 19, 1893, the *Long Island Democrat* wrote, "A peculiarity of the colored population of Queens is its avoidance of new villages. All the old villages such as Flushing, Jamaica, Westbury etc. contain many colored citizens, while new villages have scarcely any. Why? Would they rather cling to the old traditions which were settled long before the revolution? Evidently they do not care for places without a history." The engraving depicts a Jamaica farm.

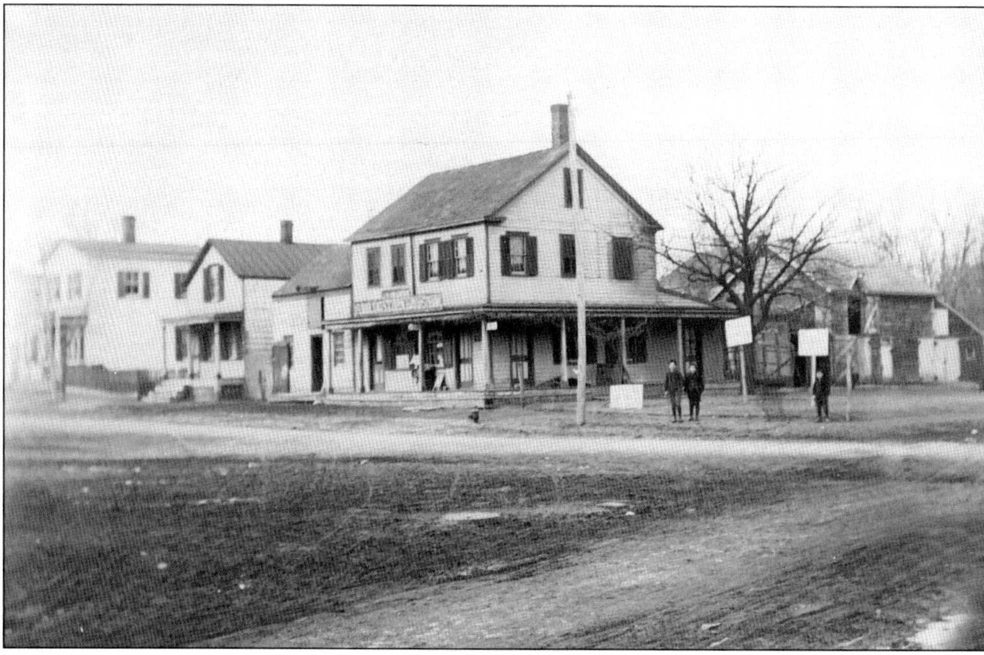

Market gardening became the principle business of the people in the rural district of the town. The increased and constantly increasing demands for garden vegetables in the city of New York made the rural area around Jamaica a busy farming community. The town was surrounded by farms. The photograph shows the J. Valentine farmhouse.

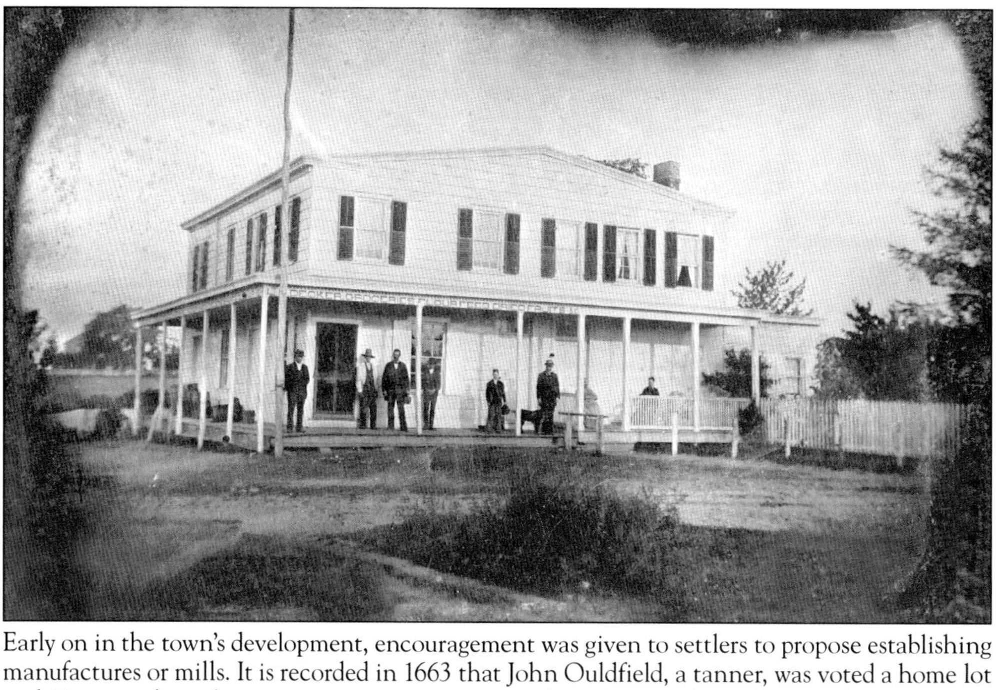

Early on in the town's development, encouragement was given to settlers to propose establishing manufactures or mills. It is recorded in 1663 that John Ouldfield, a tanner, was voted a home lot and 20 acres of meadow as an encouragement to settle and pursue his calling in the town. This tintype photograph depicts the L. Decker Grocery store. The sign on the front reads, "Flour, feed, dried fruits etc."

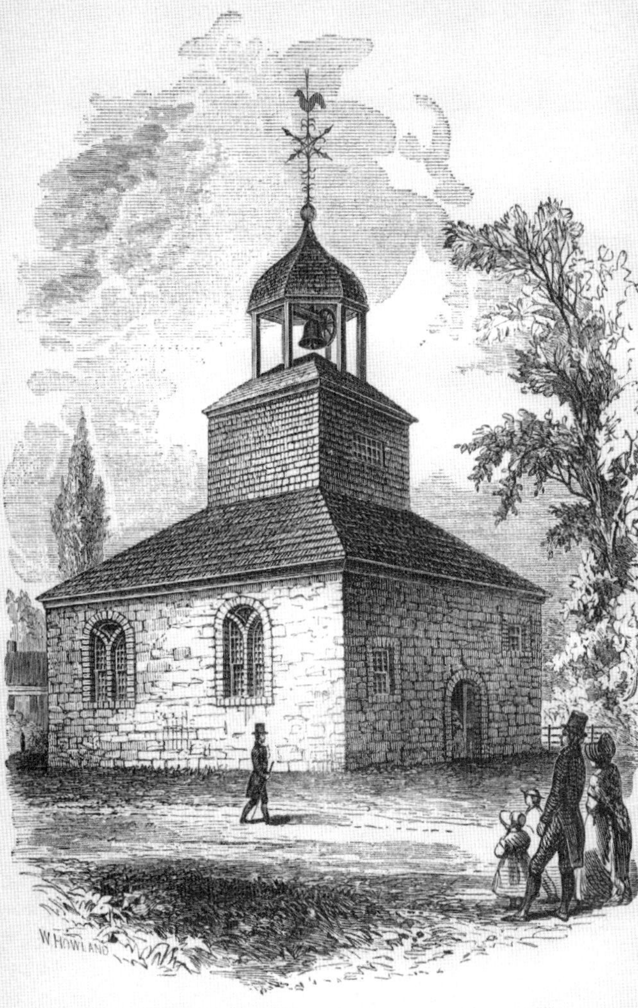

The "Old Stone Church," finished in 1699.

The first settlers to Jamaica were mostly Presbyterians or Congregationalists. Church affairs were considered and transacted at town meetings. In 1661, according to a *History of Queens County*, "some of the inhabitants petitioned Governor Stuyvesant to send a Dutch minister from New Amsterdam to preach and baptize. Reverend Samuel Drisius came to Jamaica on Saturday, January 8th. He preached two sermons and baptized eight children and two women. In 1662 the town voted to erect a minister's house, the following year they built a 20 feet square building to serve as church and town hall. In 1690 a new house, 60 by 30 feet, was built, and was succeed in 1699 by a stone building 40 feet square represented in this woodcut." It stood on Jamaica Avenue, at the head of Union Hall Street (162nd Street) called Meeting House Lane. It was taken down in 1813 having been used by Presbyterians, Episcopalian, and Dutch preachers. It was also used as a courthouse. During the American Revolution, Jamaica was occupied by British troops and American patriots, including Gen. Nathaniel Woodhull, were imprisoned here.

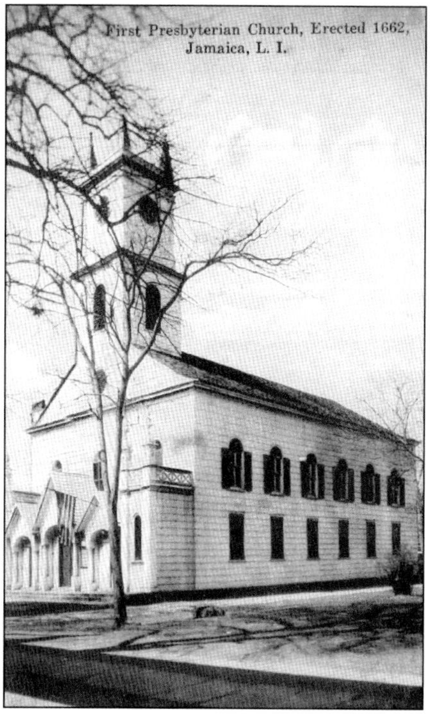

Founded in 1662, the First Presbyterian Church has a record of continuous activity to the present. Zechariah Walker was the first minister. The stone church was their first building until replaced in 1814 by a new building on Jamaica Avenue and Clinton Avenue (164th Street). When the village became part of a great metropolis, the noise of automobiles, trolleys, and elevated train caused the church to be moved further back to 164th Street in 1920.

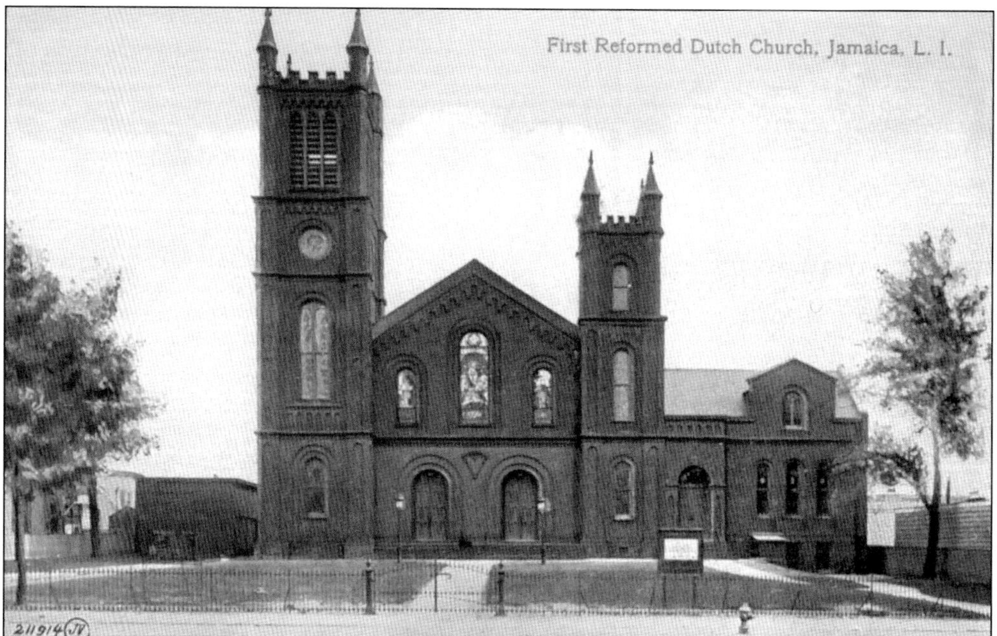

Established in 1702, a wooden octagonal building was erected in 1716 on Jamaica Avenue near 162nd Street for the First Reformed Dutch Church of Jamaica. In 1833, it was relocated to 153rd Street and Jamaica Avenue in a new Georgian-style building. Destroyed by fire in 1857, a new Romanesque Revival church designed and constructed by Sidney Young and master mason Anders Peterson opened in 1859. The congregation moved in the 1980s to Ninetieth Avenue and 159th Street. The church is now the Jamaica Center for Arts and Learning.

Established in 1702, Grace Episcopal Church was erected in 1734 along with a parish cemetery. A new church was consecrated in 1822 but was destroyed by fire in 1861. Dudley Fields designed this early English Gothic church pictured here and opened in 1862. The Rufus King family gave generously to the church for many years, donating a baptismal font, organ, Oxford Bible, bishop's chair, and more land for the cemetery.

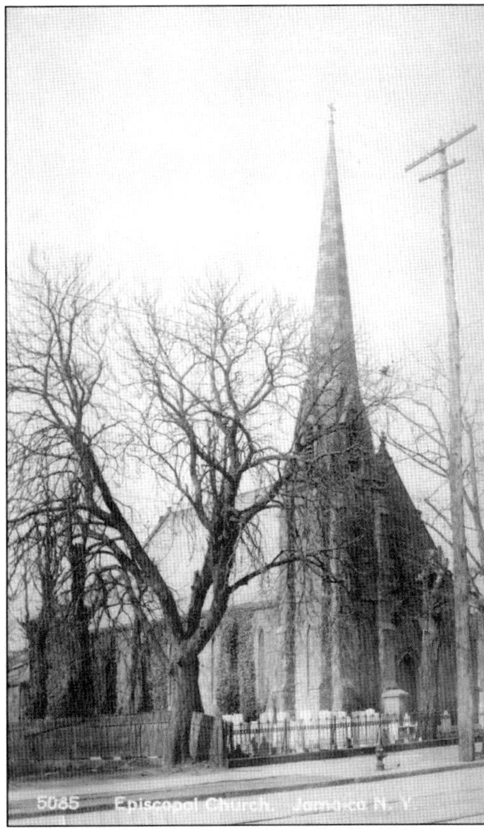

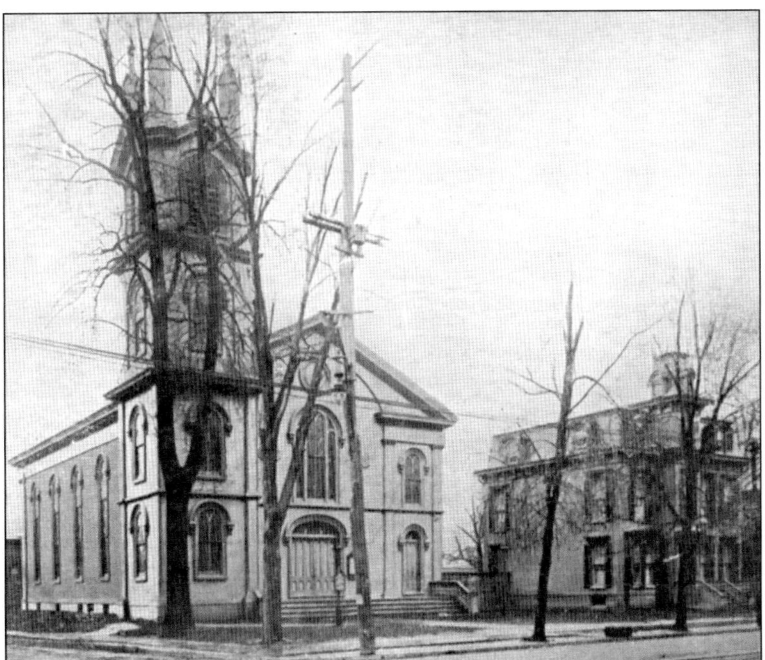

METHODIST EPISCOPAL CHURCH, JAMAICA, L. I.

Established in 1807, the Methodists built a church in 1811 on Division Street opposite the King Manor. In 1847, a new church was built at Jamaica and New York Avenues. A third church was built in 1873 at Puntine (165th Street) and Jamaica Avenues, pictured at left. In 1920, a fourth was built at Clinton Avenue (164th Street). The fifth and present church at Highland Avenue and 164th Street was dedicated in 1949.

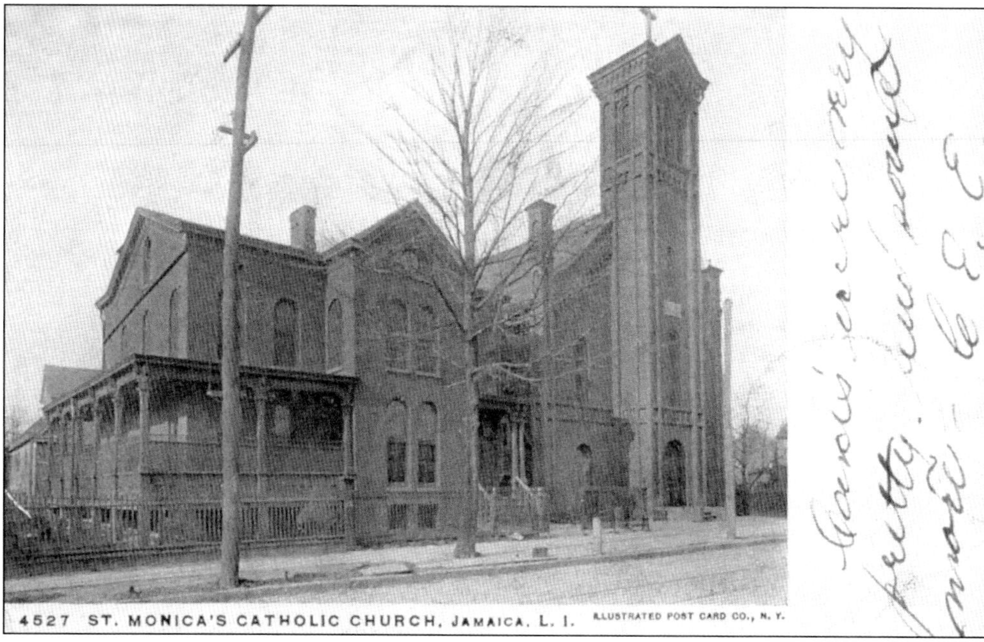

Fr. Michael Curran offered the first Mass in the home of a blacksmith in 1838. A wooden chapel was built on Washington Street (160th Street) and dedicated in 1840. In 1857, a Romanesque Revival church, pictured above, was built by contractor Anders Peterson and designated a landmark in 1979. The church's facade was saved following a destructive storm and has been incorporated into a modern day care center on the York College campus.

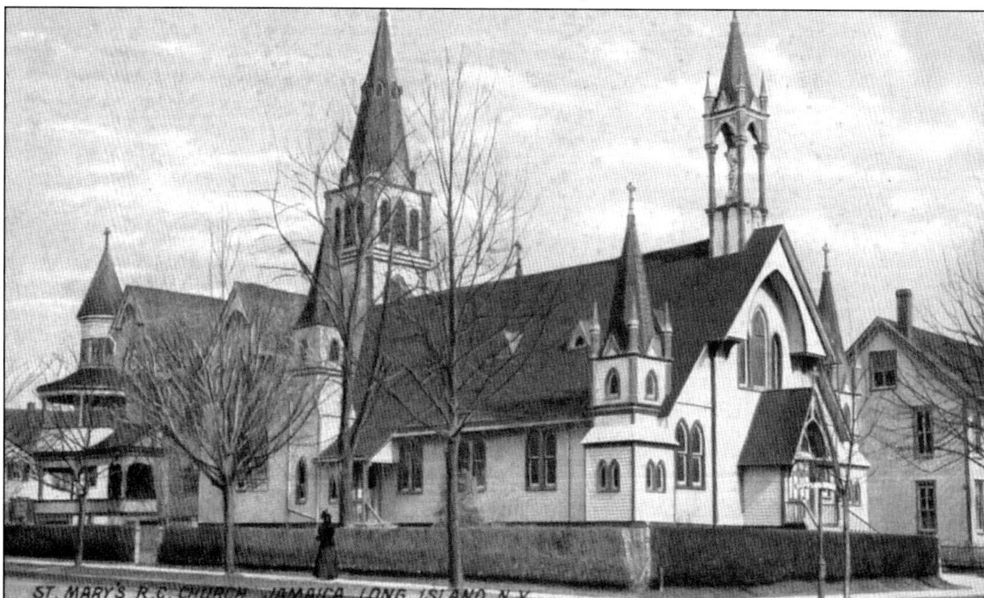

The German Catholics of Jamaica grew sufficiently to warrant a separate parish with land purchased at Shelton Avenue (Eighty-ninth Avenue) and Parsons Boulevard. Mass was said in a 1767 farmhouse on the property. In 1886, Rev. Ignatius Zeller laid the cornerstone for St. Mary's German Catholic Church, a small wooden church, enlarged in 1893 with seven steeples, pictured above. That same year he erected a two-story schoolhouse with Sisters of Saint Dominic as teachers.

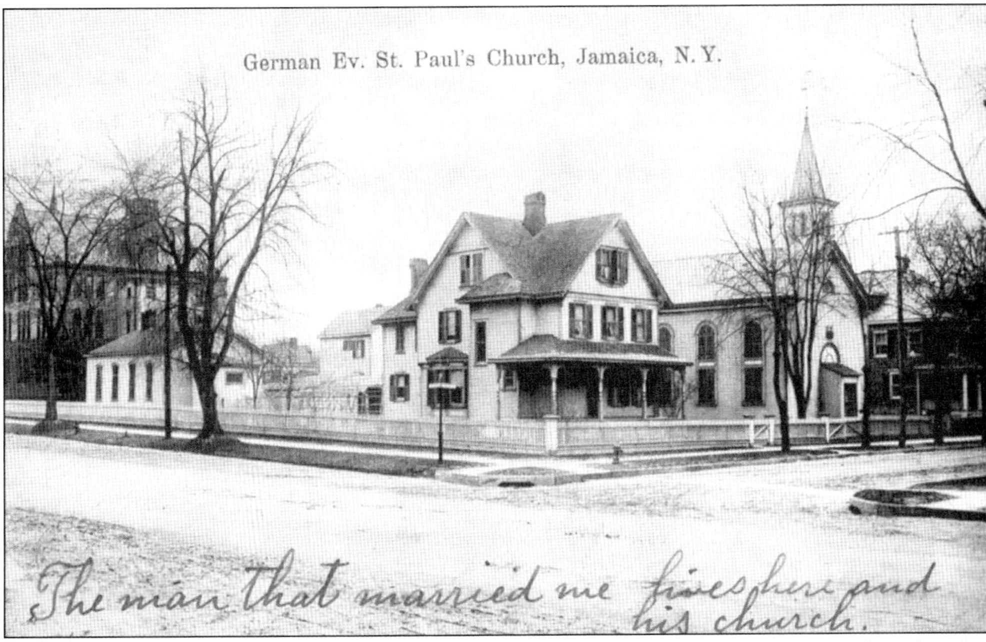

German Evangelical St. Paul's Church, pictured above, was organized in 1873. Other churches established in Jamaica include the African Methodist Episcopal Church incorporated on July 5, 1844. It was first organized about 1832 and is now known as the Allen A. M. E. Church. The Shiloh Colored Baptist Church was organized in 1847, the First Baptist Church of Jamaica organized in 1874, and St. Stephen's Colored Episcopal Church in 1903.

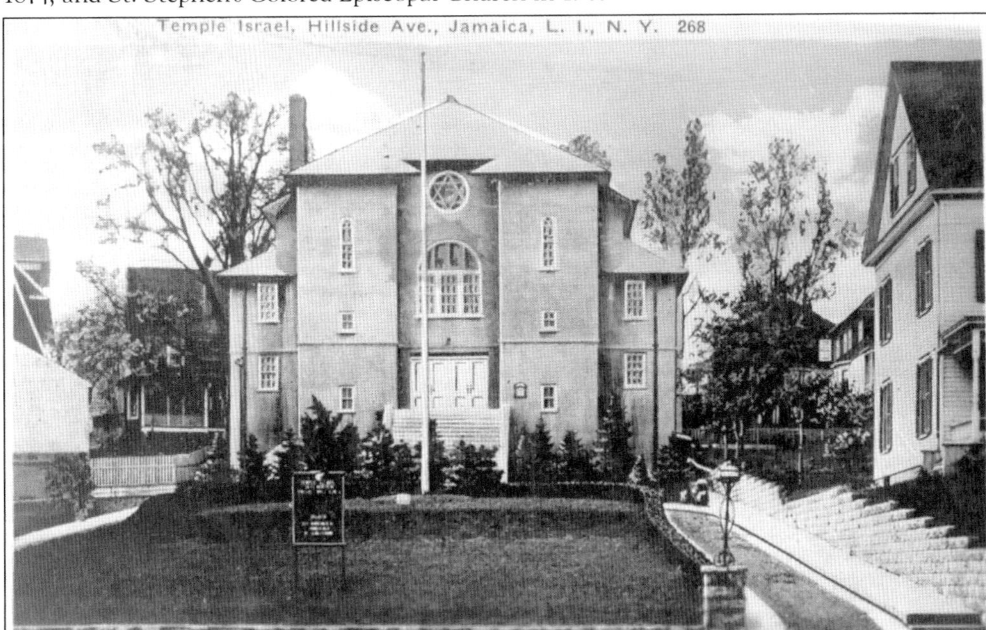

At a meeting on September 13, 1918, at the home of Mr. and Mrs. William Gold a motion was passed to form a Reform synagogue. The 1918 High Holy Days marked the beginning of services. Rabbi Lipkin was formally installed as Rabbi of Temple Israel in 1919. By 1920, a parcel of land on the north side of Hillside Avenue at 160th Street was purchased and the temple above was erected.

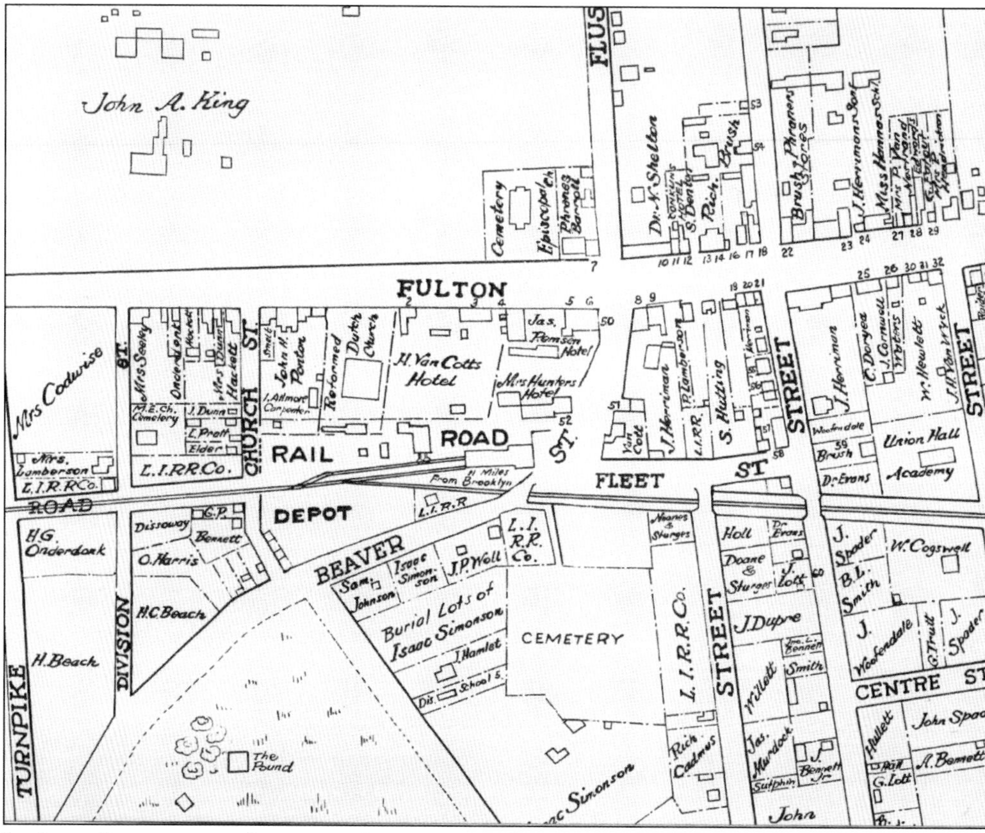

In the earliest cemetery document, the town agreed in 1668 with John Wascot to fence the burying place, 10 rods square with a sufficient five-rail fence. It is the oldest family burial ground in Queens and one of the oldest in New York City. Revolutionary war soldiers are buried here, along with many famous colonial families. The cemetery incorporated in 1879 as Prospect Cemetery and is now a designated New York City landmark.

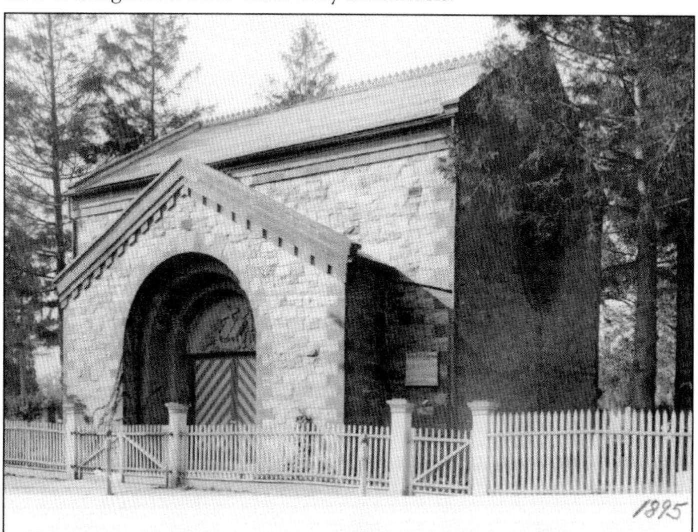

In 1857, Nicholas Ludlum bought land east of the cemetery, building the Chapel of Three Sisters in memory of his daughters, Cornelia Maria, Mary Cecelia, and Mary. The chapel is a symmetrical, one-story stone Romanesque Revival building. Restored and renovated as a performance and arts space, it is a part of the York College campus. The cemetery remains well preserved due to the care of the Prospect Cemetery Association.

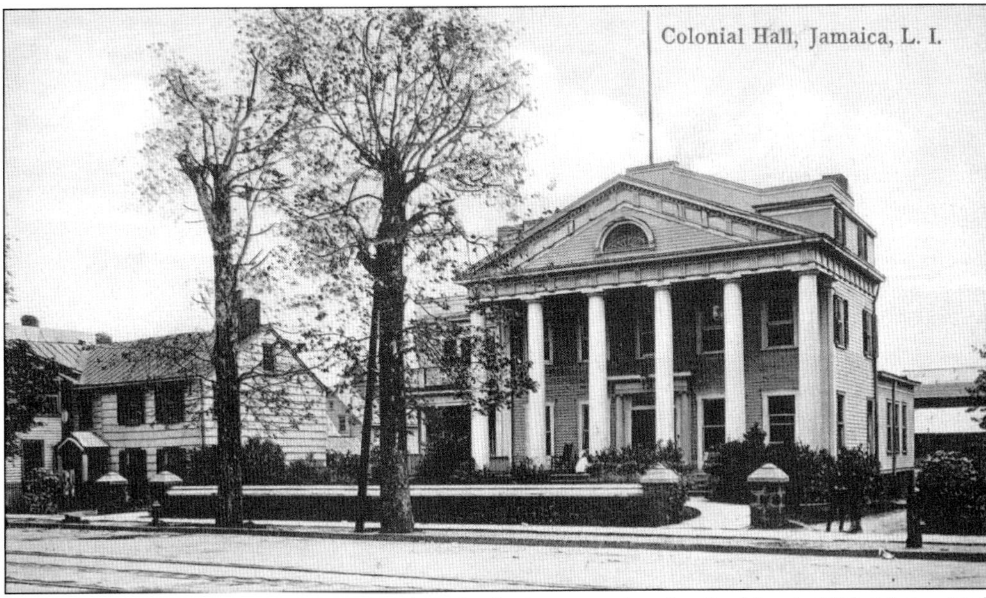

In 1676, Richard Jones opened a school in the little stone church. On May 1, 1792, Union Hall Academy, so called because a union of Jamaica, Flushing, and Newtown built it, opened on Union Hall Street (162nd Street). Jamaica became famous as an educational center with students coming from South America and even Europe. Closing in 1872, the Ladies Seminary building above became Colonial Hall, a public meeting place.

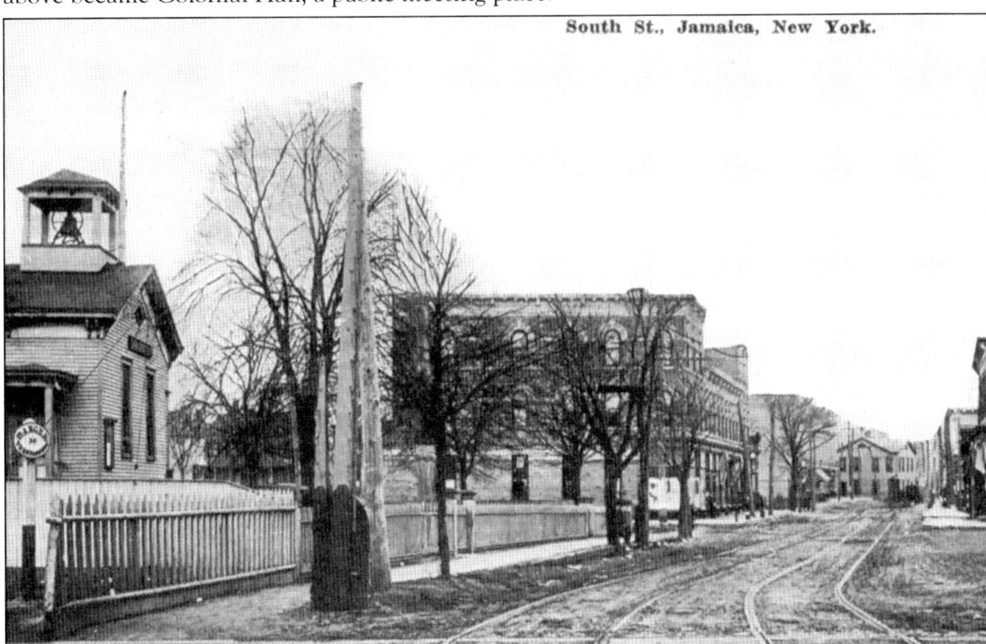

The Jamaica school district organized on July 19, 1853. A school opened on Herriman Street (161st Street) in 1854 called PS No. 1, which served the white children of Jamaica. A branch school for black children opened in rented rooms on January 17, 1854, called PS No. 2. In 1868, black children got their own school on South Street (South Road), pictured above. Schools remained segregated in New York until 1900. The site of this school is located on the York College campus.

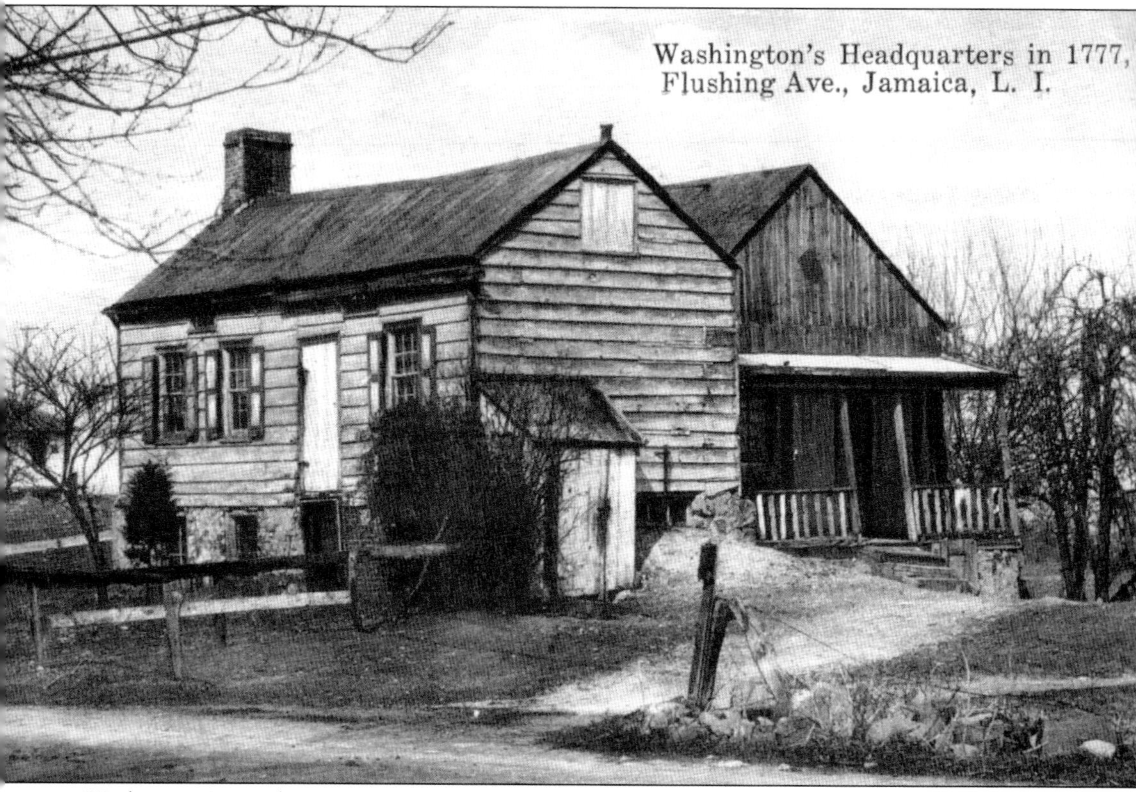

Washington's Headquarters were located on Flushing Avenue (Parsons Boulevard). The Minute Men of Jamaica was formed to defend American liberty in 1775. Among them were sons of prominent Jamaica families, such as Samuel Higbie, Isaac Baylis, Hope Rhoades, William Ludlum, Cornelius Amberman, Derick Amberman, Hendrick Hendrickson, Benjamin Everitt, Stephen Rider, Richard Betts, Daniel Skidmore, Andrew Oakley, and John Innis. Their uniform dress was a linen frock reaching below the knee, a fringe around the neck and arms, and a white feather in their hat. Following is the "Song of the Jamaica Minute Men": "Arouse, my brother Minute Men! And let us bear our chorus; the braver and the bolder, the more they will adore us. / Now to our station let us march and rendezvous with pleasure, behaving like brave Minute Men to save so great a treasure. / We'll let 'em see immediately that we are men of mettle, American boys who fear no noise, and ne'er will flinch from battle. / That Troy brood that has withstood this great and glorious jovial, if they advance, we'll make 'em dance the tune of Yankee Doodle."

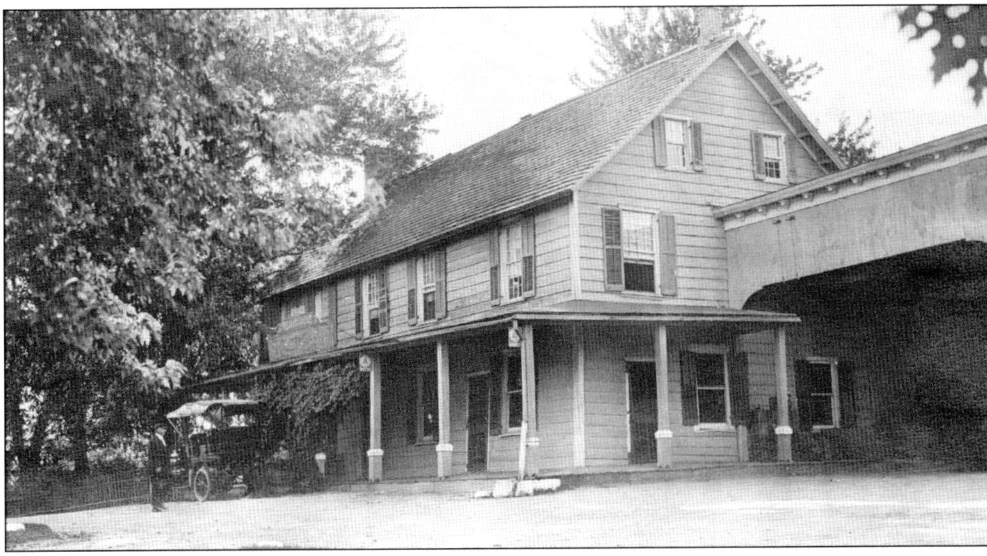

Before the Battle of Long Island in 1776, Gen. Nathaniel Woodhull was ordered "to prevent stock and other provisions from falling into British hands." His militia drove away all the cattle and awaiting orders at Carpenter's Tavern (Jamaica Avenue and 197th Street) was captured. Ordered to say, "God save the King," he replied "God save us all" and was savagely attacked. Taken to Jamaica, eventually having his arm amputated, he died on September 20, 1776.

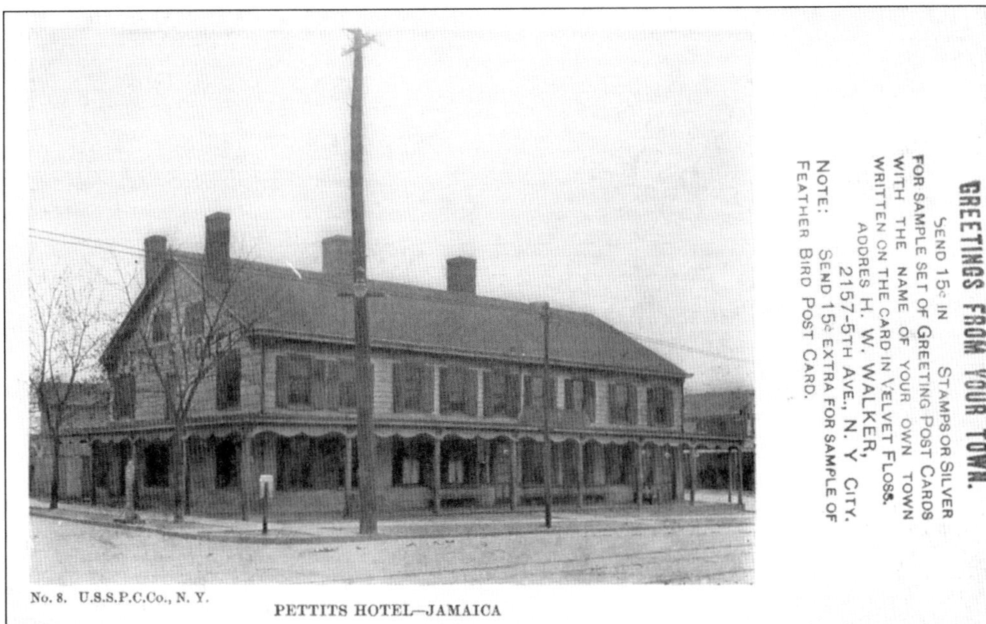

George Washington made this diary entry: "April 20, 1790 About 8 o'clock I crossed to Brooklyn and proceeded to Flat Bush—thence to Utrich—thence to Gravesend—thence through—Jamaica where we lodged at a Tavern kept by one William Warne—a pretty good and decent house." Located at the southwest corner of Parsons Boulevard and Jamaica Avenue, it had many owners. In this 1907 photograph, it is called Pettits Hotel.

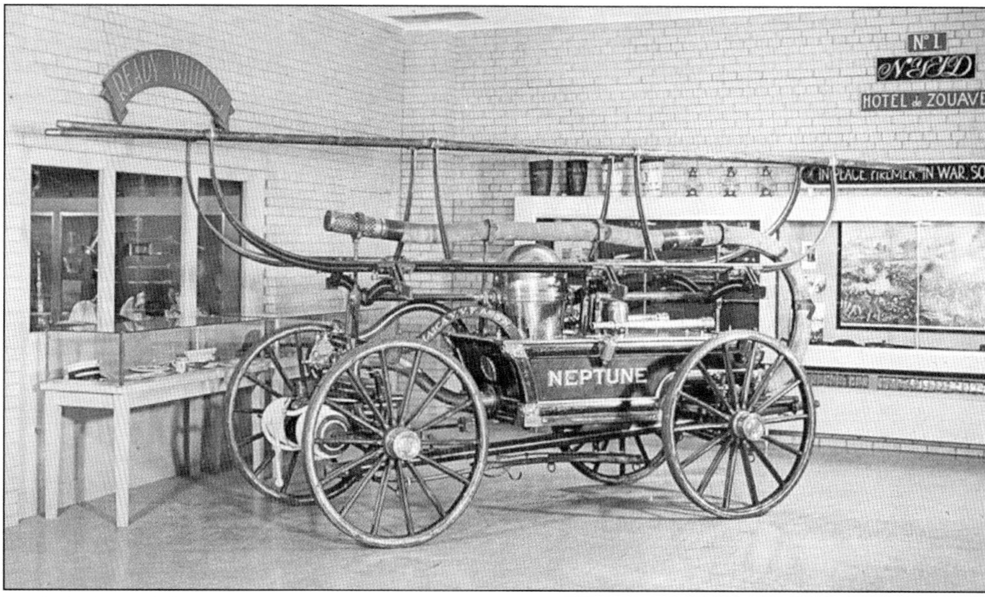

In 1797, James Waters, an owner of an engine, petitioned for a better way of extinguishing fires. Proprietors of a fire engine in Jamaica were authorized to form an organization of three to five trustees who would choose 13 volunteer firemen. This number was increased to 24. The 1863 Neptune Fire Engine of Jamaica, pictured above, is now in the American Museum of Fire Fighting in Hudson.

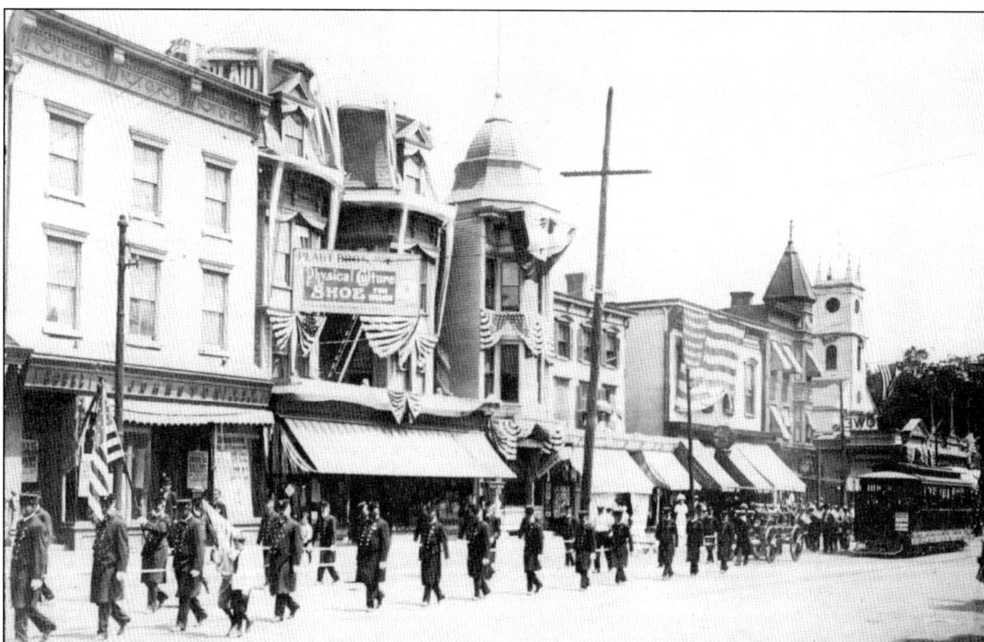

Fire companies serving Jamaica included Protection Engine Company No. 1, Neptune Engine Company No. 2, Atlantic Hook and Ladder Company, Eagle Hose Company (organized 1864 but disbanded 1871), Degrauw Hose Company No. 1, and the Continental Bucket Company. A group of firefighters march along Jamaica Avenue in this 1911 photograph with fire engine in the rear. The last building on the right is the Presbyterian church when located at 164th Street.

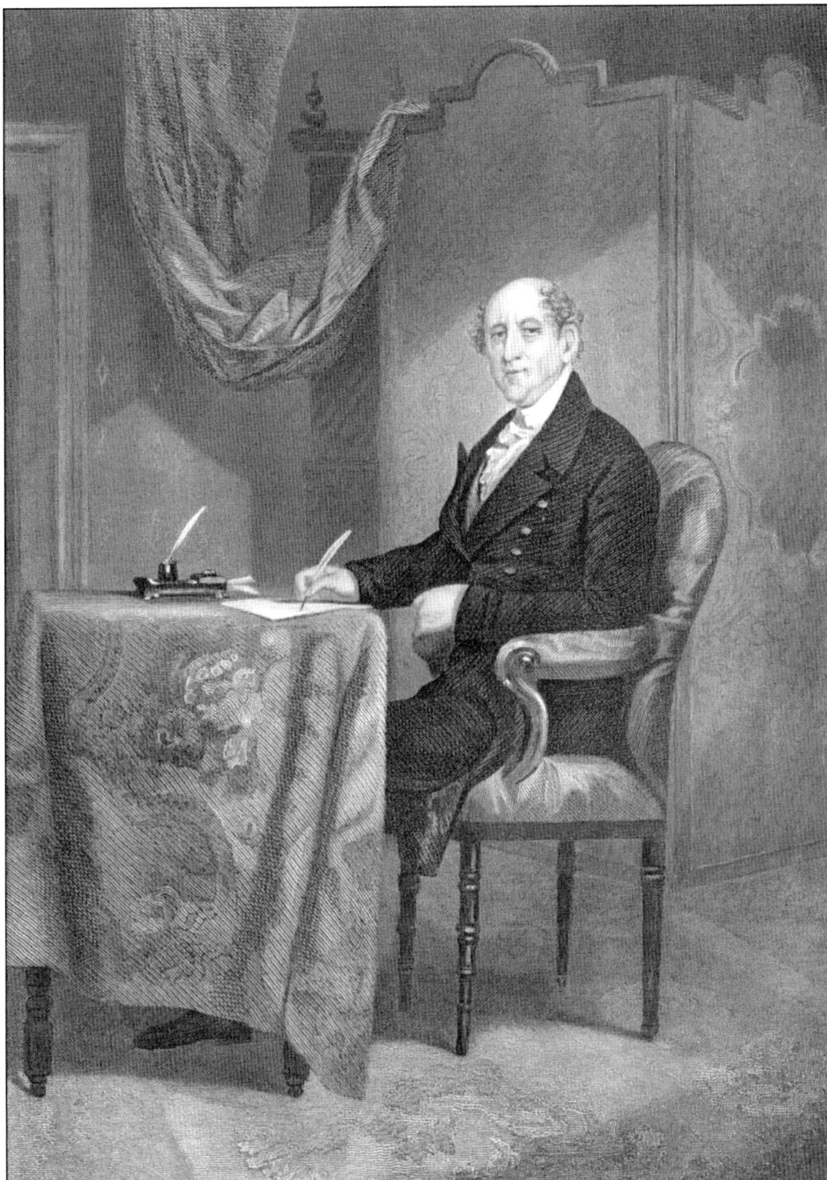

Born 1755, Rufus King graduated from Harvard and served in the American Revolution. A lawyer, he entered politics becoming a member of the Massachusetts legislature and representative in the Confederation Congress. A delegate at the 1787 Constitutional Convention, he helped draft the Constitution and was a signer and elected to the New York State Senate. From 1796 to 1803, under the administrations of George Washington, John Adams, and Thomas Jefferson, he was ambassador to England. King George III, sorry to see him leave said, "for your conduct here has been so entirely proper, both as it has regarded the interest of your own Country and of this, as to have given me perfect satisfaction." Running unsuccessfully for vice president in 1804 and 1808, he lost the 1816 presidential election to James Monroe. In the U.S. Senate he spoke against slavery, "I have yet to learn that one man can make a slave of another. If one man cannot do so, no number of individuals can have any better right to do it." These were radical words at the time and spoken 43 years before the Emancipation Proclamation.

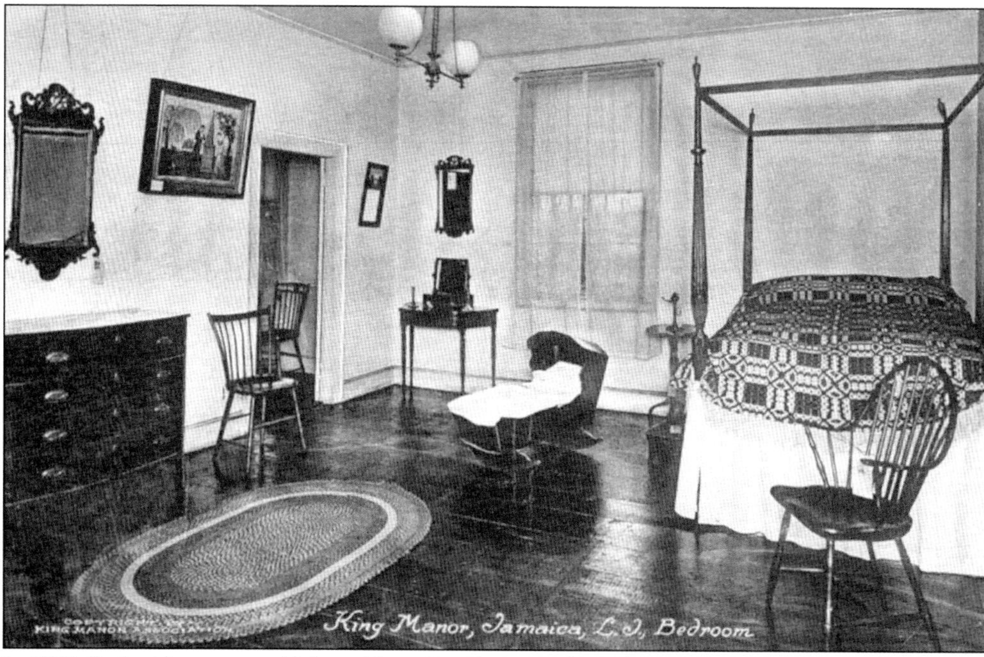

In 1786, Rufus King married Mary Alsop. Purchasing a large farm in Jamaica in 1805, he planned on retiring to this country estate. He lived here on and off until his death in 1827, buried next to his wife, who died in 1819, at Grace Episcopal Church, a block east on Jamaica Avenue. They had five sons who survived to adulthood: John, Charles, James, Edward, and Frederick.

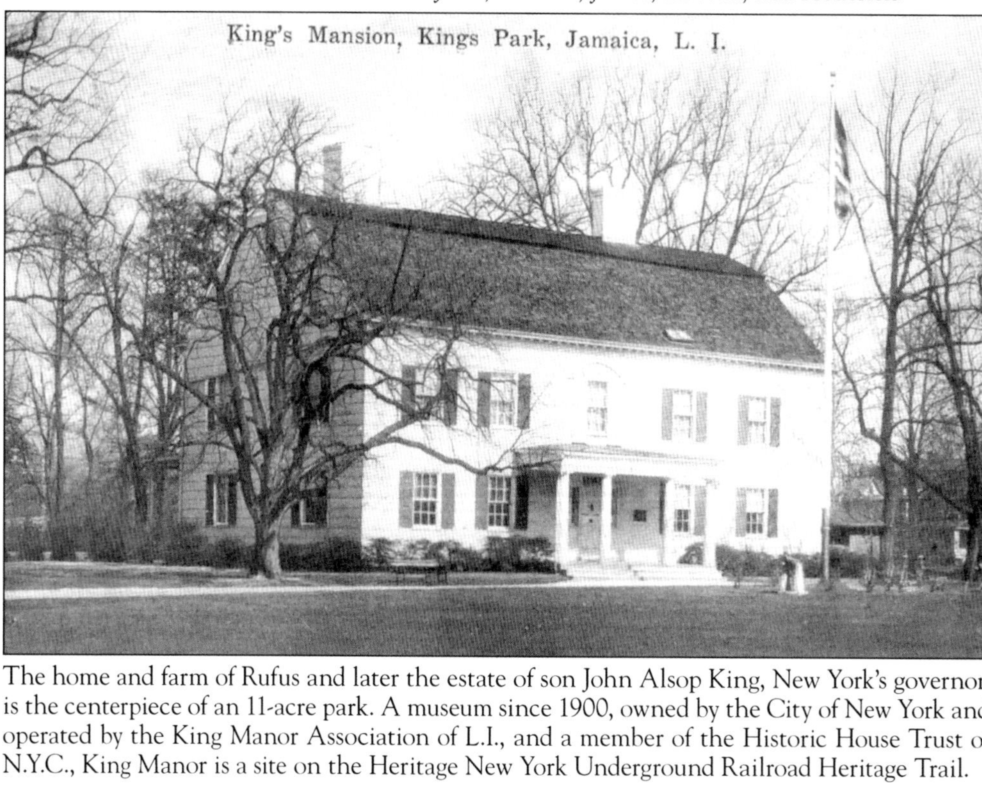

The home and farm of Rufus and later the estate of son John Alsop King, New York's governor, is the centerpiece of an 11-acre park. A museum since 1900, owned by the City of New York and operated by the King Manor Association of L.I., and a member of the Historic House Trust of N.Y.C., King Manor is a site on the Heritage New York Underground Railroad Heritage Trail.

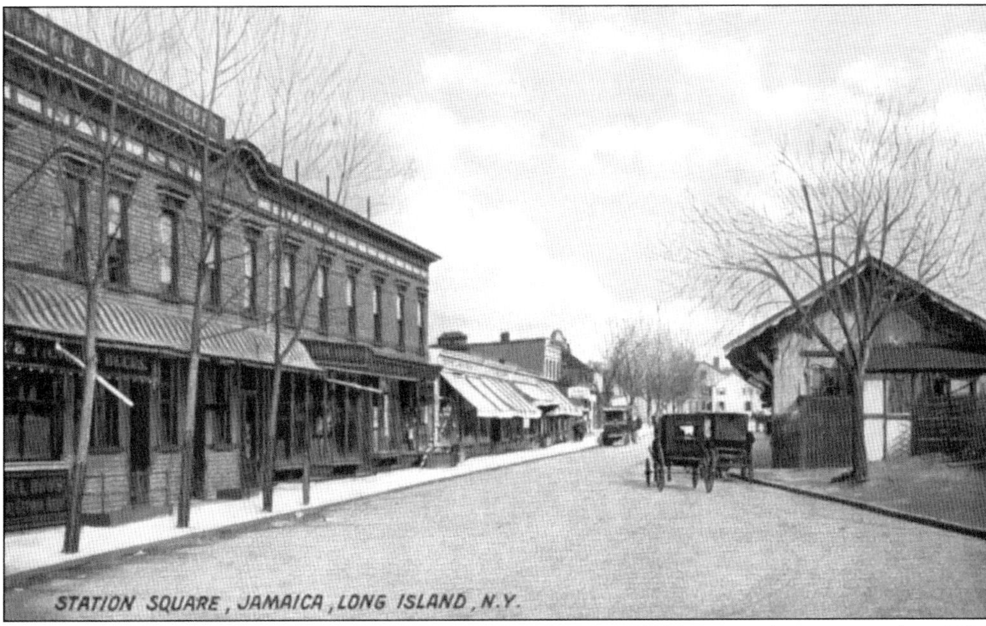

The Long Island Railroad's (LIRR) original Jamaica Station (Old Jamaica) was erected in 1836, the terminus of the LIRR. It was remodeled in 1869 and rebuilt in 1871, pictured above. In 1867, a second depot was built nearby at the South Side Railroad and was called Jamaica Beaver Street Station for the Atlantic Branch. Both stations were discontinued as stops and razed between 1912 and 1913, with a new station erected at Sutphin Boulevard.

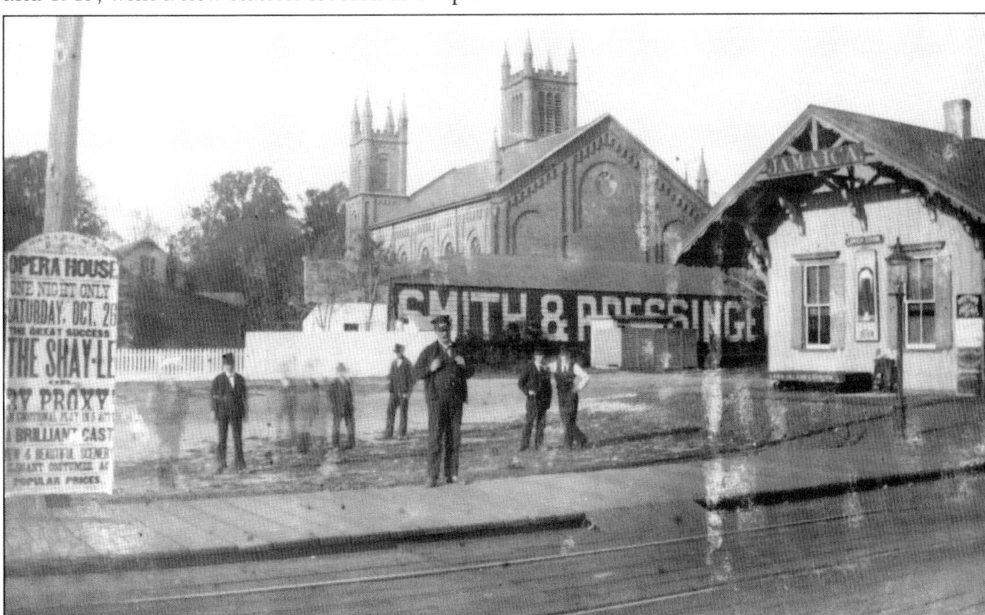

According to the *Long Island Democrat* in 1871, "A contract was made with Mr. J. B. Robertson to erect a $2000 depot 22 x 48 feet, 14 feet high with two rooms, ticket office, etc. It is to have a ladies room fitted up in neat and tasty manner, with brussels or ingrain carpet, cane seat settees, mirror, washstands, and the necessary articles for toilet use." In the background is the Dutch Reformed Church.

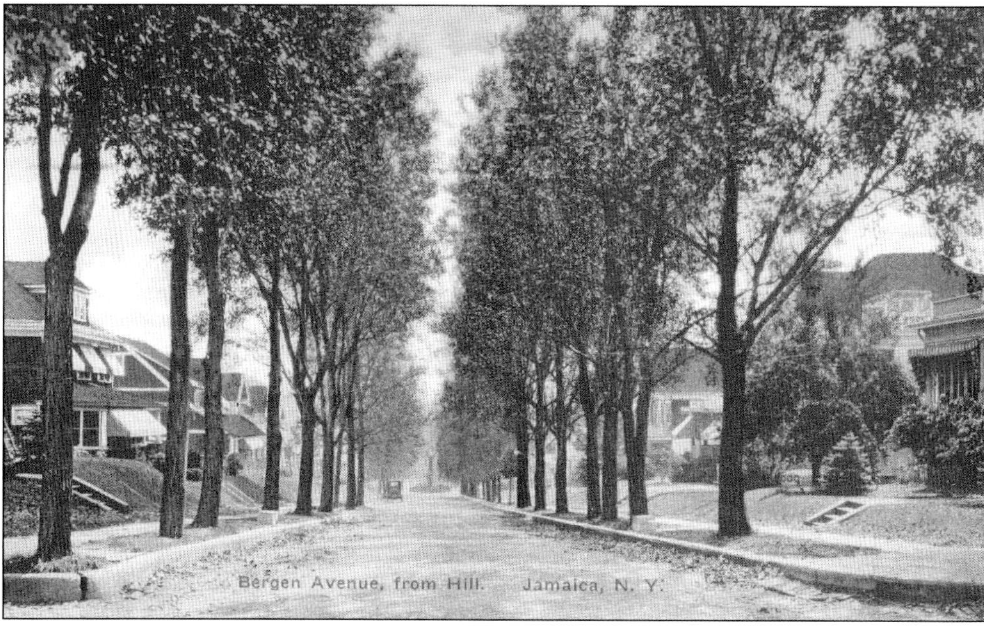

Local newspapers often published letters and poems from soldiers. "How sweet are memories. Pictures of home, happiness and bliss so pure. Mary, may I soon again be safe at home with you, my little Bella, a heaven on earth. For though imprisoned, my mind in not confined. Mary, my heart is with our child and thee." This is from James in a Virginia prison and was printed in the *Long Island Democrat* in 1861. The photograph depicts Bergen Avenue (166th Street).

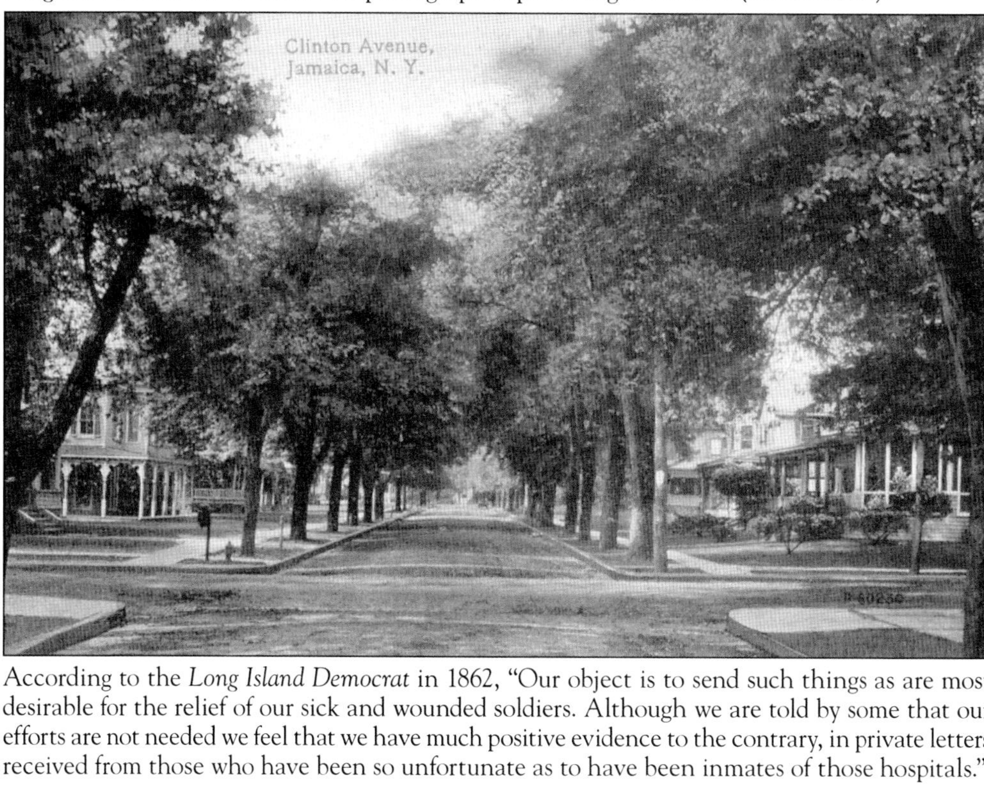

According to the *Long Island Democrat* in 1862, "Our object is to send such things as are most desirable for the relief of our sick and wounded soldiers. Although we are told by some that our efforts are not needed we feel that we have much positive evidence to the contrary, in private letters received from those who have been so unfortunate as to have been inmates of those hospitals."

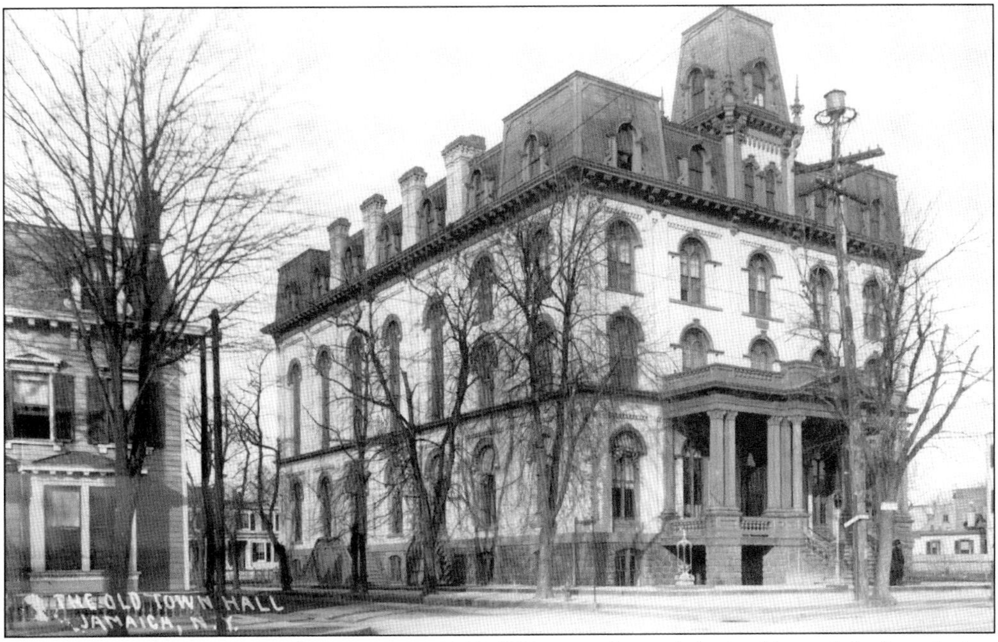

According to the *Long Island Democrat* in 1868, "We are informed the building of the foundation of the Town Hall, corner of Jamaica Avenue and Flushing Road (Parson's Boulevard)." It served as courthouse, opera house, and jail and held meeting rooms for many clubs. Among those who spoke here were suffragists Carrie Chapman Lott and Susan B. Anthony, social reformer Jacob A. Riis, and religious leader Rev. Henry W. Beecher. Performers included the noted Jubilee Singers.

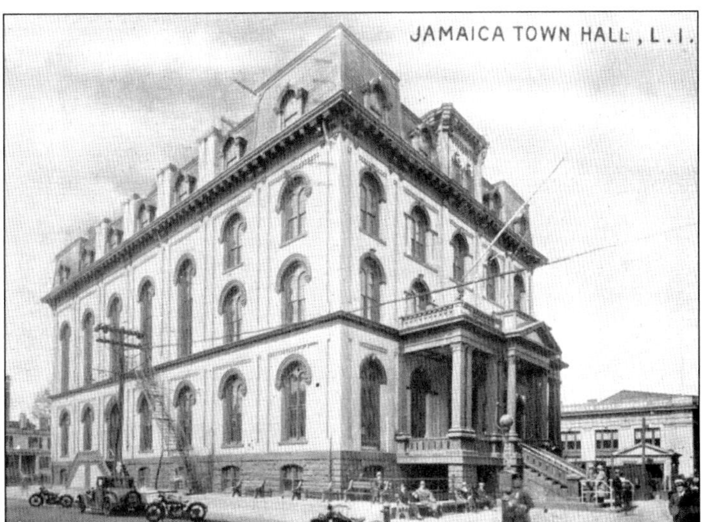

Jamaica became an important 19th-century trading center for farmers. The Village Charter was obtained in 1841, but a more efficient one was granted in 1855 with William J. Cogswell as first president. After the 1898 consolidation of the five boroughs, the hall became the municipal courthouse, sheriff's office, and traffic court. This eclectic Victorian structure, with a rusticated base, classical porch, and a mansard roof was razed in 1941.

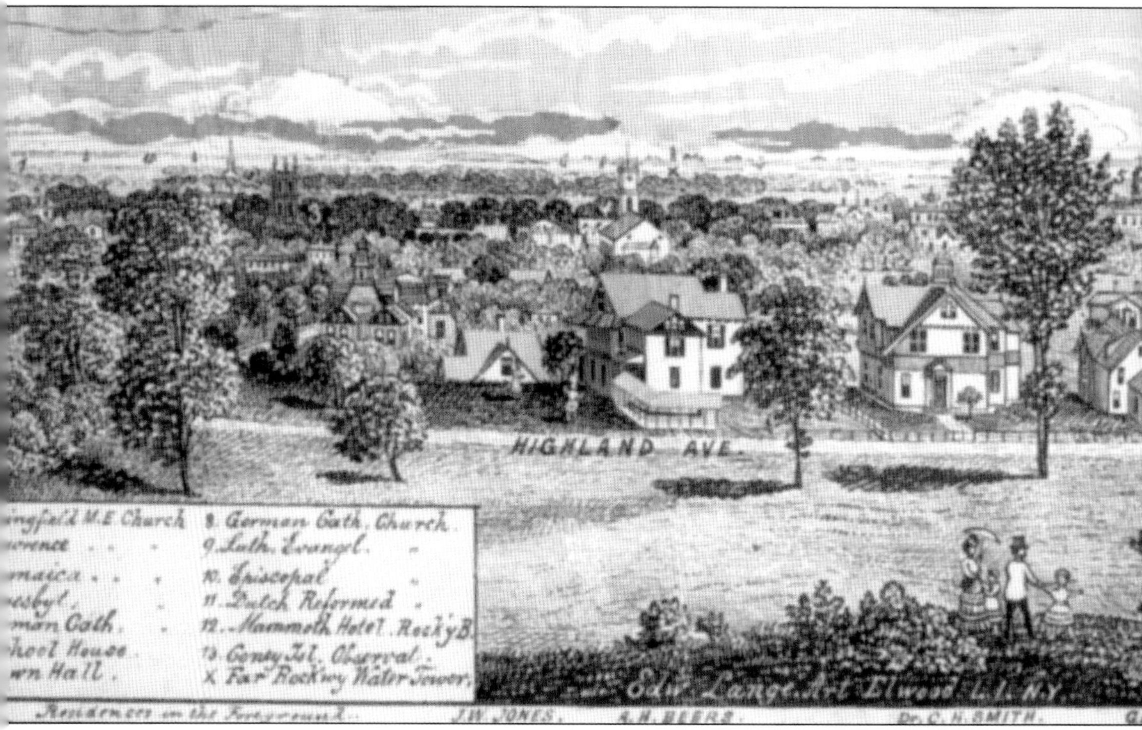

On May 29, 1883, the *Long Island Democrat* printed, "Thursday night many people went to the hills to view the fireworks of the newly opened Brooklyn Bridge. At this great distance the rockets and colored lights being distinctly visible. Some of the younger spectators being either of sharper sight, or of more imagination, professed to see figure pieces and all sorts of fiery devices." Highland

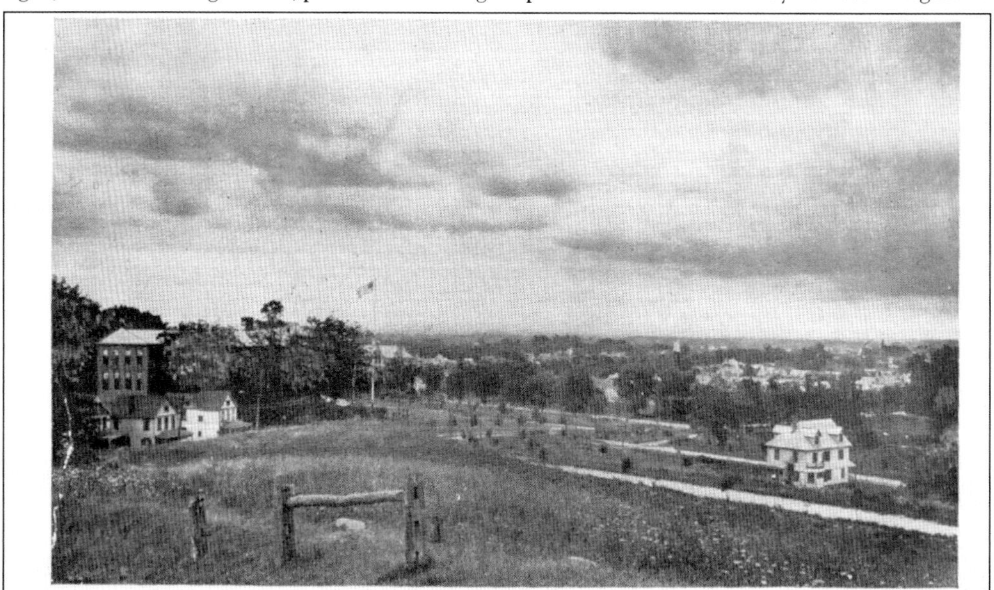

Prospect Hill was located west of Highland Park. The brick building to the left is the Normal School located at Hillside Avenue and Parsons Boulevard, today the site of Hillcrest High School. The white house in the foreground on the right can be seen in the next photograph on the left.

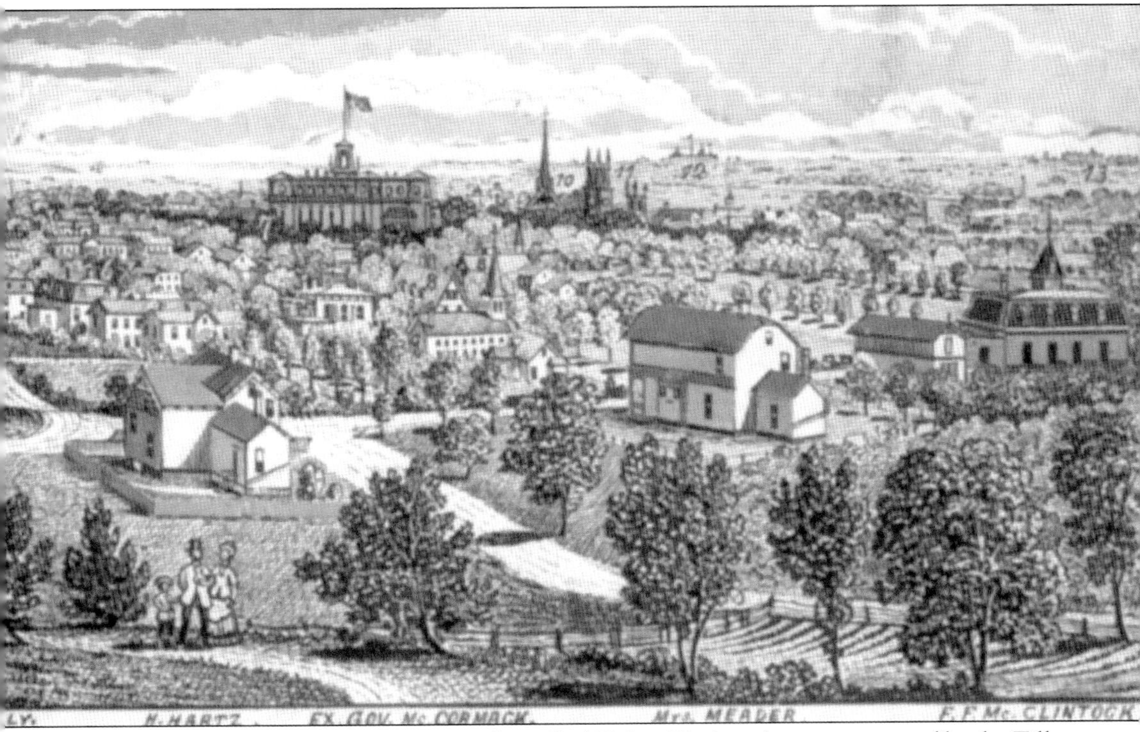

Park with Goose Pond at the center was also called Upland Park and was once owned by the Tilly family. When their son, Capt. George Tilly, was killed in the Philippines in 1899, it was renamed in his honor and located at 165th Street and Highland Avenue in Jamaica Hills.

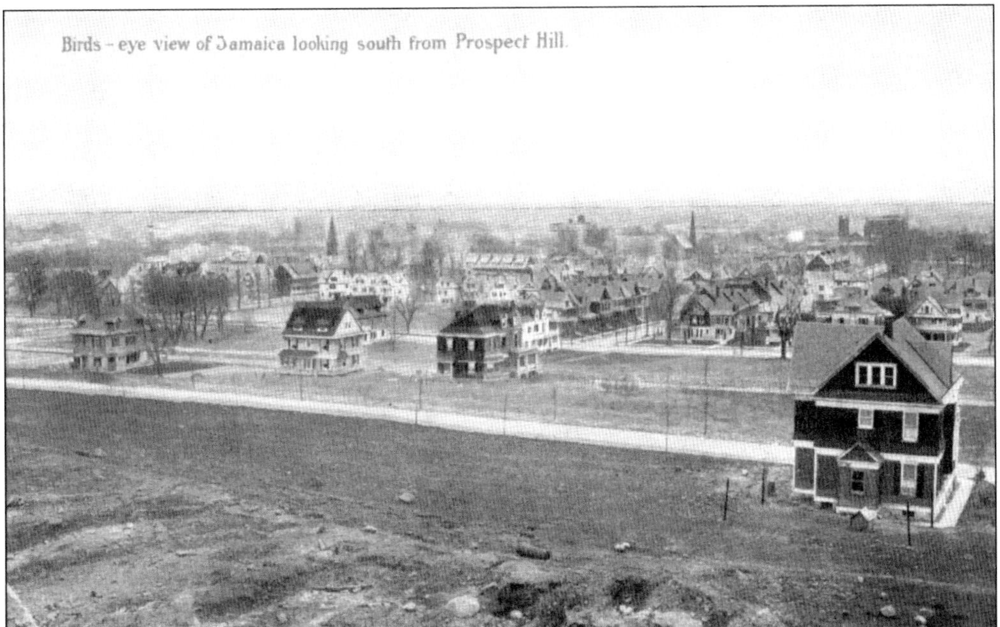

A number of the landmarks, numbered in the above 1887 engraving, are visible: Jamaica Town Hall in the distance and the steeples of two churches—St. Mary German Catholic Church and Grace Episcopal Church. To the right is the bell tower of the Dutch Reformed Church.

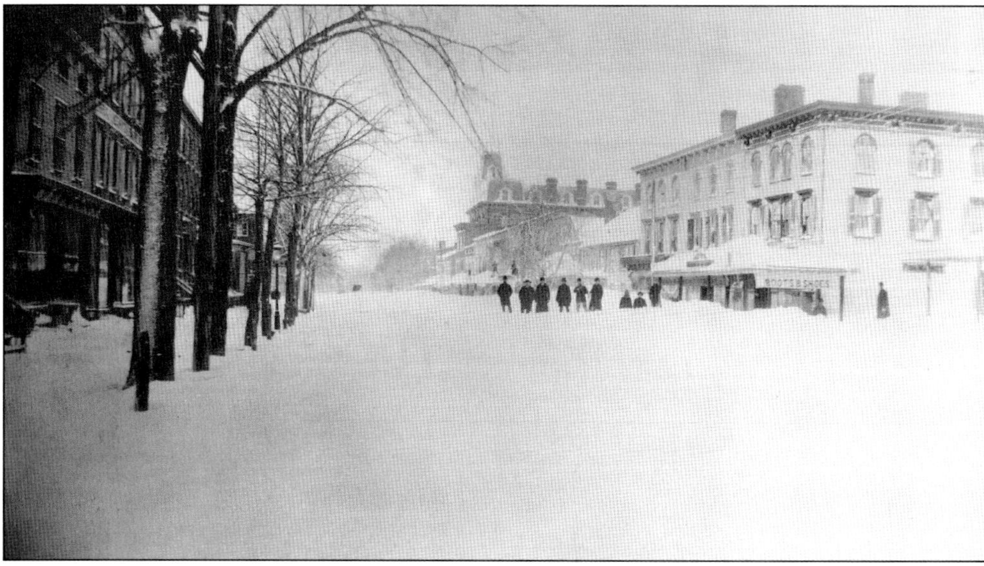

Looking west on Jamaica Avenue, town hall is in distance in this view from the blizzard of 1888. According to the *Long Island Democrat*, "The snow was found in many many places waist deep. Jamaica was snowed in. In front of Edward's Bakery a drift had formed 12 feet in height and so on down the north side of Jamaica Avenue, 10 feet was about the general rule to Town Hall and beyond."

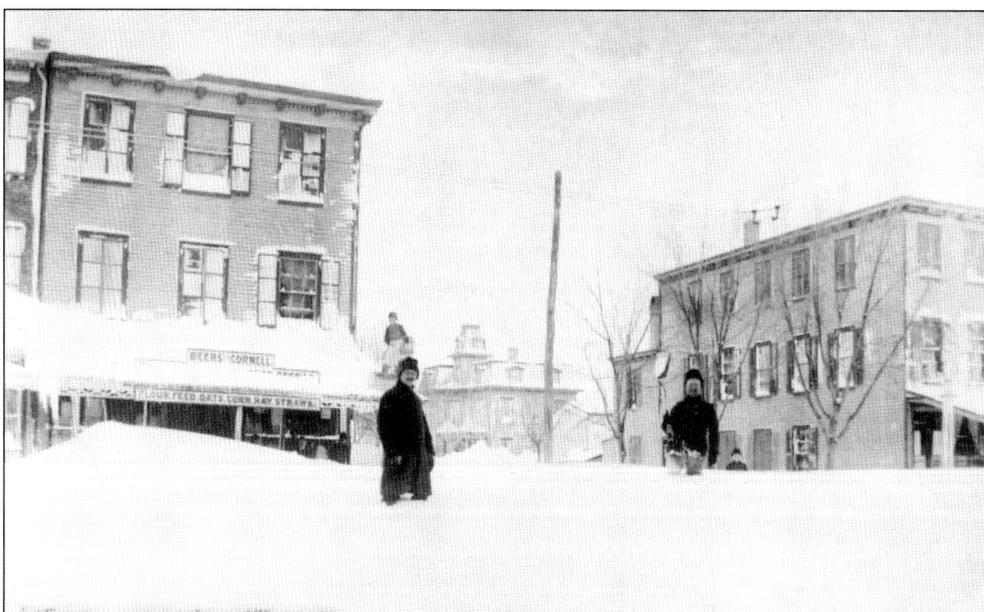

According to the *Long Island Democrat*, "Fred Coe, the milkman was compelled to shelter his horse under Beer & Cornell's shed, and delivered milk on foot. Philip and Leander Faber dug a tunnel in front of their father's shoe store and many ladies and gents went through it, and will have in years to come the story to relate of going under the snow."

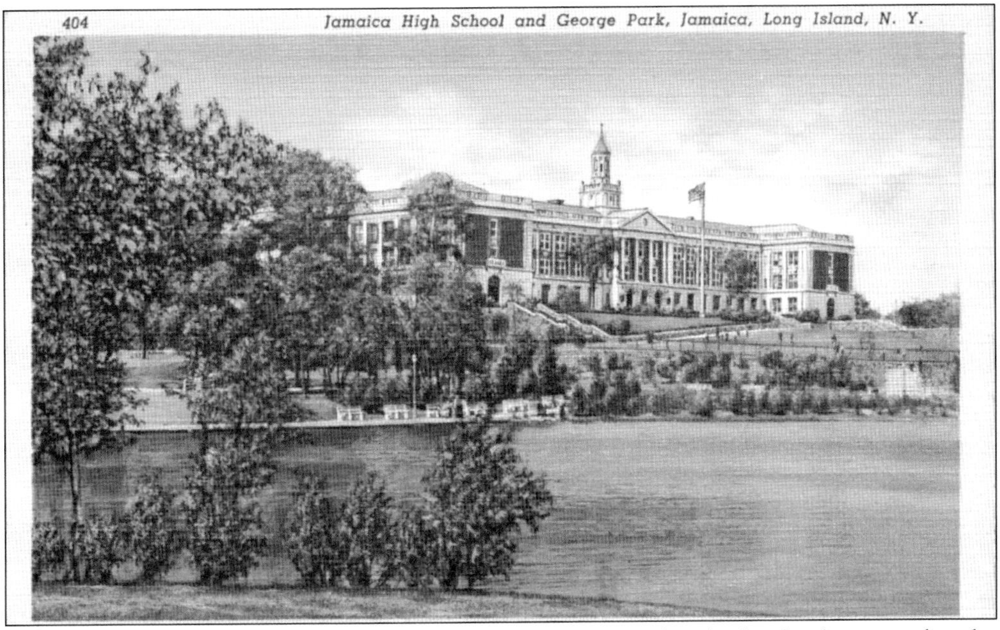

On December 14, 1892, the Board of Regents granted a charter for a high school; it started in the 1854 school building on Heriman Street (161st Street). The first high school building was open in 1896 on Hillside Avenue and 162nd Street. A new building, pictured above, was built in 1925 and opened 1927 on 168th Street and Gothic Drive. The Georgian Revival building designed by William Gompert was designated a city landmark in 2009.

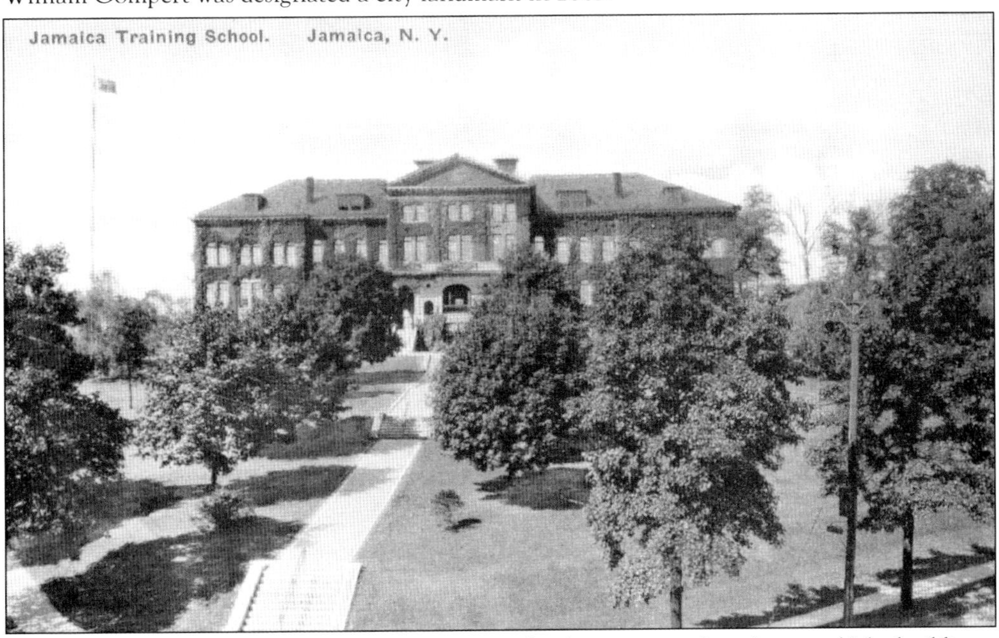

The Jamaica State Normal School opened in 1897 for the training of teachers, and "the buildings, which are surrounded by spacious lawns, are situated in a forest grove on the crest of a long range of hills overlooking the town and facing the ocean," stated the *Long Island Farmer*. It stood on Flushing Road (Parsons Boulevard) and Hillside Avenue and was torn down in the early 1970s. In 1974, Hillcrest High School was built on the site.

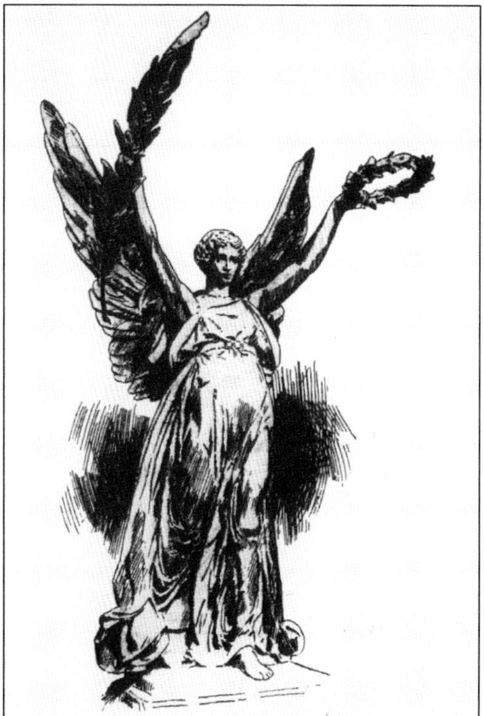

Jamaica Soldiers and Sailors Monument.

Designed by F. Wellington Ruckstuhl, the Soldiers and Sailors Civil War Monument depicts Victory alighting from the clouds. Her drapery filled with the rushing wind giving motion to the figure. She holds a palm branch symbolizing fame and a crown of laurel symbolizing immortality. The face has the expression of triumph. It is an apotheosis of the soldiers of Jamaica who, having died in battle for their country, will live victorious in history.

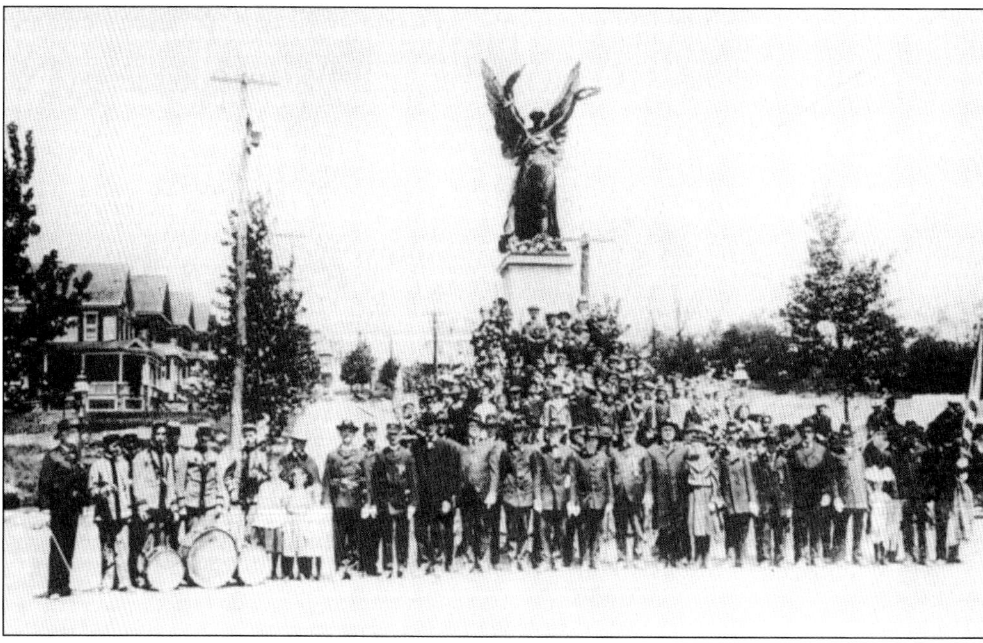

The monument was erected at Hillside Avenue and Merrick Boulevard and unveiled on May 30, 1896. The parade's grand marshal was Thomas S. Rider, who had enlisted at the age of 19 and the orator was Col. John Fleming. The granite pedestal with dates 1861–1865 was designed by Julius Harder. In 1960, it was moved to a park at Hillside Avenue and 175th Street. This photograph shows a 1907 Memorial Day event.

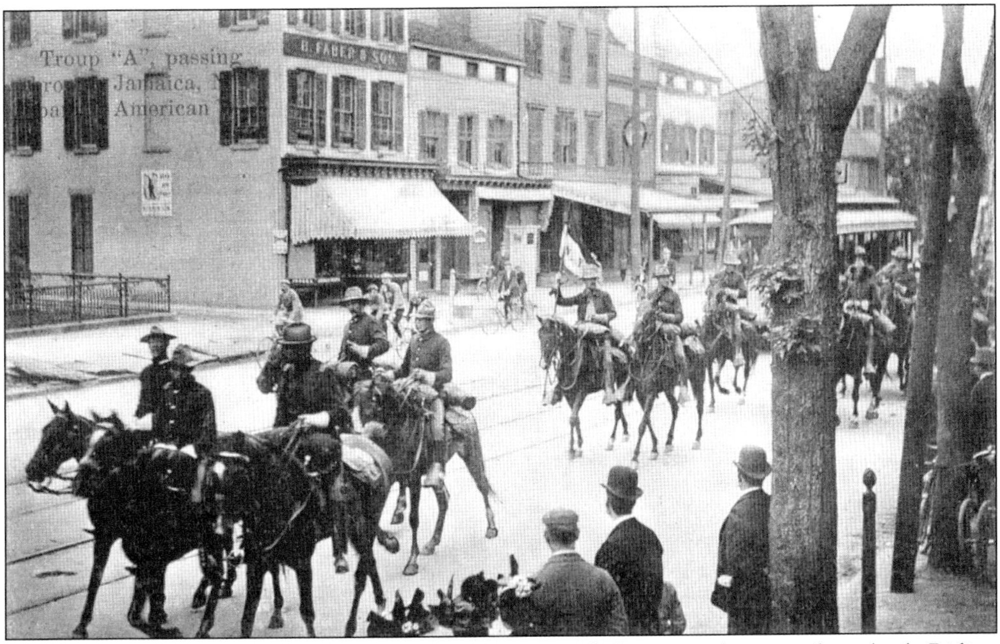

Here the residents of Jamaica line Jamaica Avenue to watch Company A pass on horseback. Riding west, they are about to pass in front of the Jamaica Town Hall whose garden fence is seen across the street. Note the old-fashioned hitching post in the foreground for tying one's horse.

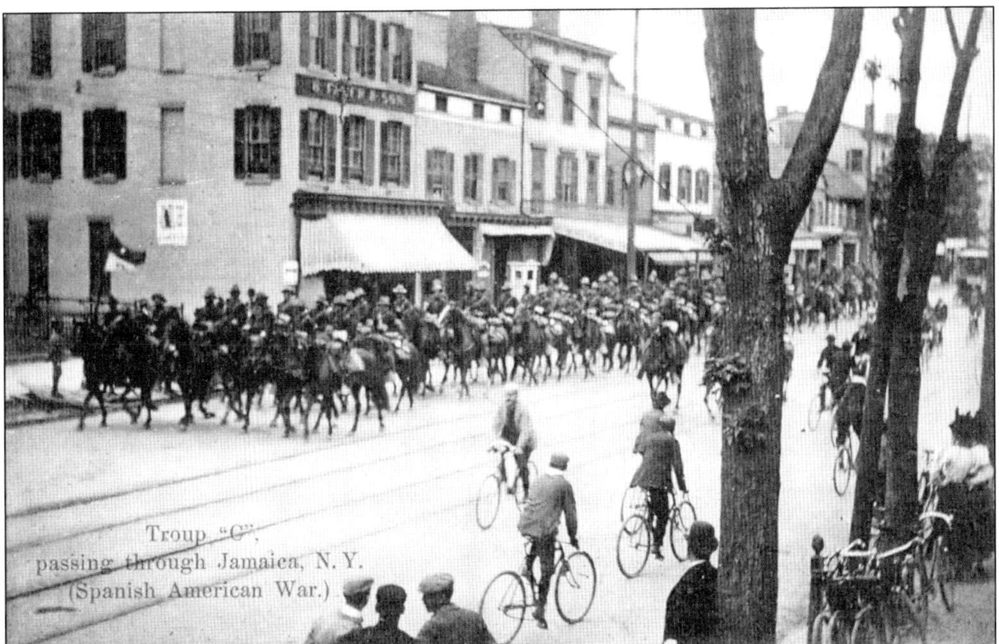

Company C passes along Jamaica Avenue. Note the other means of transportation of the day. The use of bicycles had gained popularity at the end of the 19th century. A monument to the Spanish American War can be found just north of the town in the community of Jamaica Hills in Captain Tilly Park. The photographs on this page date to 1898.

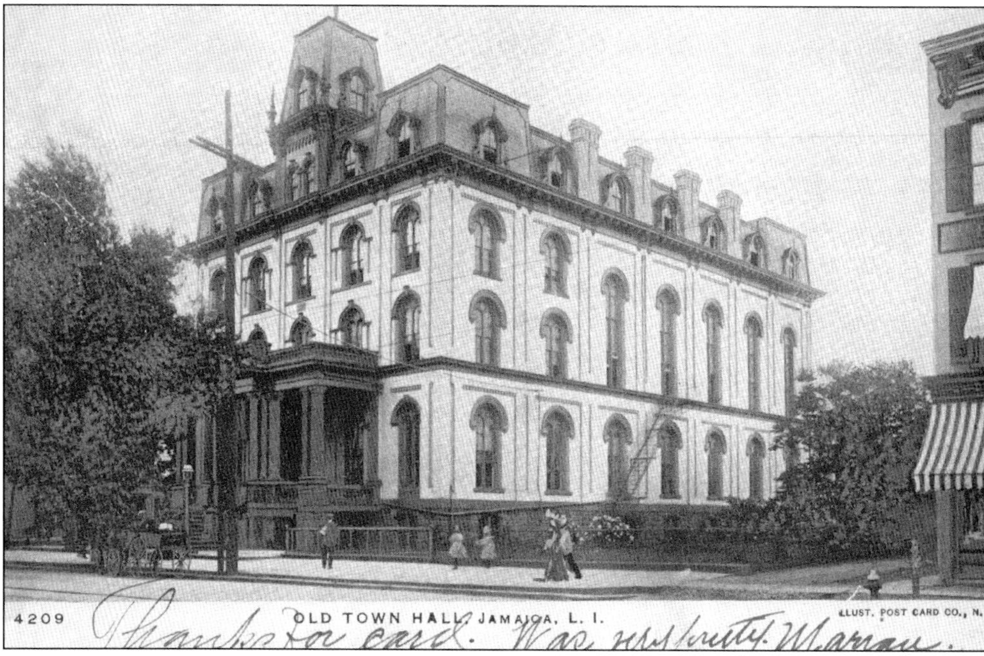

According to the *Long Island Democrat* in 1888, "A committee is in charge of establishing a temporary hospital. If the hospital is located in our Town Hall it seems that there will be some trouble, several clubs have decided to vacate as soon as it is placed there. Small-pox, typhoid fever, or the piercing screams of persons undergoing amputation will be everything but pleasant to endure thus their decision."

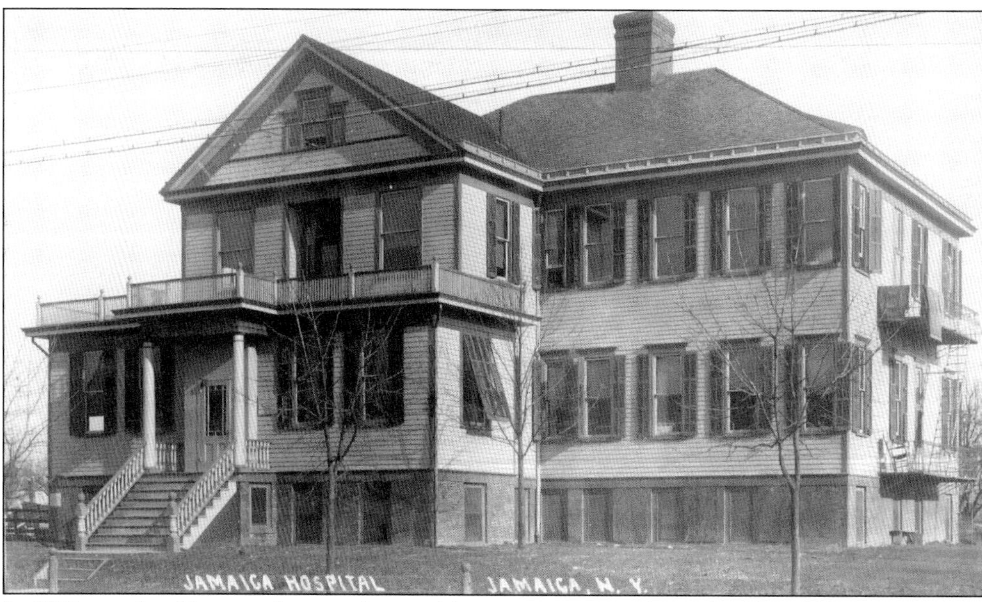

In 1883, people of Jamaica foresaw the need for an institution where the ill could be made well. A Hospital Fair raised $179.40, and a temporary hospital opened in 1891 in rented space at Jamaica Avenue and Canal Street (168th Street). The first permanent hospital, pictured above, was opened in 1898 at New York Avenue (Guy Brewer Boulevard). In 1924, a larger hospital opened on Van Wyck Boulevard (Expressway).

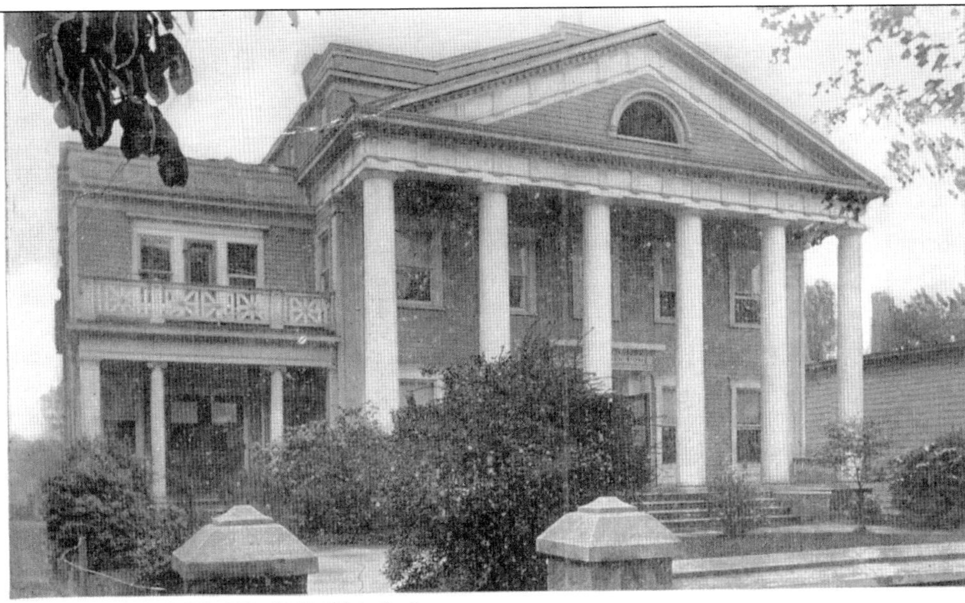

PUBLIC LIBRARY, JAMAICA, L. I.

The first Queens library was founded in 1858 in Flushing as a subscription service and became a free circulation library in 1869. In 1901, the city government proposed a charter joining all libraries in Queens into the Queens Borough Public Library. A Jamaica branch opened in 1906 in an antebellum schoolhouse and in 1911 moved to Colonial Hall, formerly the Ladies Seminary, pictured above.

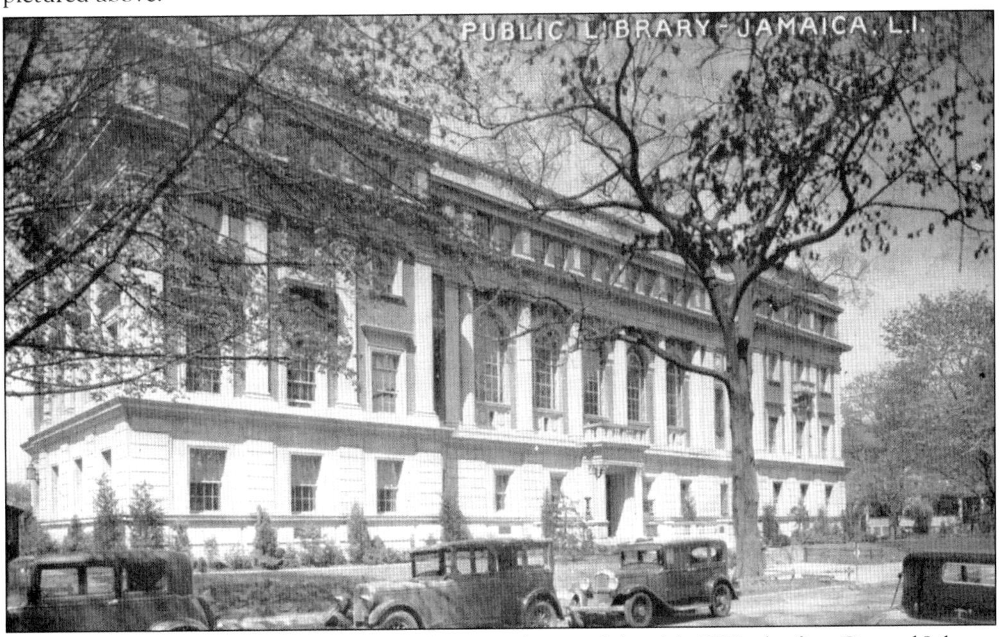

Located on Parsons Boulevard, pictured above, and opened April 1, 1930, the first Central Library was designed by R. F. Schirmer and J. W. Schmidt featuring marble staircases, bronze railings, high vaulted ceilings, and ornate chandeliers. Becoming inadequate to service the needs of the library, it moved to a new building on Merrick Boulevard, which was dedicated on April 11, 1966, and designed by the architects York and Sawyer, Kiff, Colean, Voss, and Souder.

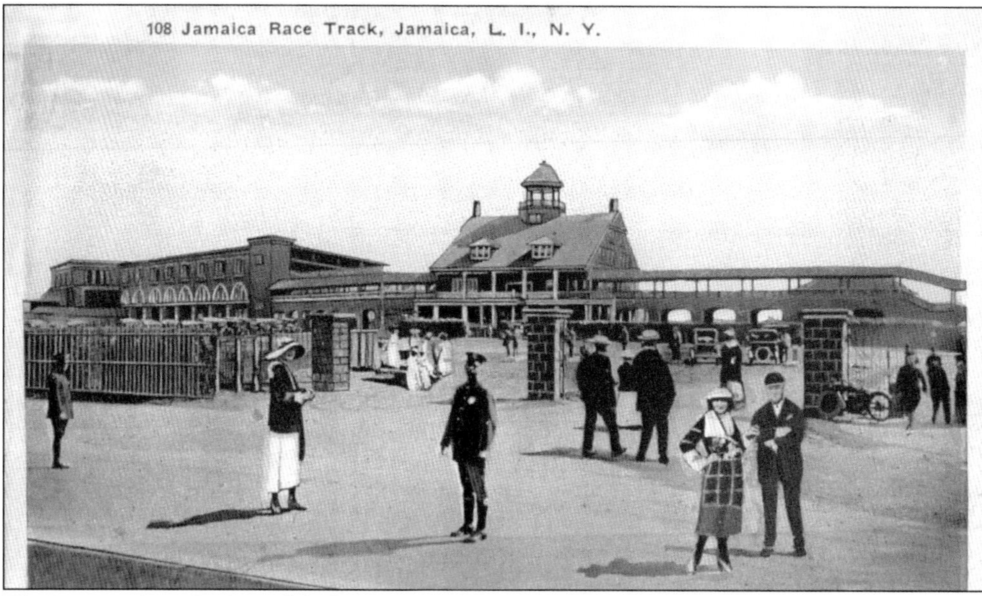

The Metropolitan Jockey Club (later Jamaica Race Track) opened on April 27 1903, attended by Lillian Russell, "Diamond Jim" Brady, and John F. "Bet-a-million" Gates. This and the Queens County Jockey Club (Aqueduct) provided convenient outlets for sportsmen and their money. The racetrack was closed in 1959 and demolished. On the property a residential cooperative designed by architect Herman Jessor and called Rochdale Village, after the English town of Rochdale, was built.

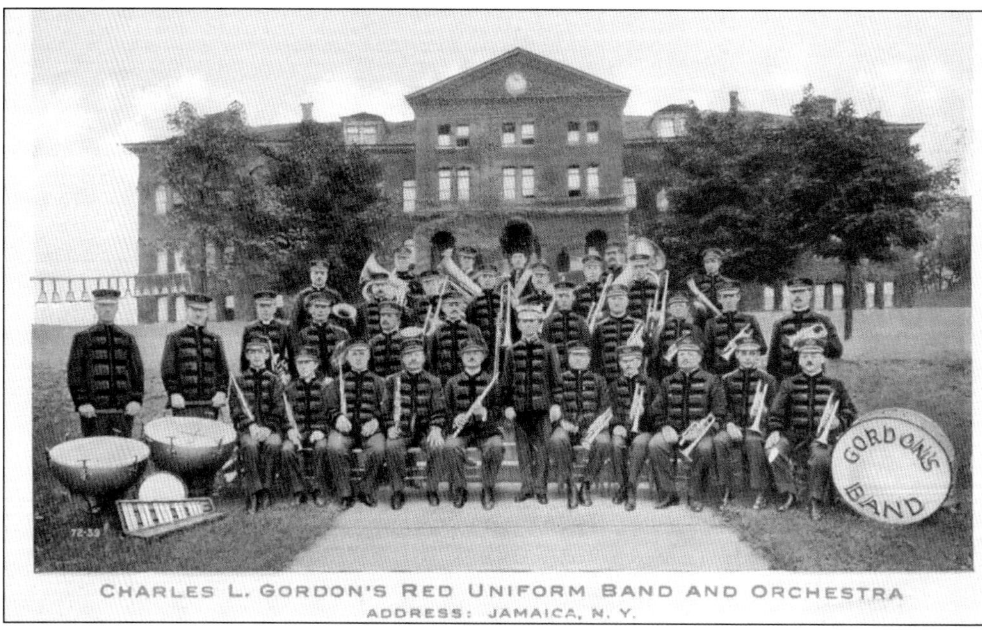

Music was always a part of the community. "The concert given by the Crescent Band of this village was a grand success. The large room of the Town Hall was filled by the friends of the members of the Band and our villagers. Under the leadership of Prof. E. Gerber, some fine music was rendered," according to the February 16, 1886, *Long Island Democrat*. Gordon's Band is pictured by the Jamaica State Normal School in 1914.

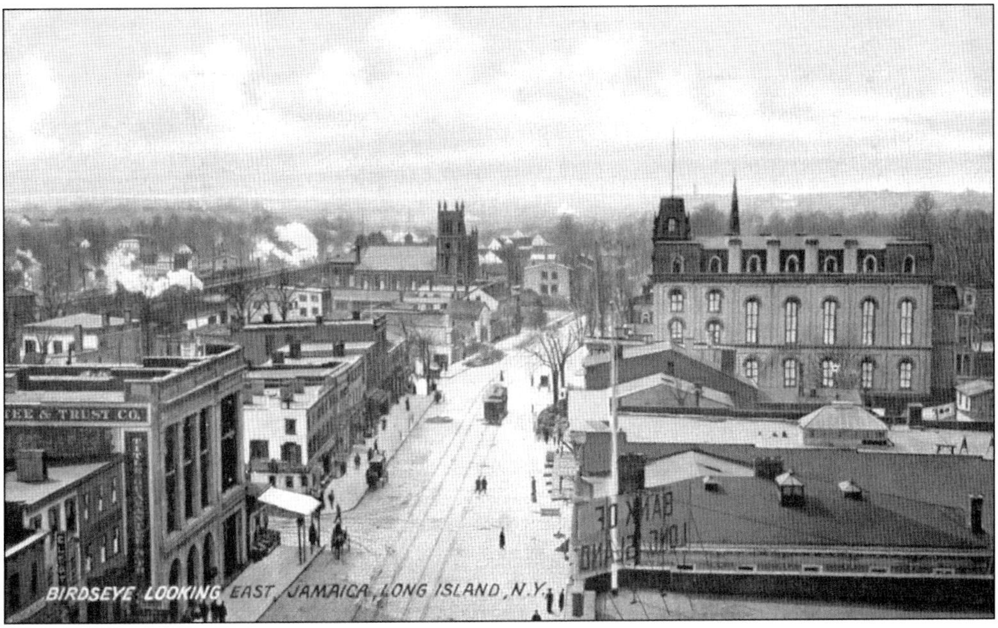

This mislabeled postcard looks west, not east. Jamaica Town Hall is on the right, and behind it is the steeple of Grace Episcopal Church. To the left are the towers of the Dutch Reform Church. Behind the church was located the Jamaica Train Depot. Near to the trolley in the center is the location of the hotel where George Washington spent an enjoyable night in 1790.

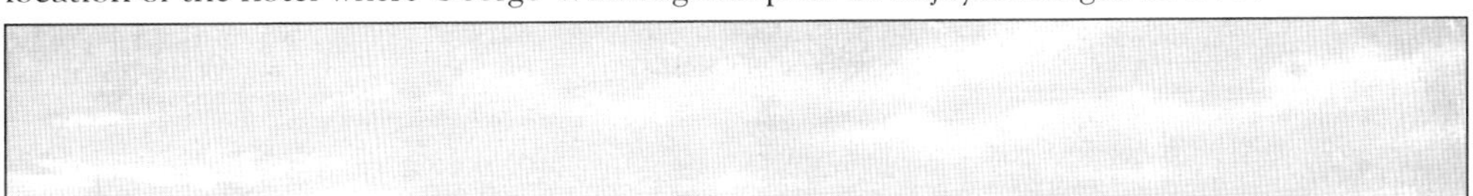

This mislabeled postcard looks east, not west. In the foreground is the First Presbyterian Church founded in 1662, the oldest continuously serving Presbyterian church in America. In the distance on the right is the First Methodist Church. The building to the right with the circular drive is Colonial Hall and was the Ladies Seminary of Union Hall Academy. In 1868, Gen. Tom Thumb made a special appearance at Union Hall Academy.

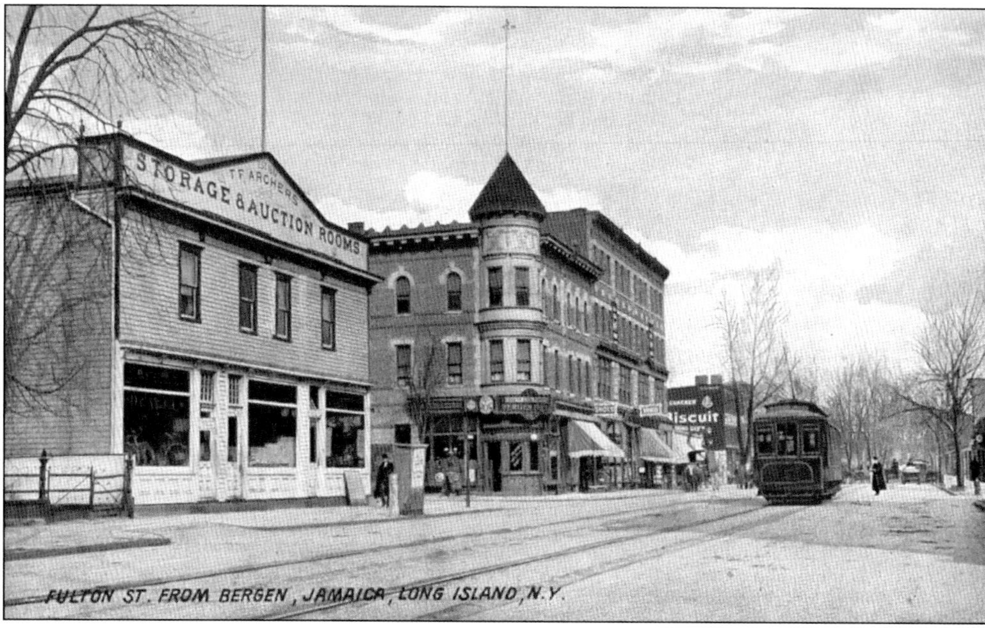

Theodore Archer, born in 1837, became a builder and real estate speculator in Long Island City. Wiped out by the panic of 1873, he came to Jamaica and resumed his real estate speculations, becoming one of the most extensive dealers and auctioneers of land on Long Island. Upon his death, Archer Avenue was named to honor his memory. These buildings were located on the corner of Fulton Street (Jamaica Avenue) and Bergen Avenue (Merrick Boulevard).

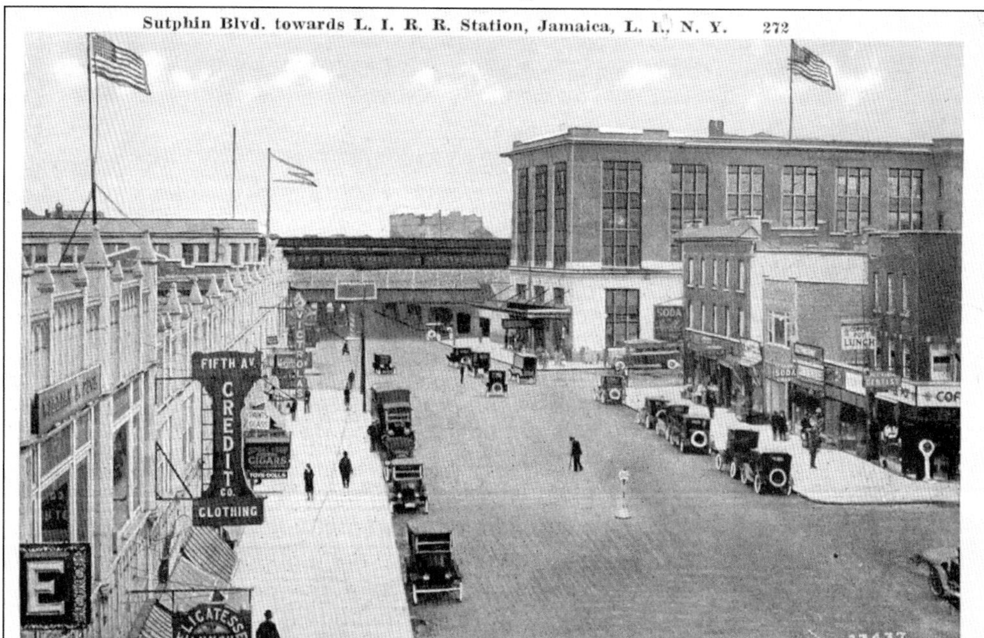

To the right is the brick LIRR station. John Henry Sutphin was another well-known Jamaica resident who was honored with a street named after him. He served as deputy county clerk of Queens and formed the Jamaica Saving Bank and was its president. A philanthropist, he gave away $2 million to those in need, paying rent for 55 families and asking for nothing in return.

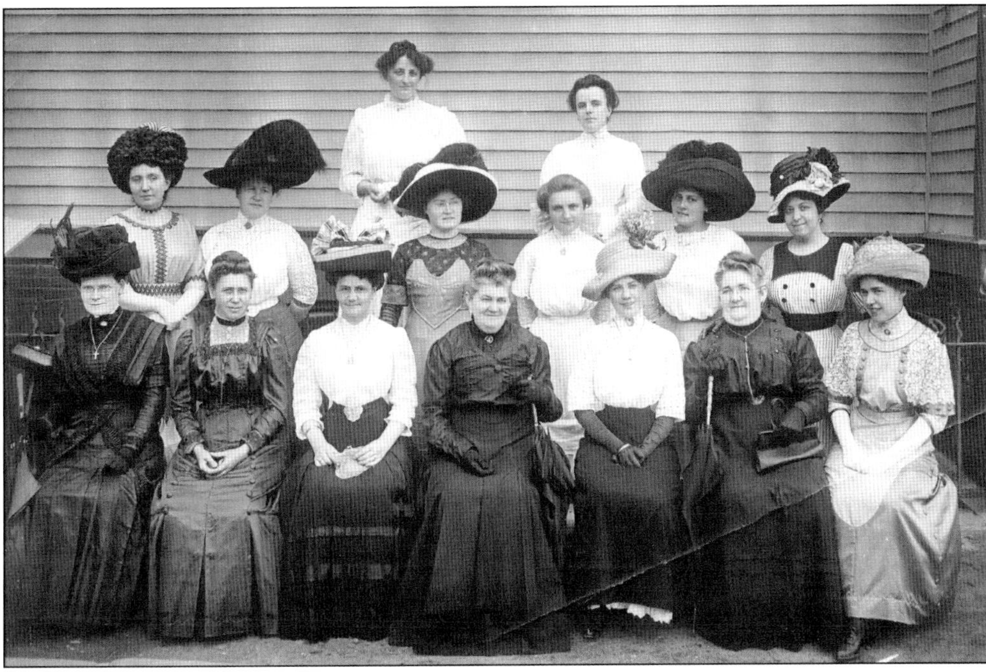

This photograph is by Jamaica photographer Frederick Weber of the Ladies Society of Saint Mary's Catholic Church. Jamaica had many clubs, including the Jamaica Rod and Gun Club established in 1875; the Jamaica Women's Club of 1880; the King's Manor Association devoted to historic preservation; the Cleff Club, a musical association of 1898; and the Jamaica Camera Club of 1904. The King's Daughters of the Grace Episcopal Church were instrumental in the organization of Jamaica Hospital.

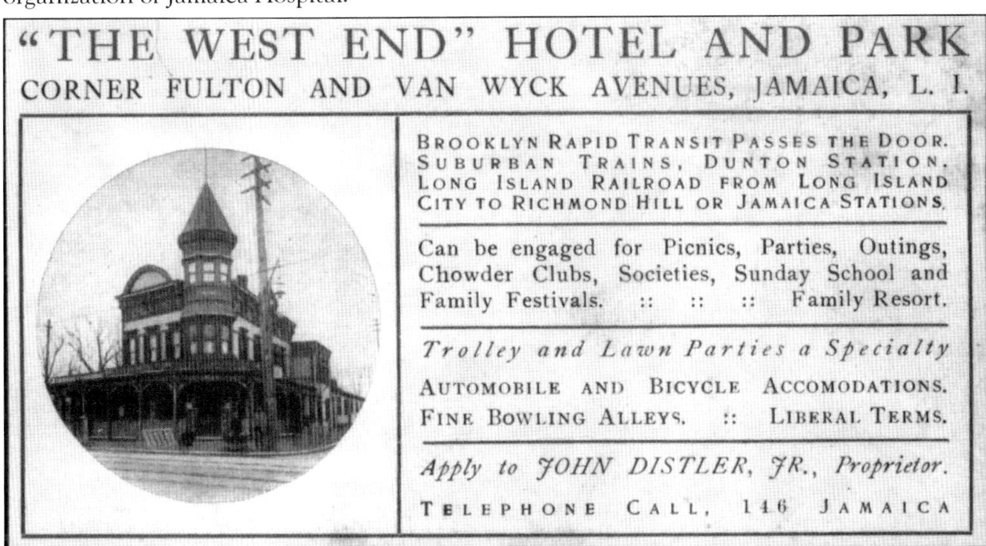

John Distler was the successful owner of the West End Hotel, located at Jamaica (Fulton) Avenue and Van Wyck Avenue (Expressway), that boasted fine dining and entertainment. It had a large dance pavilion and a parklike setting. Today the location of this hotel would be in the center of the busy Van Wyck Expressway traffic. The once narrow Van Wyck Avenue was widened into a major expressway.

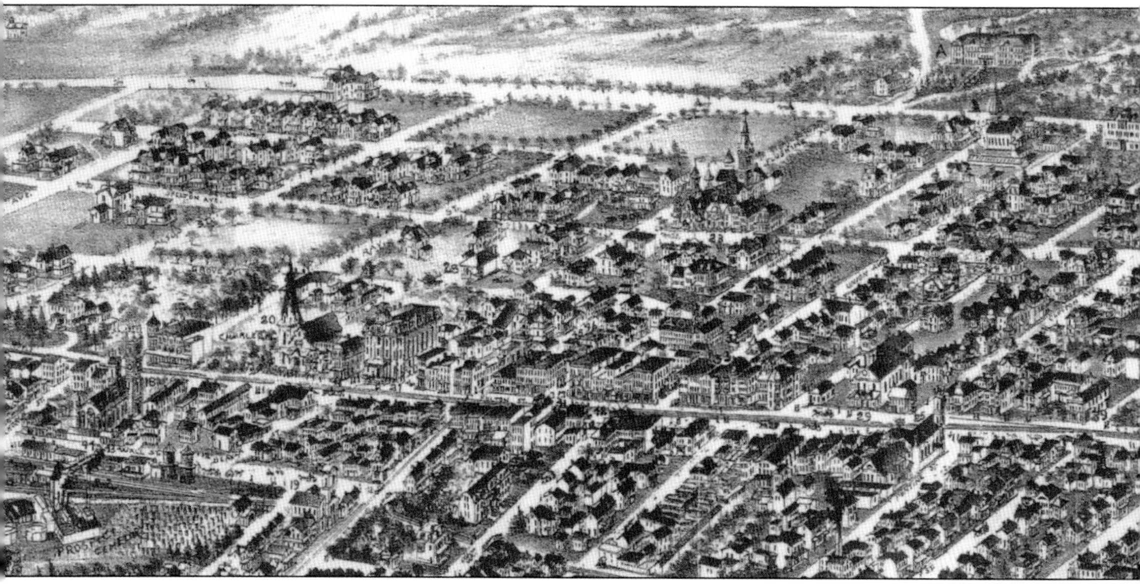

This is the heart of the Jamaica community. In the foreground is Jamaica Avenue and above it is Hillside Avenue. At top right is the Jamaica State Normal School (Labeled A). To the right is Jamaica High School, and next to it, No. 24, is the Church of St. Paul. Starting at the left along Jamaica Avenue is the home of Rufus King with circular drive; the Dutch Reformed church across the street is No. 18; and Grace Episcopal Church is No. 20. The next structure is the town hall, No. 21, located at the corner of Flushing Avenue (Parsons Boulevard). Behind it is the Baptist church, No. 28. Further back to the right is St. Mary's German Catholic Church, No. 23. Back on Jamaica Avenue with No. 29 is the Presbyterian church, and across the street is the Methodist Church, No. 25. At bottom left is Prospect Cemetery, and next to it, No. 19, is Saint Monica's Catholic Church.

Two

The Daughter Village
Jamaica Estates

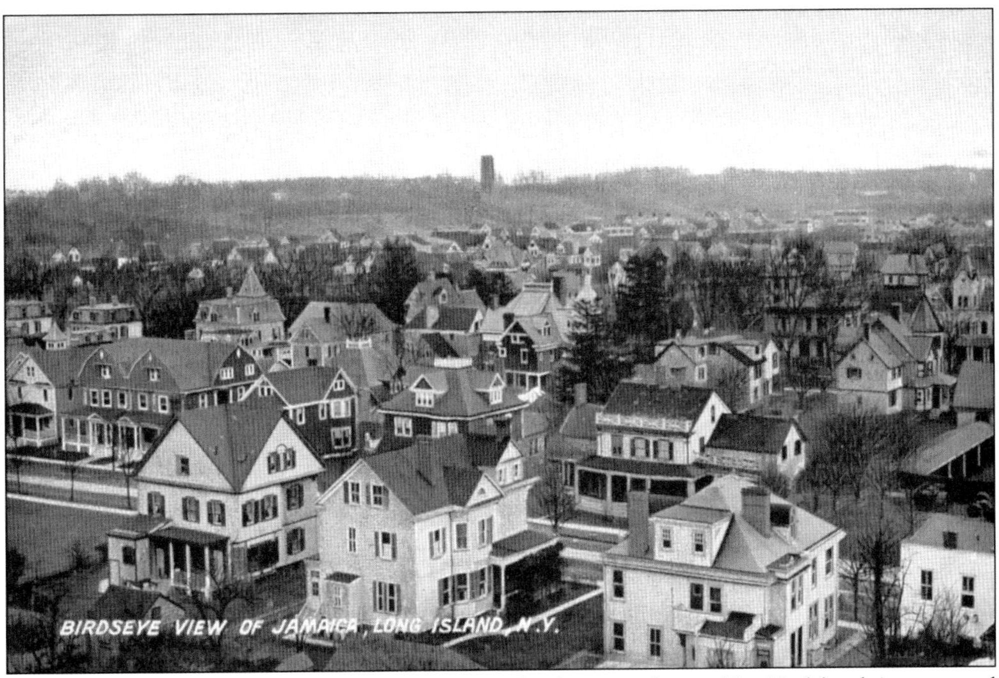

The hilly area to the right of the water tower in the distance (located by Highland Avenue and Homelawn Street today) is the future home of Jamaica Estates. The forest-covered hills served the Jamaica community as their playground. In the summer, hiking, picnics, swimming, and opossum hunting occurred. In winter, sledding down the slopes and ice-skating on the frozen ponds were popular.

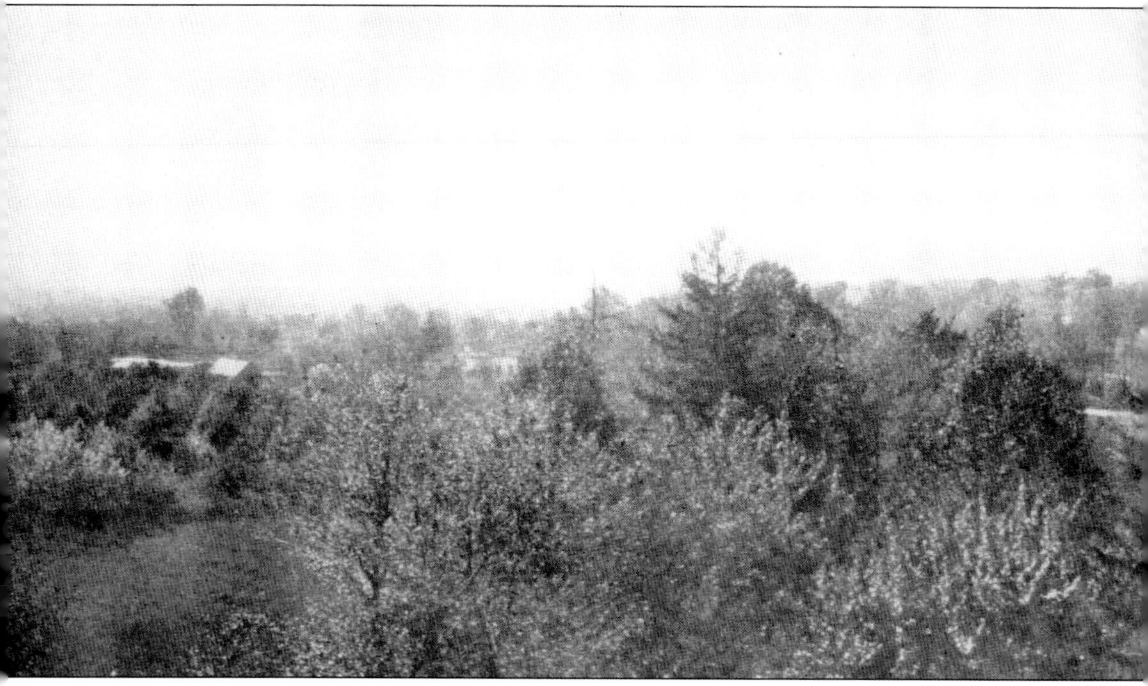

The Ice Age stopped here 10,000 years ago, creating the terminal moraine stretching across Staten Island, Brooklyn, and Queens. As a glacier moved, it eroded the landscape by abrasion and picked up material such as soil, rocks, and massive boulders that were carried inside the ice. It is estimated

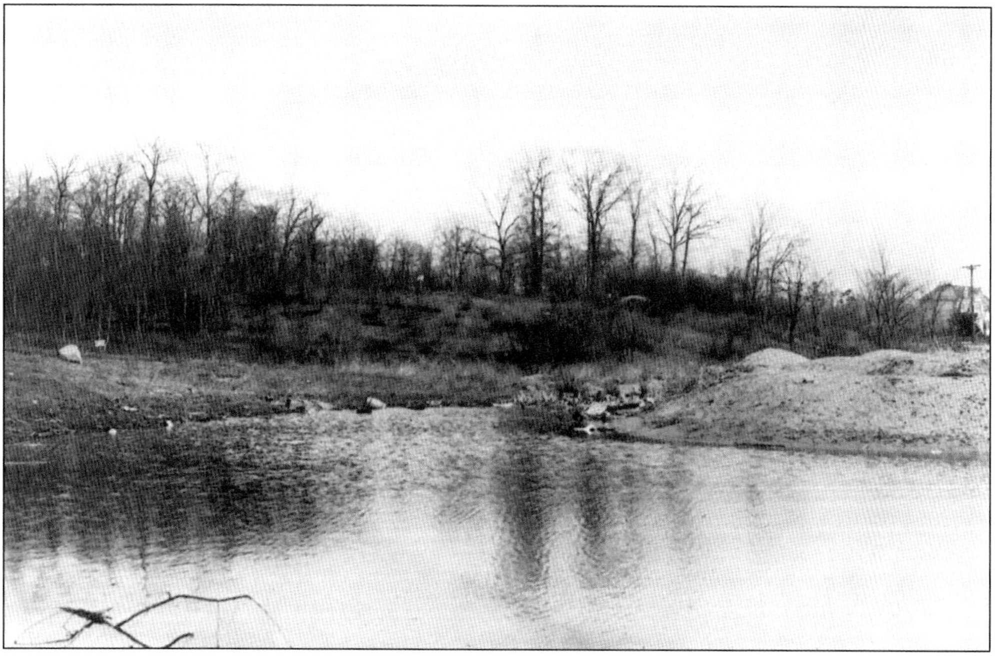

This glacial pond, called Redder's Pond and having a size of 2 to 3 acres, was once located near the head of present-day Homelawn Street. Now drained, the Grand Central Parkway runs through this pond today. (Courtesy of the Queens Borough Public Library, Long Island Division, Eugene L. Armbruster Collection.)

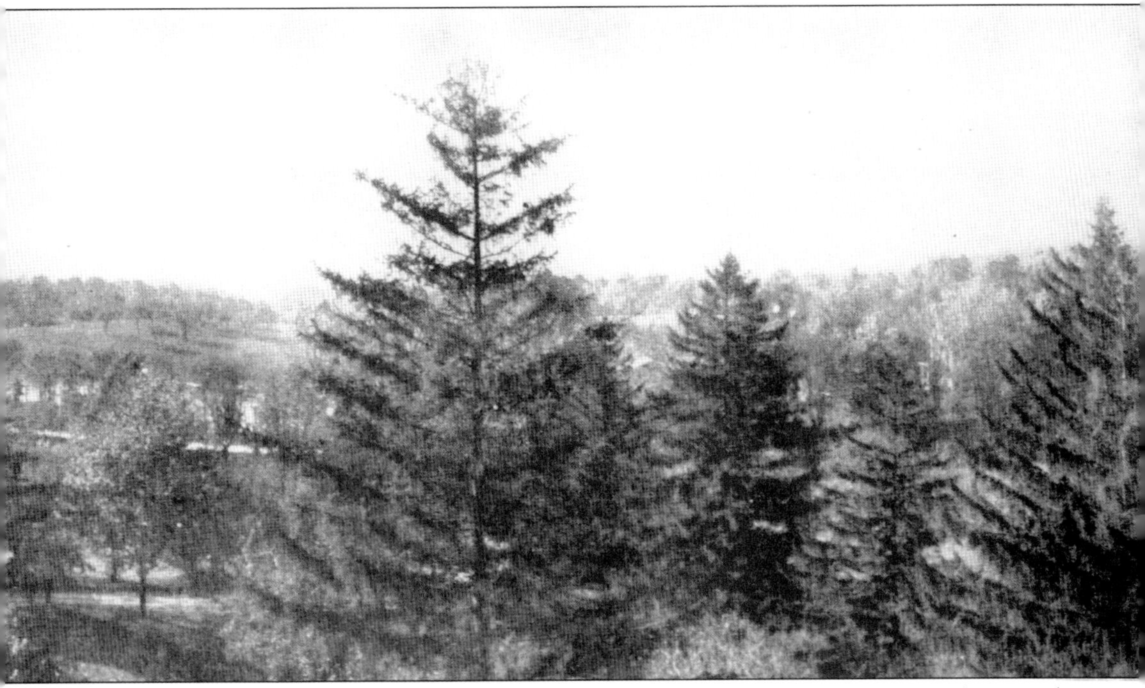

that the glacier was over a mile high. When the glacier stopped and melted, the materials trapped in the ice were deposited at the end of the glacier forming the hilly terminal moraine. The melting of the glaciers created a washout that leveled the land all the way to Jamaica Bay.

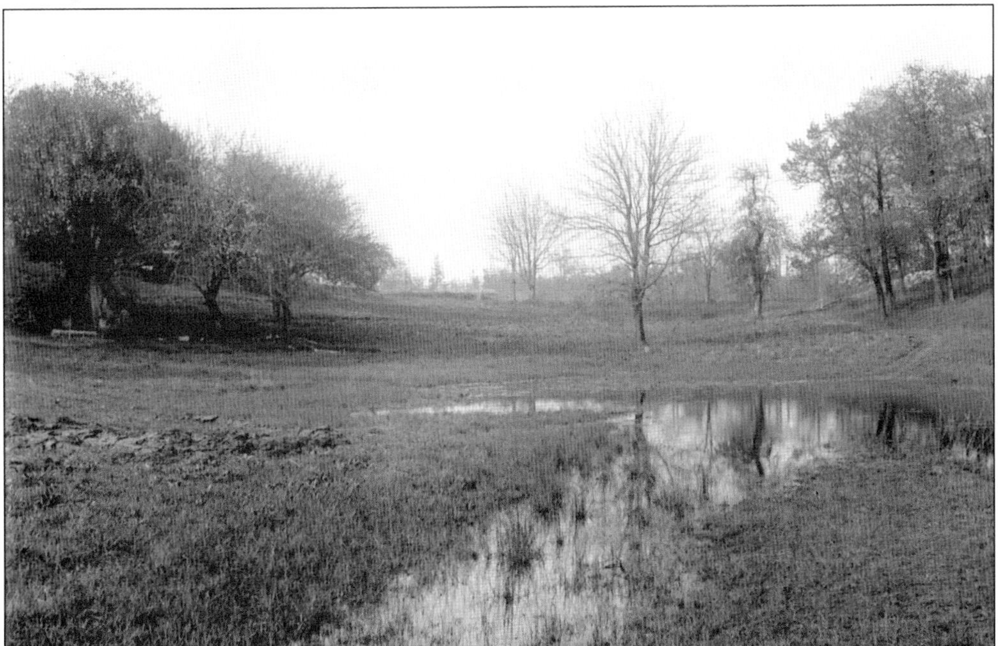

According to the *New York Times* on January 6, 1908, "Three persons lost their lives in the icy waters of Redder's Pond due to the treacherous condition of the ice covering the pond." (Courtesy of the Queens Borough Public Library, Long Island Division, George Winans Collection.)

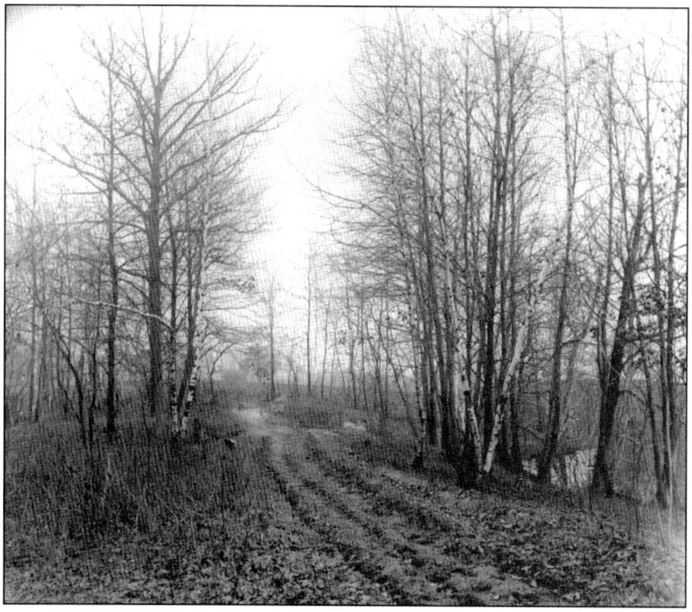

This tree-lined path was located in the hills north of Jamaica. The area that became Jamaica Estates offered an escape from the congestion of the crowded cities. (Courtesy of the Queens Borough Public Library, Long Island Division, George Winans Collection.)

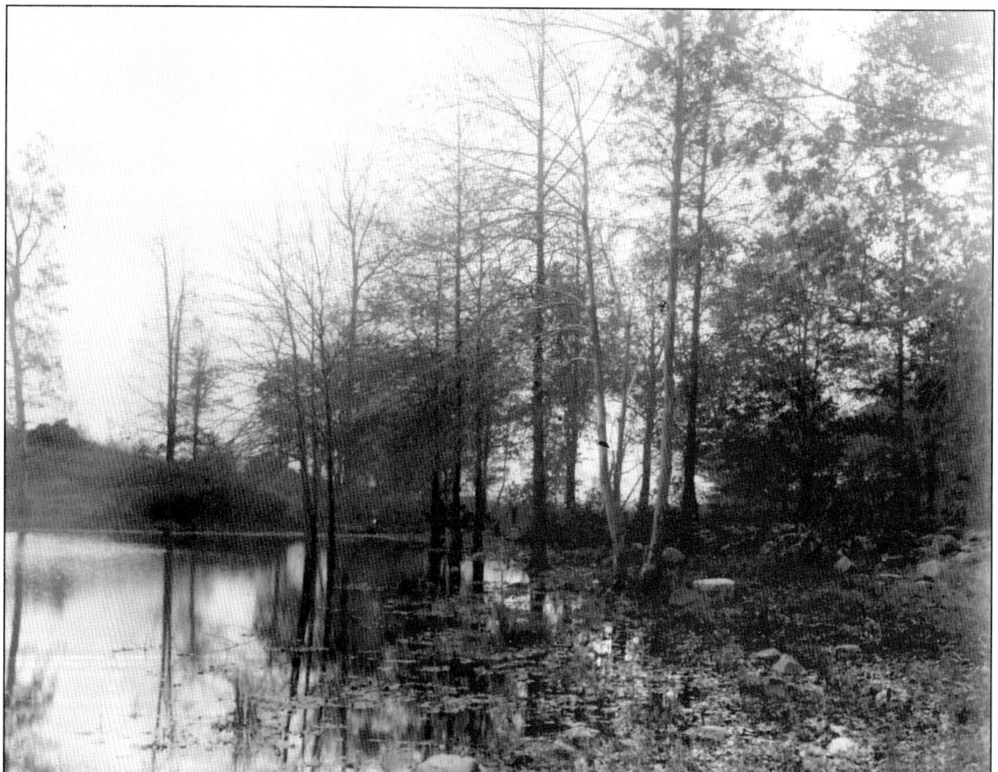

According to the *Long Island Democrat* on October 27, 1874, "Mark Oswald went hunting in the woods and observed a large black snake. He exclaimed, 'There's a snake!' Reversing his gun he struck the snake, discharging a quantity of shot into his brain and through the top of his skull, killing him instantly." (Courtesy of the Queens Borough Public Library, Long Island Division, George Winans Collection.)

This 1903 photograph by Amy Phelps was taken in the woods north of Jamaica. According to the *Long Island Democrat* on August 6, 1867, "The ladies whose words are like dewdrops to thirsty flowers, or as the sweet perfume of the honey suckle were out in full force, and made the woods ring loud and clear with their musical tones." (Courtesy of the Queens Borough Public Library, Long Island Division, George Winans Collection.)

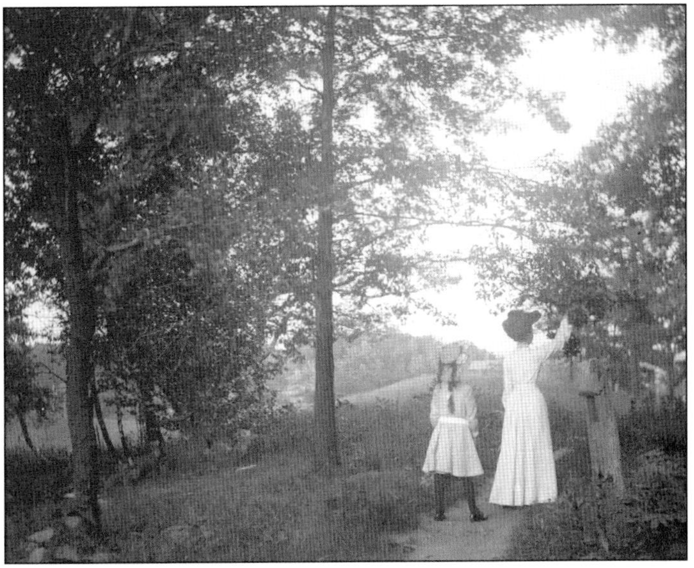

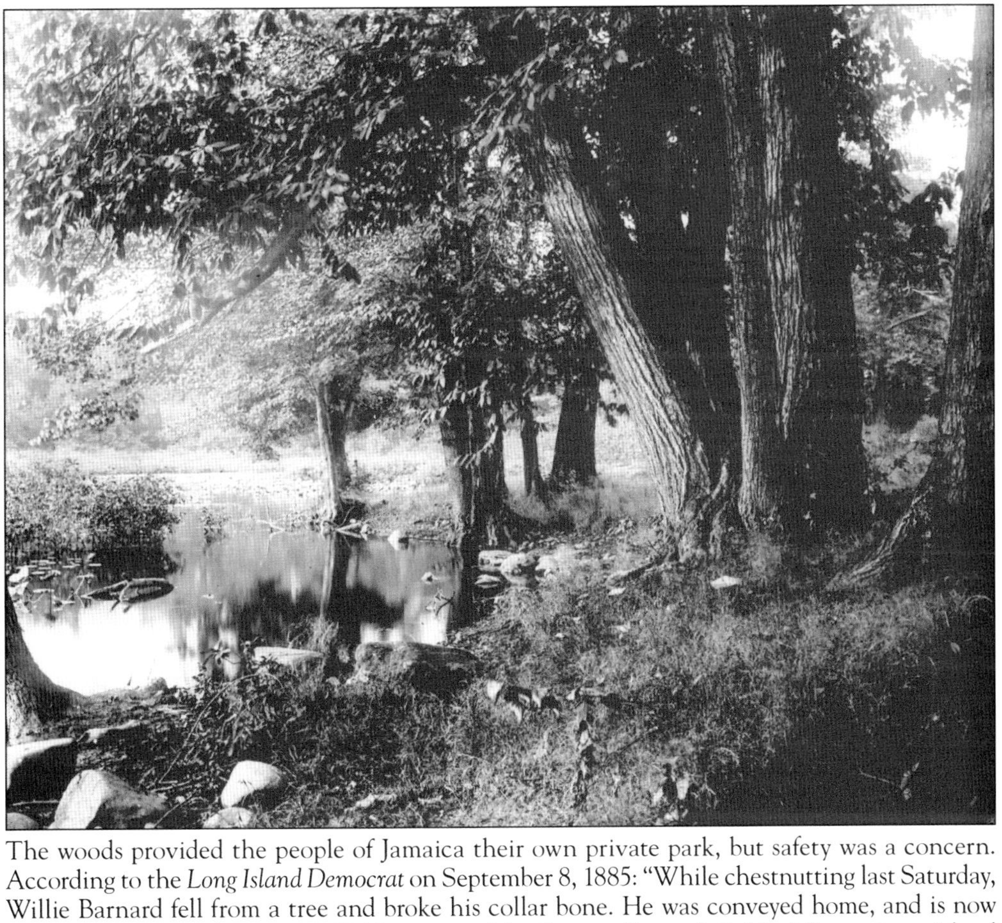

The woods provided the people of Jamaica their own private park, but safety was a concern. According to the *Long Island Democrat* on September 8, 1885: "While chestnutting last Saturday, Willie Barnard fell from a tree and broke his collar bone. He was conveyed home, and is now doing as well as can be expected." (Courtesy of the Queens Borough Public Library, Long Island Division, George Winans Collection.)

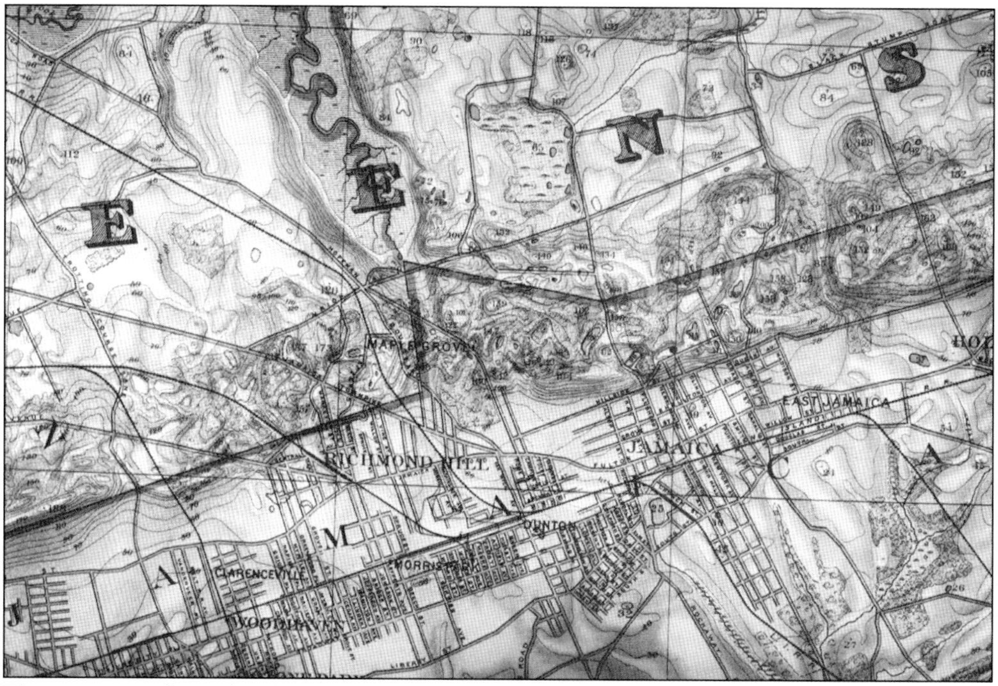

This 1892 map shows the elevation of the Terminal Moraine north of Jamaica. Maple Grove refers to the cemetery of the same name, now in Kew Gardens. Some towns like Clarenceville, Morris Park, Dunton, and East Jamaica have ceased to exist. The Jamaica Estates community began north of what was called East Jamaica at the right. Note the glacial ponds that once dotted the area.

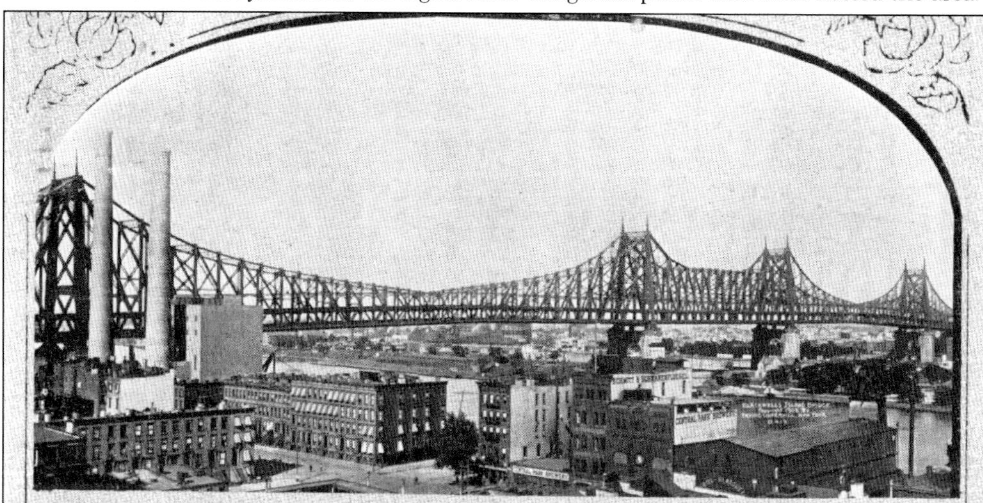

Proposals for a bridge linking Manhattan to Queens were first made in 1838. Construction began in 1903 and completed in 1909 due to delays from the collapse of an incomplete span during a windstorm and from labor unrest. The bridge cost $18 million and 50 lives. It opened the development of Queens to land speculators who realized that having a country home while working in the city was now possible.

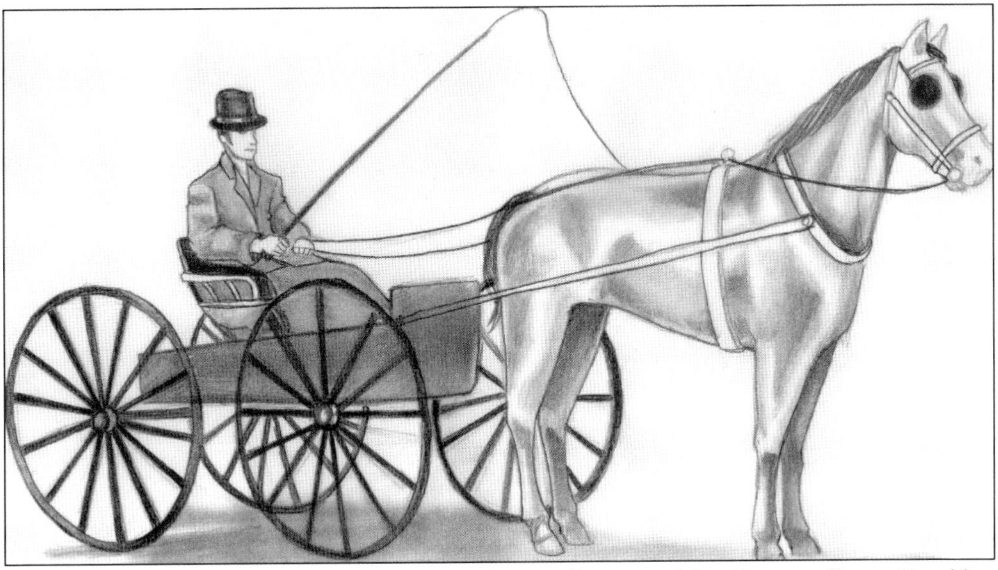

Born in Illinois, March 24, 1865, Ernestus Gulick opened a successful real estate office in Brooklyn in 1883. Creator of the Ernestus Gulick Company, he was also founder and first president of the Jamaica Estates Corporation. According to Gulick in the *New York Times* on January 5, 1908, "The physical joining of Manhattan Island with Long Island by tunnels and bridges must cause a rise in values which no financial depression can possibly stop." (Illustration by Kem Boatwright.)

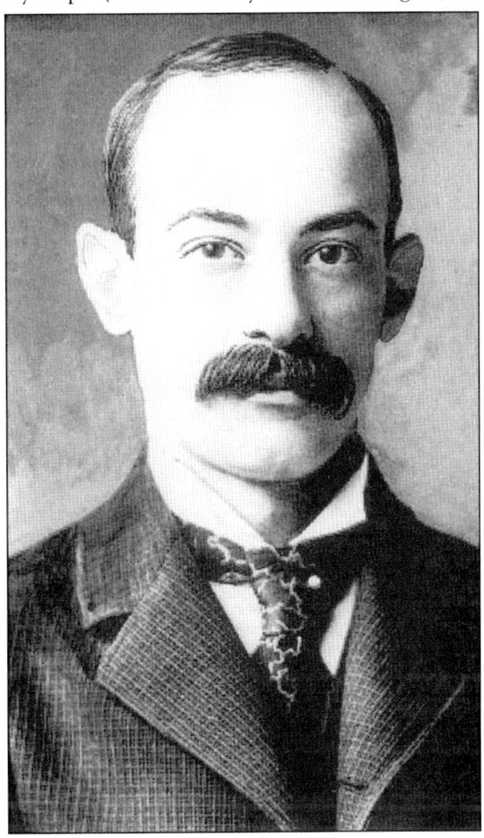

Born in 1874, by the age of 33 Felix Isman had amassed a fortune estimated at $30 million. He was a noted real estate speculator and a theatrical manager and stunned New Yorkers in 1902 by spending $1.55 million for property on the southeast corner of Fifth Avenue and Forty-second Street. Isman's famous doctrine was, "You can be 75 percent wrong and still make money in Manhattan real estate."

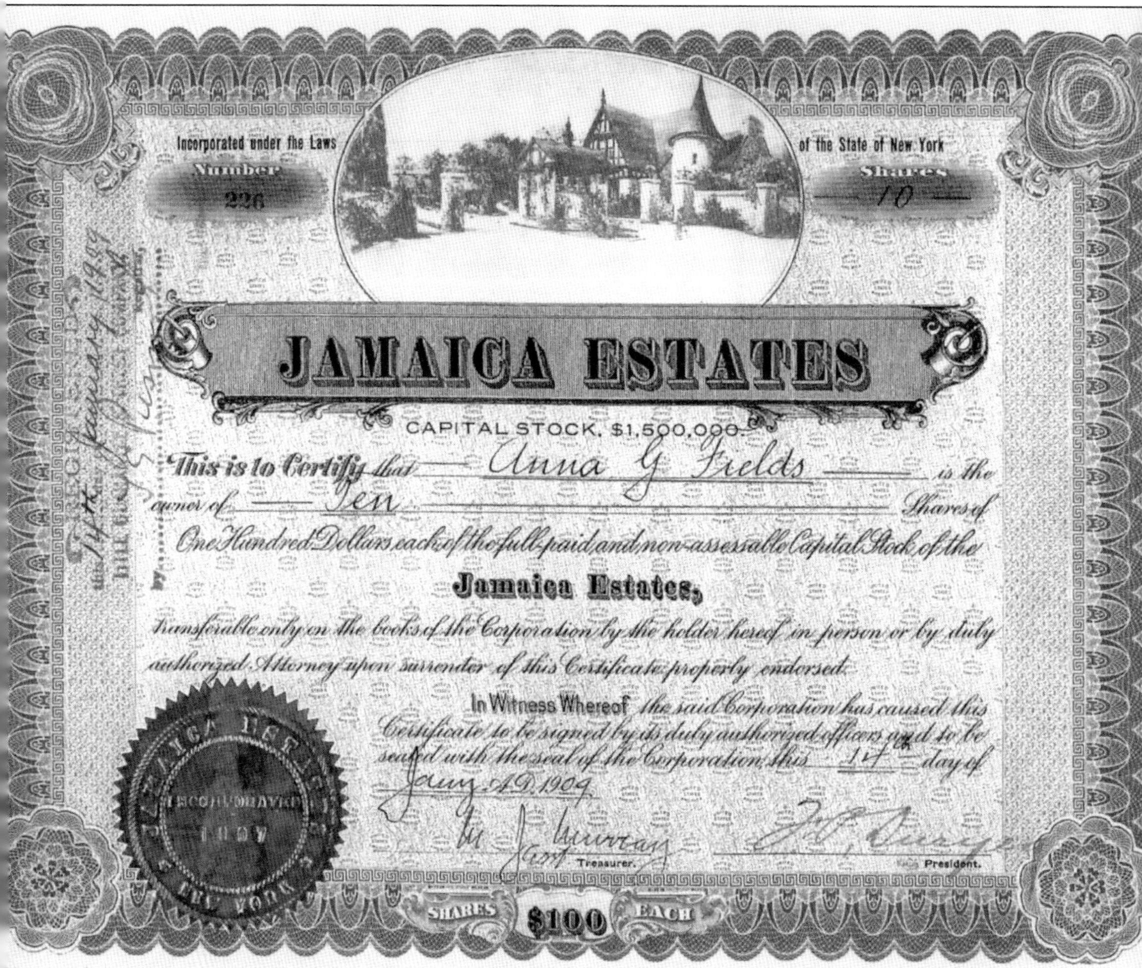

Incorporated under the Laws of the State of New York

Number 226

Shares 10

JAMAICA ESTATES

CAPITAL STOCK, $1,500,000.

This is to Certify that Anna G Fields is the owner of Ten Shares of One Hundred Dollars each of the full paid and non-assessable Capital Stock of the

Jamaica Estates,

transferable only on the books of the Corporation by the holder hereof in person or by duly authorized Attorney upon surrender of this Certificate properly endorsed.

In Witness Whereof the said Corporation has caused this Certificate to be signed by its duly authorized officers and to be sealed with the seal of the Corporation this 14th day of Jany A.D. 1909

Treasurer.

President.

SHARES $100 EACH

According to the *Long Island Farmer* on August 13, 1907, "The initial step in what promises to be an important realty development in Jamaica has been taken in the incorporation of Jamaica Estates in the offices of the Ernestus Gulick Company last week." This stock certificate to Anna G. Fields for 10 shares is signed by then Jamaica Estates vice president Franklin P. Duryea on January 14, 1909. On the golden seal are the words, "Jamaica Estates, New York Incorporated 1907."

An August 11, 1907, *New York Times* article lists Ernestus Gulick and Felix Isman of the Jamaica Estates Corporation as the "moving spirits" who will develop 500 acres or 8,000 city lots north of Jamaica. It was to be a "Long Island Tuxedo Park." The entrance lodge was designed by John Petit of Kirby, Petit, and Green, and the street system was designed by landscape designer Charles Leavitt. Timothy L. Woodruff and Michael J. Degnon are mentioned.

TO DEVELOP 8,000 LOTS.

Plans of Messrs. Gulick and Isman Involving Large Tract at Jamaica.

Ernestus Gulick and Felix Isman of Philadelphia are the moving spirits in the new Jamaica Estates Corporation, which will immediately open and improve a 500-acre tract, some 8,000 city lots, on high ground at Jamaica.

It is the intention of the promoters to make the place a Long Island Tuxedo, and the thorough way in which this is to be done is evidenced by the drawings for the stone entrance lodge at Hillside Avenue Boulevard, which have been prepared for Jamaica Estates by John J. Petit, of Kirby, Petit & Green. The lodge will cost $50,000. A wide boulevard is being opened across Jamaica Estates, connecting with Hillside Avenue, the main motor car thoroughfare from this city to all Long Island, and at this intersection the attractive lodge is to be built. The boulevard is to be paved and parked, while Charles W. Leavitt, the landscape architect, has devised an unusually attractive street system.

Besides Major Gulick and Mr. Isman, those interested in Jamaica Estates are Franklin P. Duryea, Clayton C. Goss, George J. Smith, ex-Gov. Myron T. Herrick of Ohio, ex-Controller Edward M. Grout, Timothy L. Woodruff, and Michael J. Degnon.

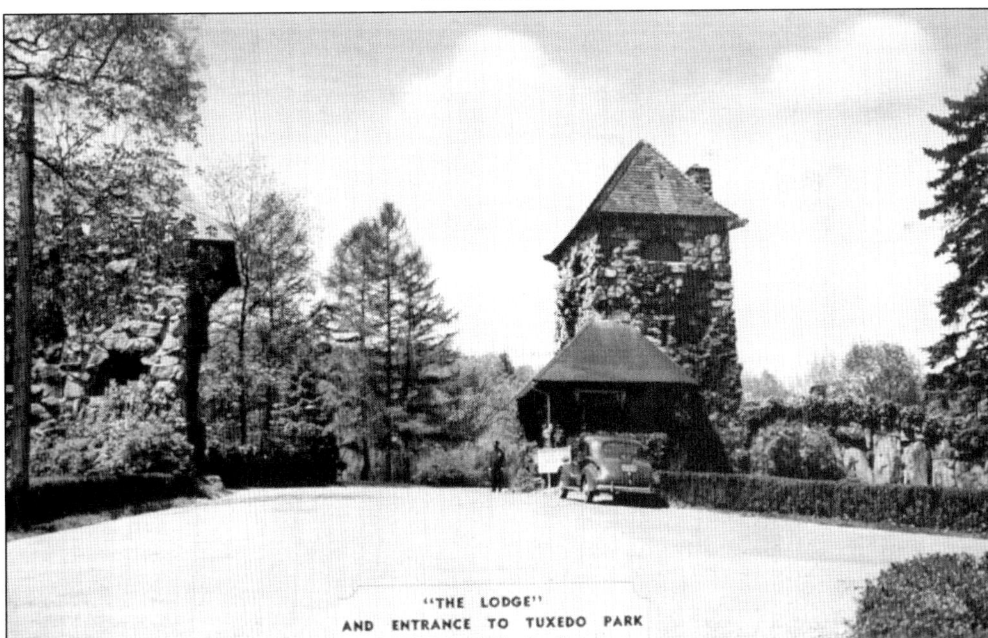

Tuxedo Park was developed as a resort for blue blood society, the financial, industrial, and social leaders of the day in 1885. Some 20 miles of roads, a gate, a clubhouse, and three dams were created and were the model for Jamaica Estates. The evening attire known as the tuxedo, takes its name from Tuxedo Park, where it was said to have been worn for the first time in America.

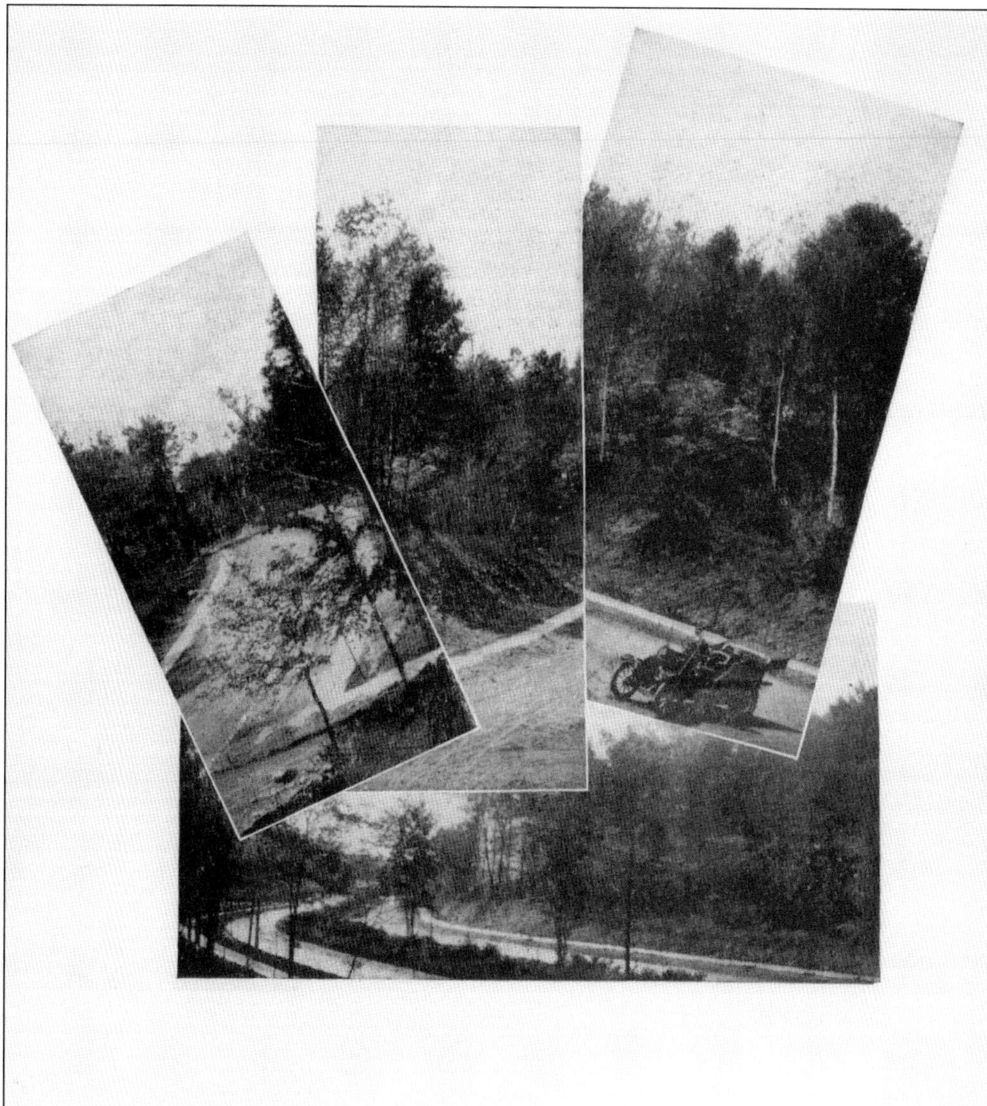

According to the *New York Times* on May 31, 1908, "The residential park, laid out and developed idealistically, with an eye to beauty and exclusiveness rather than to profitable economy of space, has become the most pleasing and attractive feature of the building up of Long Island as a land of homes. The idea is now being carried out in various parts of the island. First of all the developer finds the spot desired and purchases it as it stands, with its virgin beauty unmarred. He is prepared and ready to spend a big pot of money in preserving and improving the natural beauties of his holding before even attempting to market a single foot of the land. If there exists a pretty vista, his care is to preserve it, rather than destroy it by selling a plot or two to advantage. On the wooded heights north of Jamaica the Jamaica Estates Company, of which Ernestus Gulick is President and Felix Isman Vice President, is making a beautiful residential park."

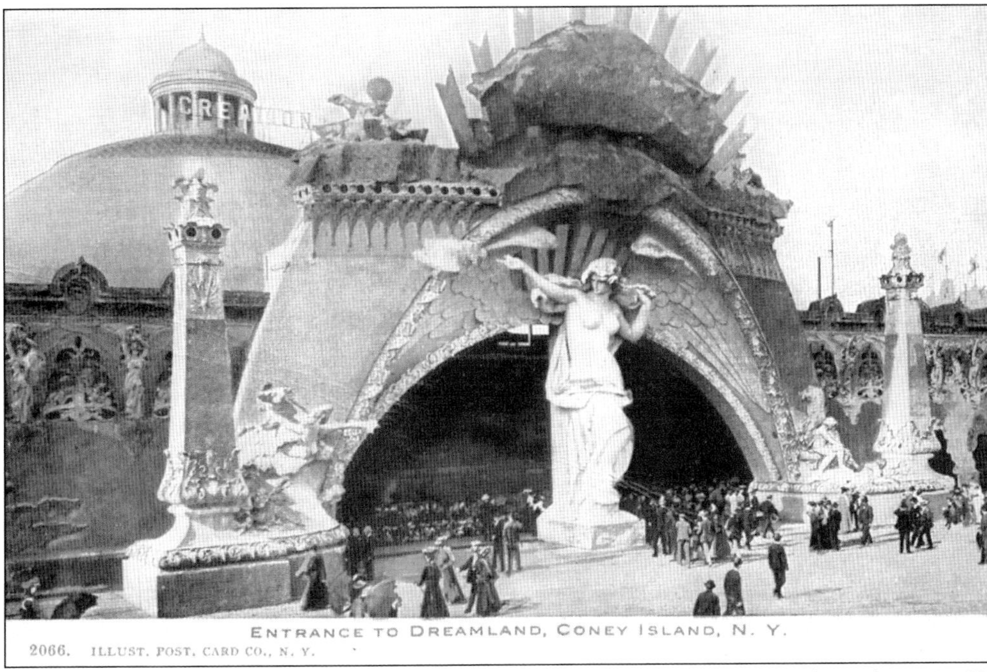

Architect John C. Petit (1870–1923) established a practice in Brooklyn during the early 1890s. He was a partner in the architectural firm of Kirby, Petit, and Green, active during the first decade of the 20th century. They designed the American Bank Note Company in New York City and the historic Hearst Building in San Francisco. In 1904, they designed the amusement park Dreamland at Coney Island with the elaborate entrance shown above.

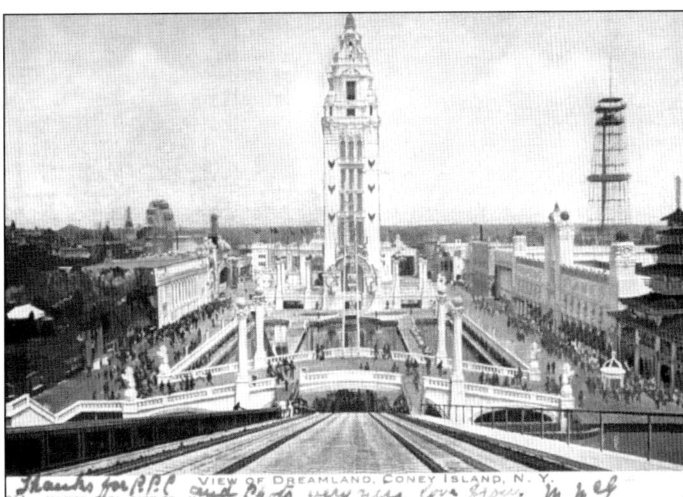

The architects were given free rein to design this park. A central lagoon was surrounded with broad avenues that offered wonderful ocean views and cooling sea breezes. At high tide, the floodgates were opened, filling the central lagoon with fresh saltwater. The buildings were designed in a variety of architectural styles that contained a variety of attractions. A Japanese pagoda can be seen at the right.

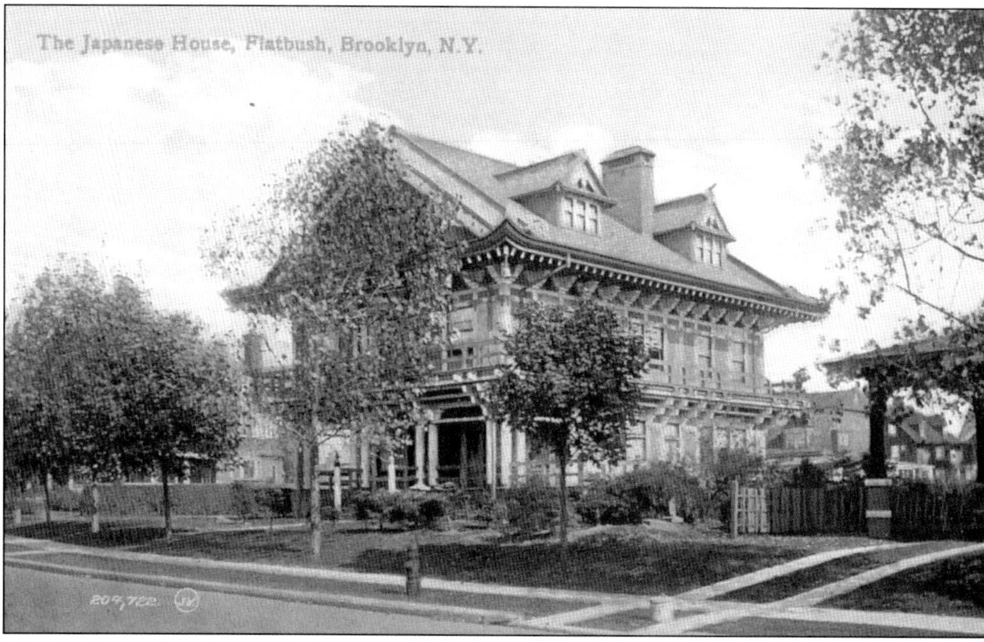

John C. Petit is best known for his residential work in Brooklyn's Prospect South Historic District. He was the official architect employed by the developer of this area and several of his designs were published in *Architects' and Builders' Magazine*. Between Church Avenue and Albemarle Road is his most famous residential work—the Japanese House.

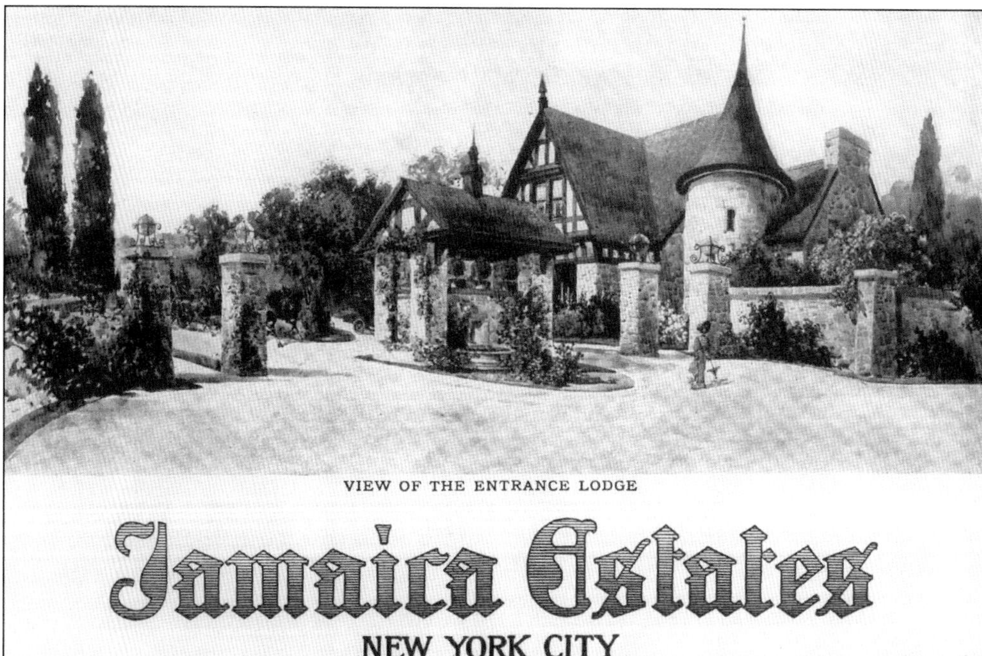

Architect Petit designed the $50,000 entrance at Hillside Avenue. According to a *New York Times* article on May 3, 1908, "In keeping with the generally high character of improvements planned by the Jamaica Estates Corporation is the new Elizabethan Lodge, with imposing pillars and gateways, just completed at the entrance to the property."

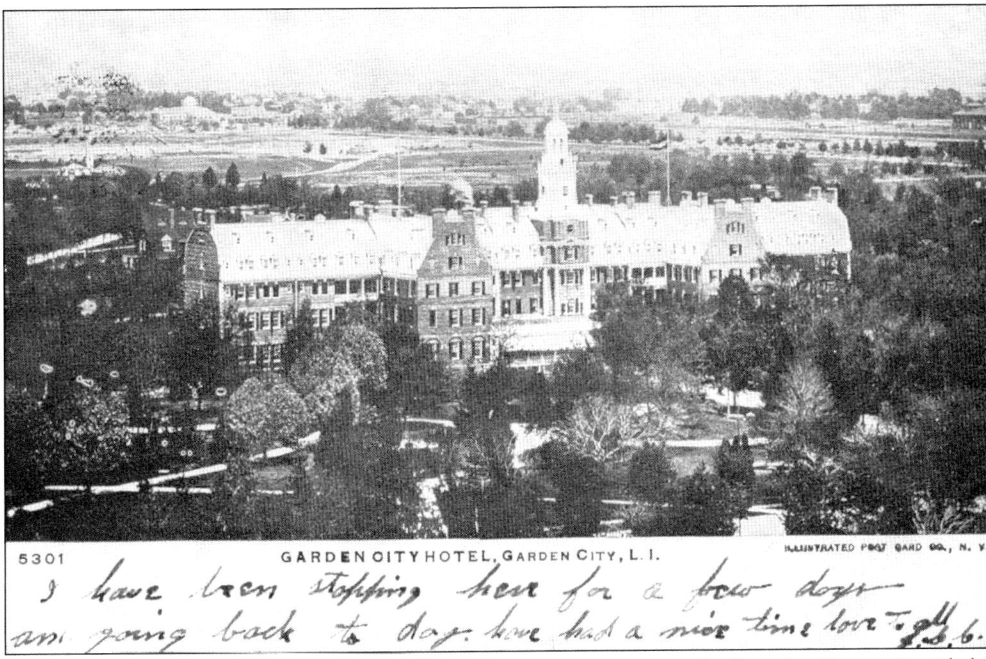

"Charles Leavitt has devised an unusually attractive street system for Jamaica Estates," said the *New York Times* on August 11, 1907. Describing himself as a "landscape engineer, designer of public parks, country clubs, racetracks and large private estates," he designed elaborate gardens on Long Island and New Jersey, federal parks in Cuba, and hotels in Puerto Rico. Leavitt did much of the initial town planning for Garden City, New York, and West Palm Beach, Florida.

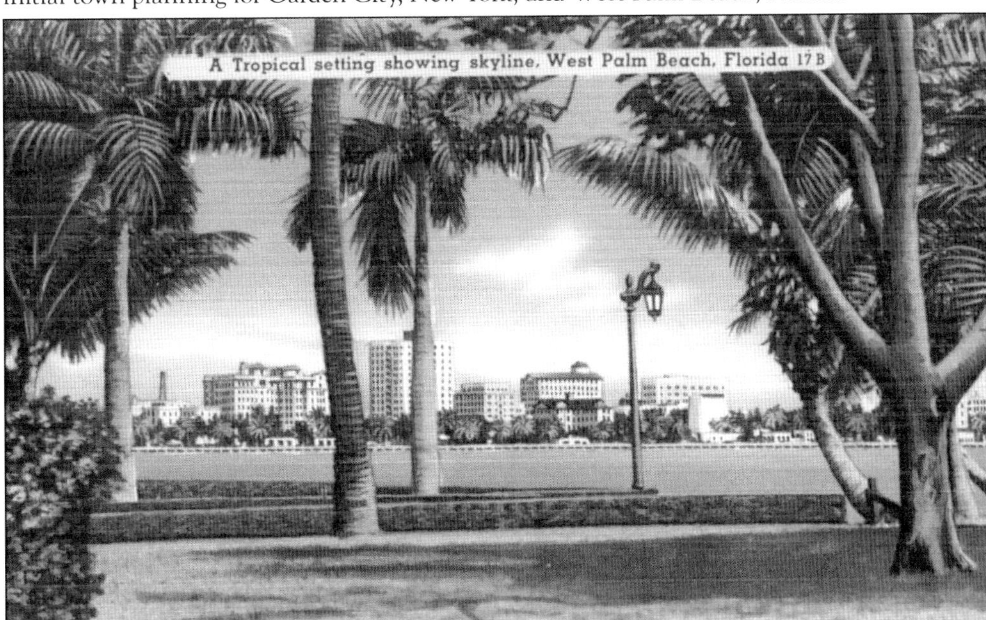

New York publisher Julius David Stern called Charles Wellford Leavitt (1871–1928) "a rare combination of engineer, artist, and diplomat." Leavitt was one of the preeminent landscape architects of his era and helped found the study of landscape architecture at New York City's Columbia University.

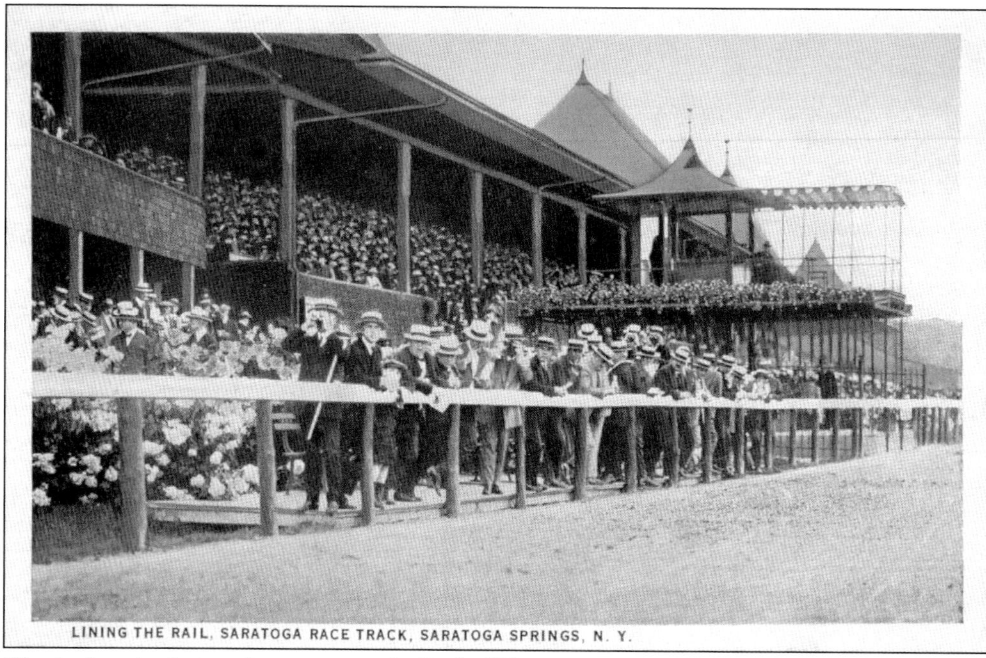

Charles Leavitt designed race courses for Foxhall Kenne, a racetrack owner, including the Empire City Race Track, as well as the tracks at Saratoga, Sheepshead Bay, Belmont Park, Toronto, Montreal, and Winnipeg. On March 6, 1904, the *New York Times* reported, "The Belmont Race Track covers a square mile and offers every facility for the sport and comfort—A Grand Stand seating 12,000 people, a spacious Clubhouse and Tunnels under the Track to the Infield."

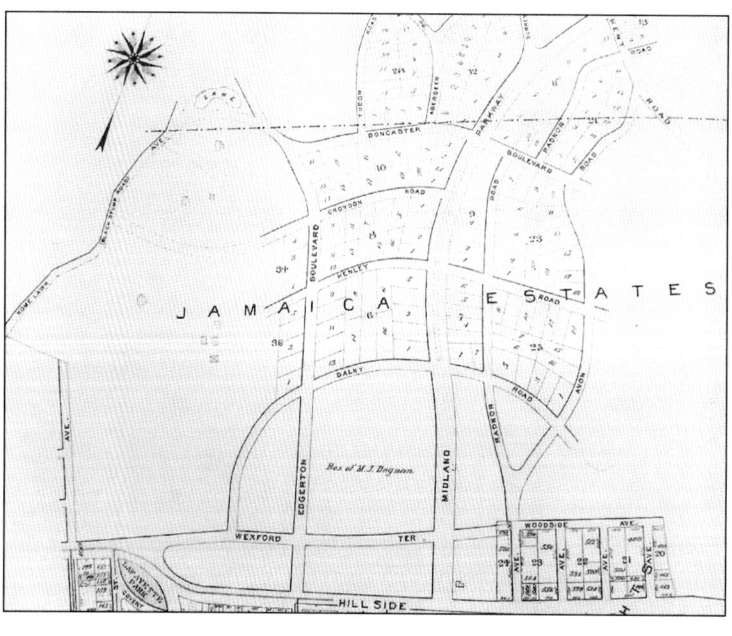

On August 13, 1907, the *Long Island Farmer* reported, "Charles Leavitt, the landscape architect of the tract, has devised a variegated plan of side streets that seem more like park drives than the average residence street of city folk. The fact that the land has high elevation and also that it is exquisitely wooded has been an advantage to the landscape architect."

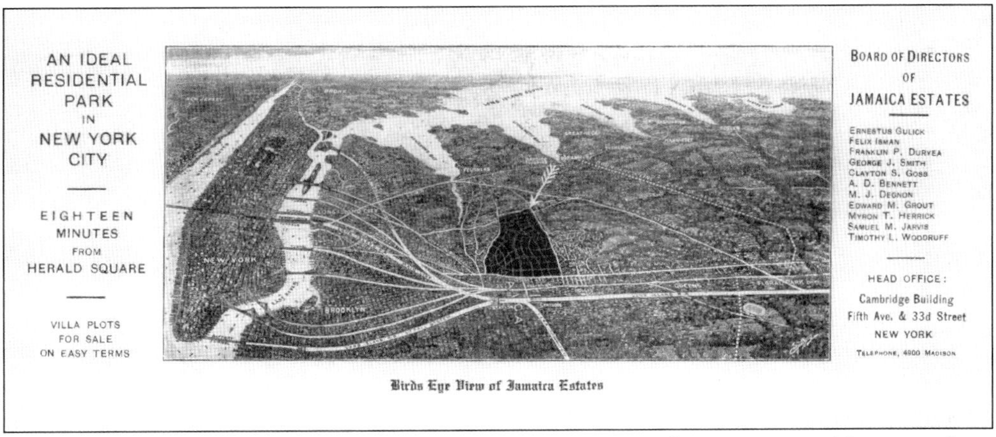

This 1908 map of Jamaica Estates shows lines of transportation only a convenient 18 minutes from Herald Square. Jamaica Estates was "An Ideal Residential Park in New York City." Among the names of the board of directors are the following: officers Franklin Duryea, second vice president; Clayton Goss, secretary; and George Smith, treasurer. The office was located at Fifth Avenue and Thirty-third Street. The reverse of this blotter is seen on the next page.

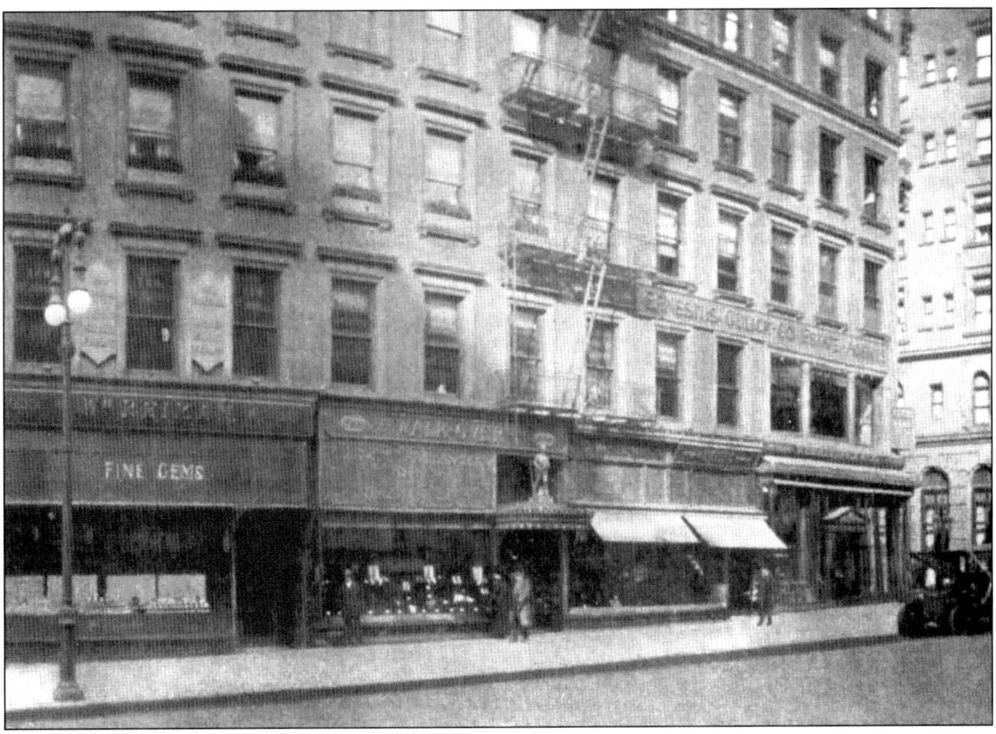

On June 27, 1907, the *New York Times* reported, "The Ernestus Gulick Company has leased from the Gorham Company the first floor of the Cambridge Building, 334 Fifth Avenue, at Thirty-third Street. The Jamaica Estates company will be located here." Ernestus Gulick's office is on the corner at the right and his name, in raised letters, can be seen mounted above the second floor windows.

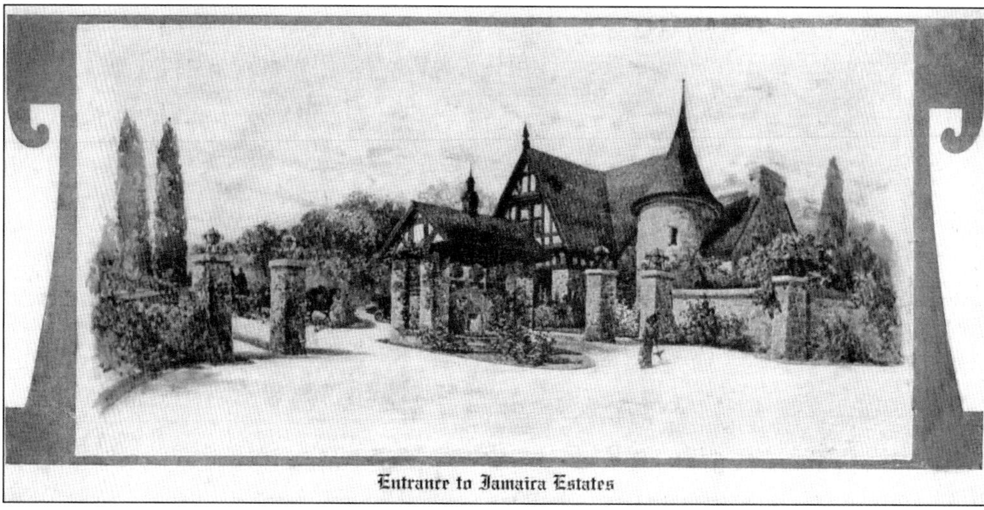

This 1908 blotter depicts the Jamaica Estates entrance. An ink blotter was designed to pick up extra ink on a handwritten document with the goal of preventing smears and bleeds. According to the *Long Island Farmer* on August 13, 1907, "Drawing for the stone entrance lodge at Hillside Avenue will cost $50,000 and will be erected in the picturesque fashion adopted in providing entrances to English country estates."

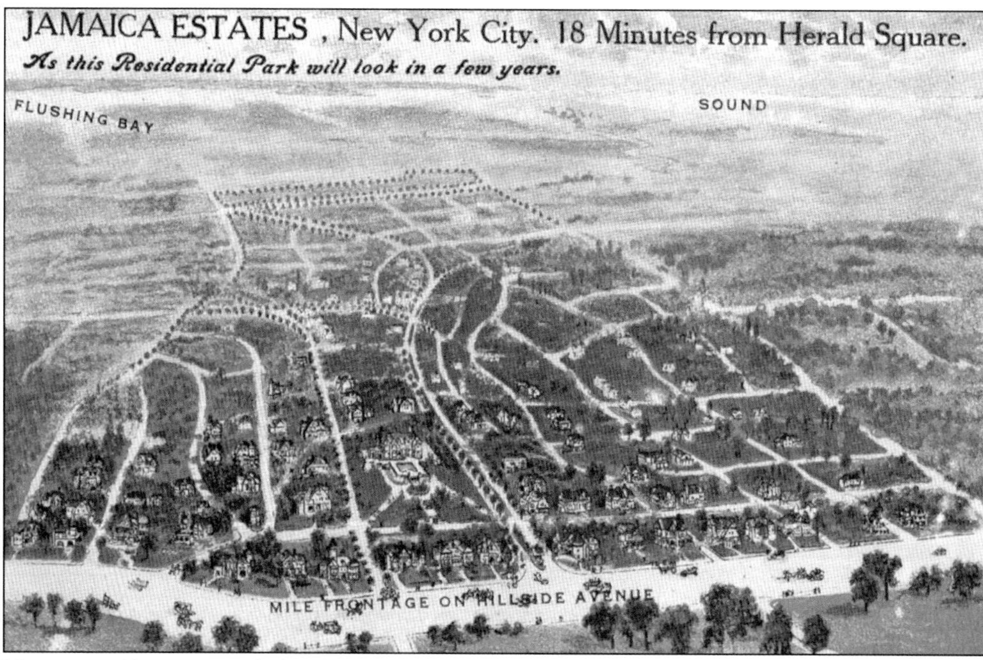

Here is an illustration of what Jamaica Estates will look like in a few years. The large mansion in center belongs to Michael J. Degnon. On September 1, 1907, the *New York Times* reported, "An entire block of sixteen acres has been secured by Michael J. Degnon, contractor for the 42 Street tunnels to Long Island City. He intends to erect a large house in the fall. The house will cost over $50,000."

A New York City subway builder and philanthropist, Michael John Degnon (1856–1925) created one of the largest construction companies in the country, building five sections of the New York City subway in 1904, including the city hall to the Battery section. Towering 6 feet 4 inches tall, his capacity for work was unlimited, but he was known for his good temper, tact, and genial manners. (Illustration by Kem Boatwright.)

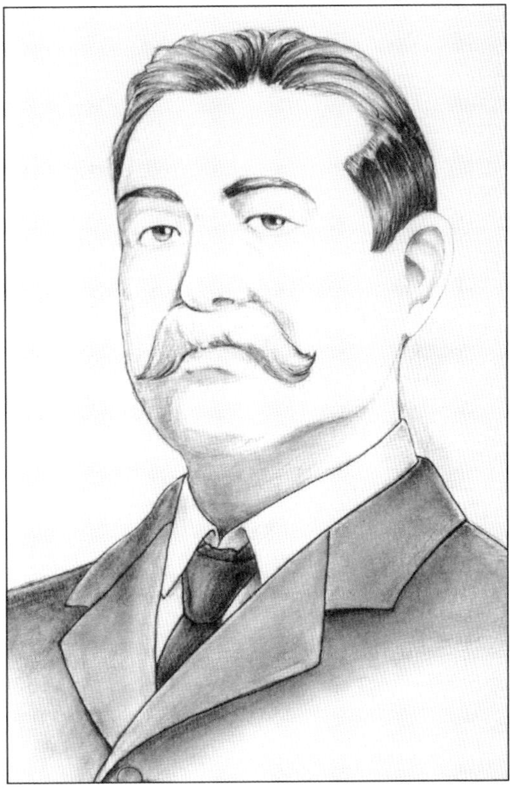

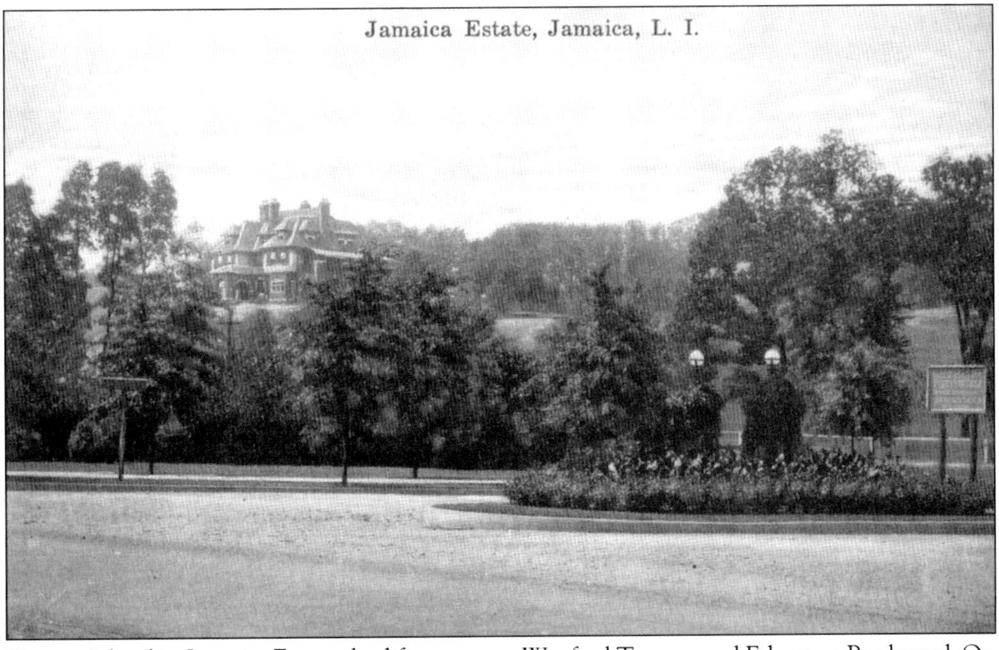

Degnon's land in Jamaica Estates had frontage on Wexford Terrace and Edgerton Boulevard. On July 24, 1910, the *New York Times* reported, "Degnon's handsome residence at Jamaica Estates is practically finished and he expects to occupy it in September. Most of the grading and terrace work is done, and the house presents a very imposing appearance from Hillside Avenue."

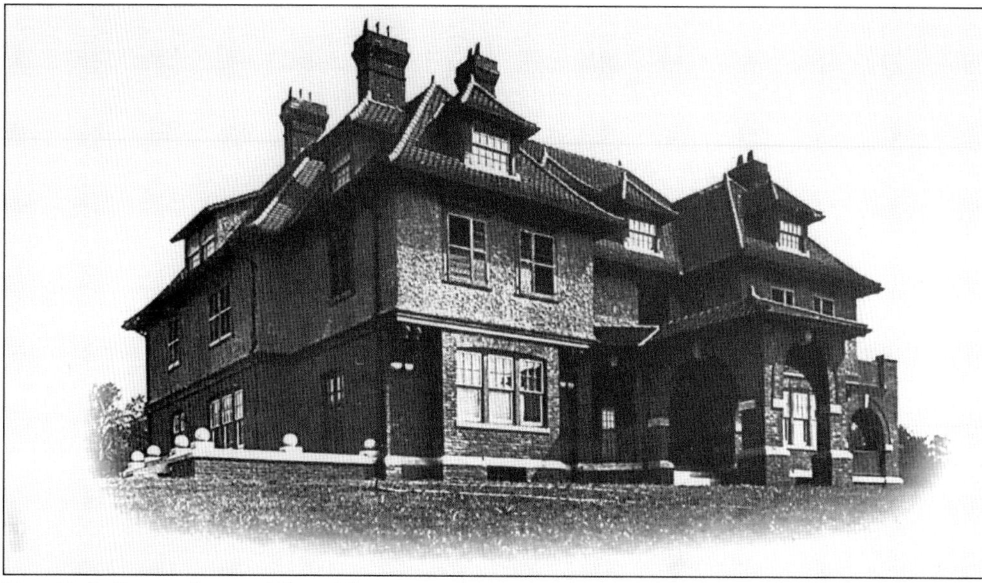

New York City architect Albert Thompson (1871–1952) was the architect for the 71st Regiment Armory in New York City; the Jamaica, New York, children's courthouse; homes in the Jamaica Estates area; and the old Queens Borough Hall on Hunters Point Avenue, Long Island.

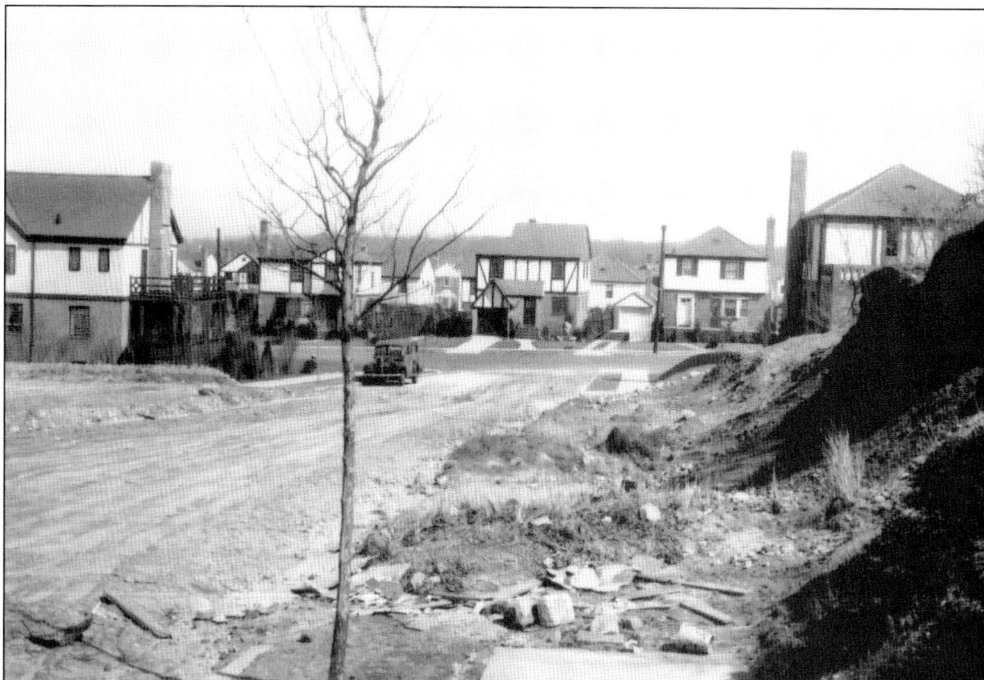

According to the January 19, 1908, issue of the *New York Times*, "The Gulick Company announces that contracts have been signed with the Degnon Company for improving the entire 8,000 lots in Jamaica Estates including a modern system of sewers, macadamized streets, sidewalks, a water supply, and electric and gas lighting systems. A force of several hundred men to work immediately." This photograph of Troon Road looks east to 188th Street in 1930. (Courtesy of Q Gardens Gallery.)

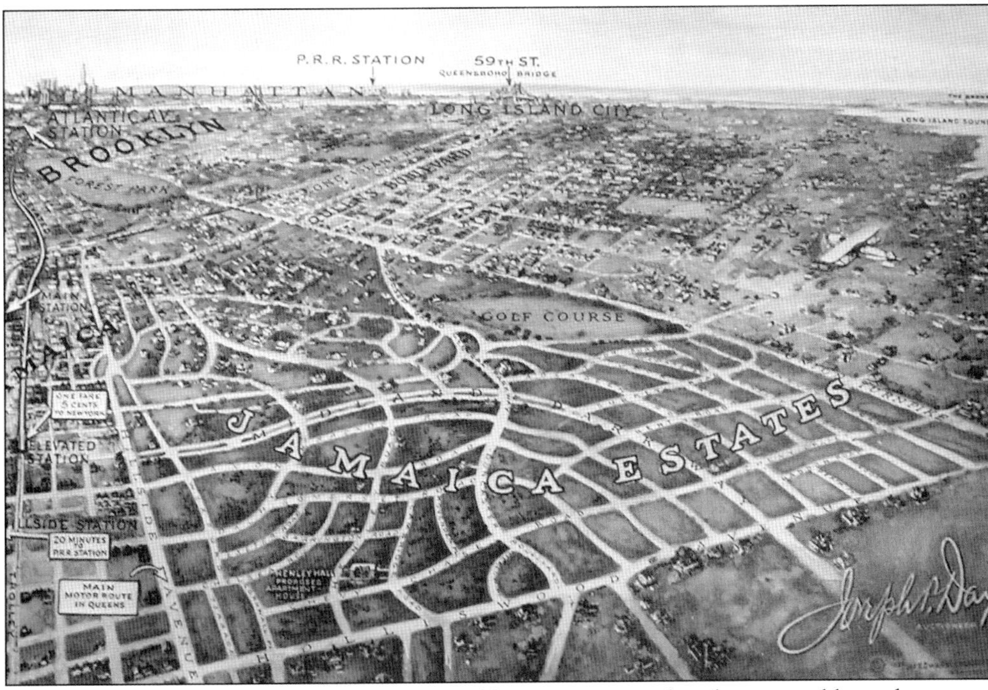

From the beginning, Jamaica Estates had a golf course as part of its design, visible in the center. On January 19, 1908, the *New York Times* reported, "Engineers are now are work on the new golf course which is to be laid out on the Jamaica Estates property. The course has been laid out under the supervision of Willie Tucker, who planned the links at Ardaley, St. Andrew's and other important clubs."

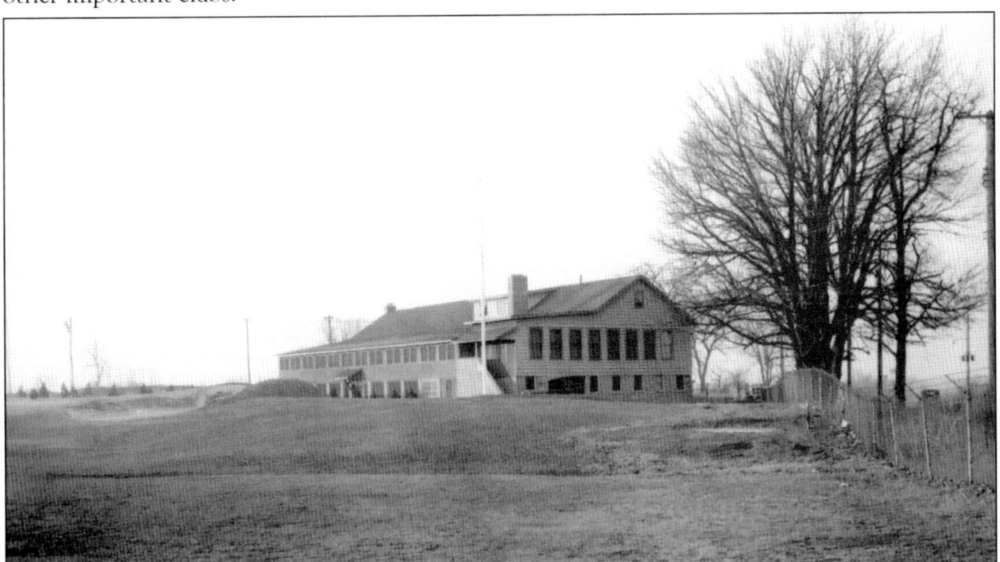

The Jamaica Estates Golf Course became known as the Hillcrest Golf Course. A 1924 Hillcrest brochure boasted, "It is an eighteen-hole course fully completed and second to none. The links were designed and built under the supervision of Devereux Emmett, the eminent golf architect." On February 11, 1936, the Vincentian University of Saint John University purchased the 100-acre Hillcrest Golf Course for their campus. (Courtesy of Q Gardens Gallery.)

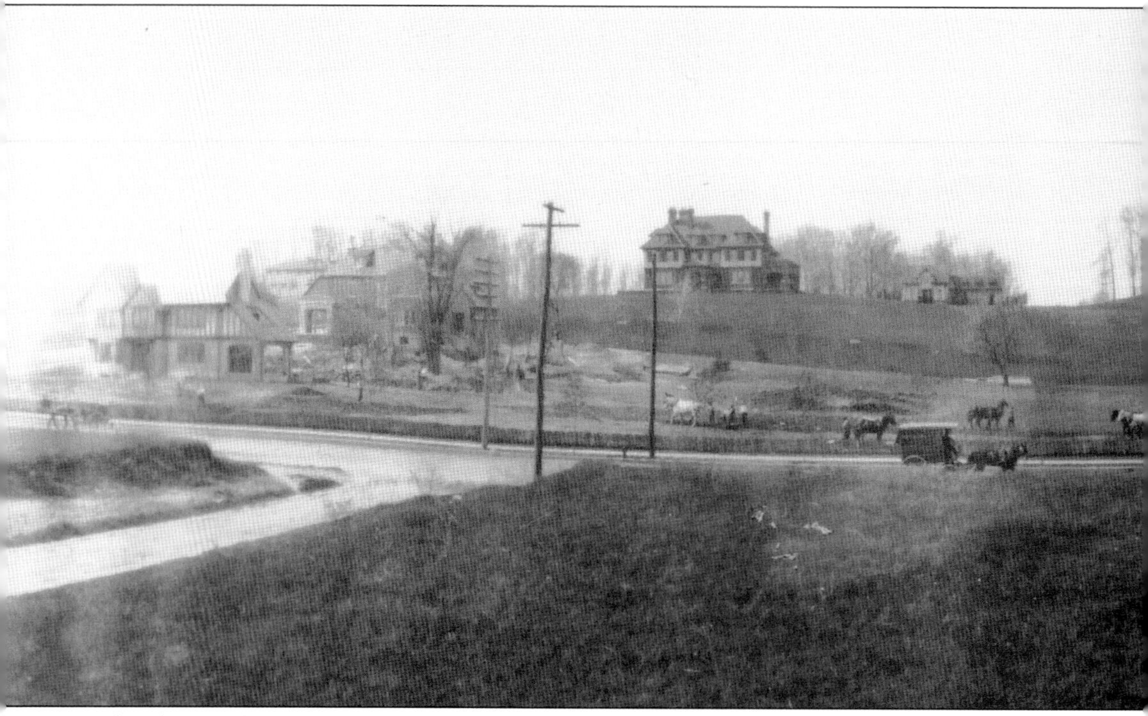

Taken by noted Jamaica photographer Frederick Webber looking north on Hillside Avenue, the street at left is 179th and at the right 179th Place. At the top of the hill is the Degnon House.

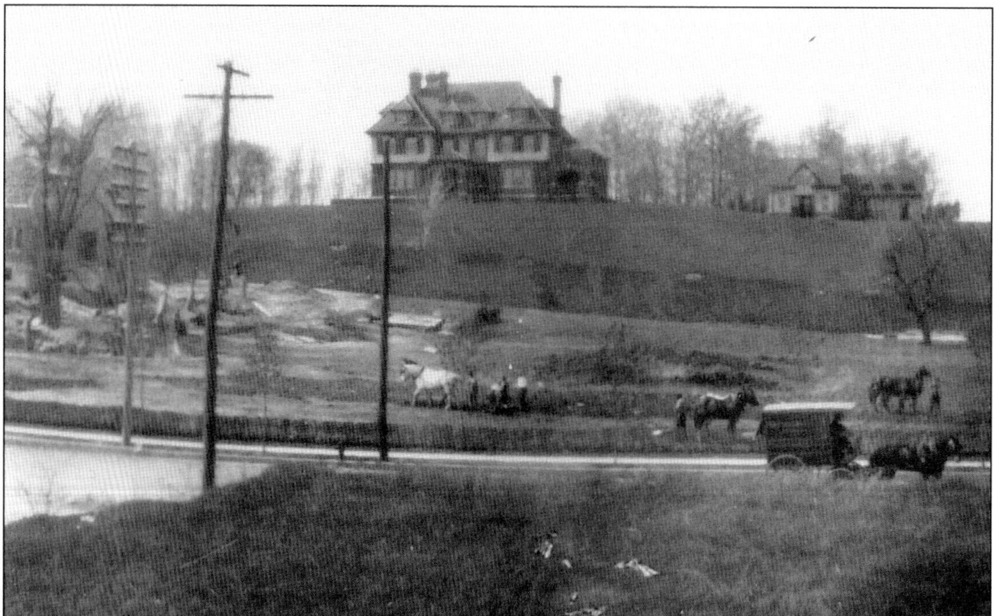

On June 12, 1910, the *New York Times* reported, "Splendid progress has been made and this tract is one of the show places of Hillside Avenue. Six more houses are to be started with Jamaica Estates this coming week. Among the recent sales are a plot, 60 by 120, on the south side of Midland Parkway and a plot 76 by 165, on the north side of Dalny Road."

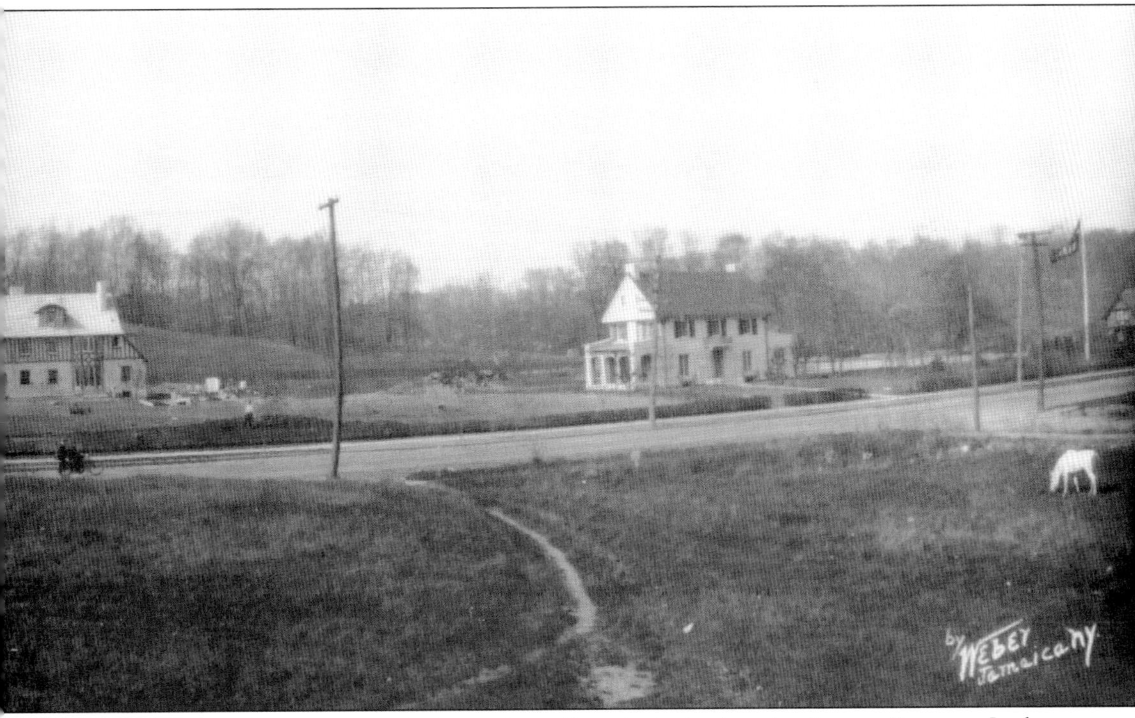

The building to the extreme right beyond the flagpole is the Jamaica Estates Entrance Lodge. Next to the white house at the right are the Jamaica Estates tennis courts.

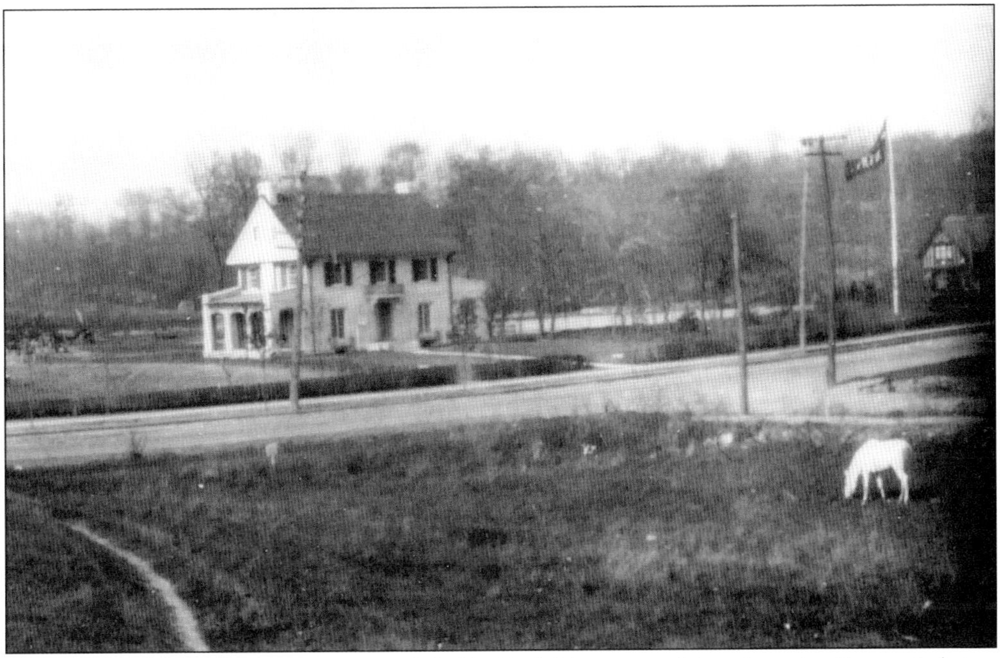

According to the *New York Times* on July 31, 1910, "A tennis club at Jamaica Estates is being organized by the residents and purchasers there, and already great progress is being made. There are to be four courts, two of grass and two of dirt, to be located on the Hillside Avenue frontage, just west of Midland Parkway and opposite the lodge."

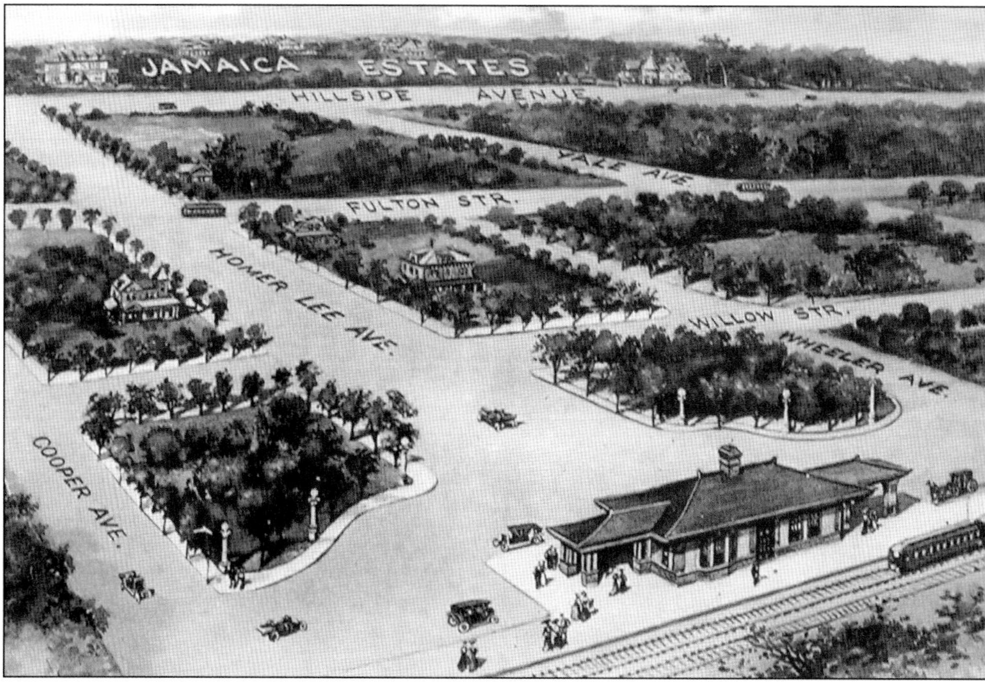

"Arrangements made by the Long Island Railroad and Jamaica Estates, for the immediate construction of a Passenger Express Station. Jamaica Estates has purchased two solid blocks between the railroad and Fulton Street (Jamaica Avenue), as well as property along Homer Lee Avenue (178th Street)," reported the *Jamaica Estates Circular* on August 1, 1910. The cost of the property was $94,000 and was done so that a person getting off at the new station would be on Jamaica Estates property.

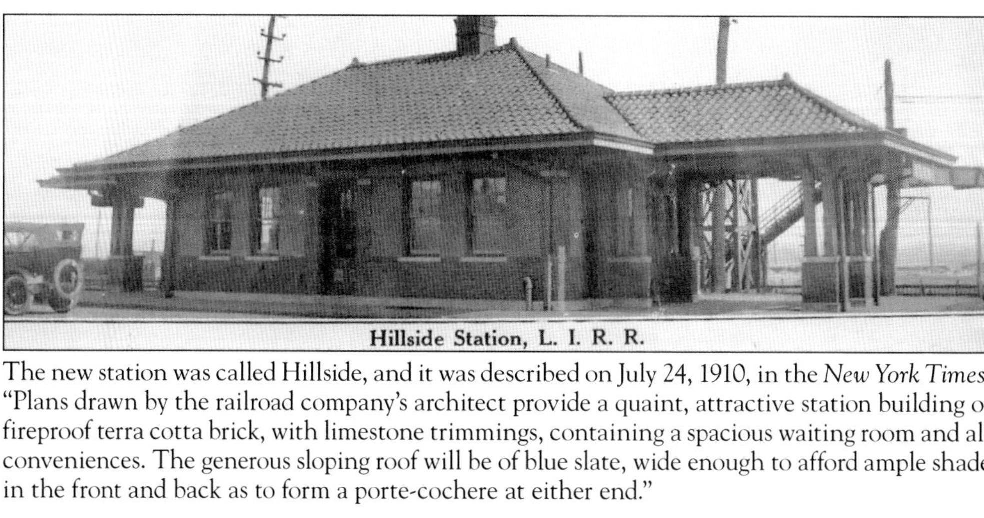

The new station was called Hillside, and it was described on July 24, 1910, in the *New York Times*: "Plans drawn by the railroad company's architect provide a quaint, attractive station building of fireproof terra cotta brick, with limestone trimmings, containing a spacious waiting room and all conveniences. The generous sloping roof will be of blue slate, wide enough to afford ample shade in the front and back as to form a porte-cochere at either end."

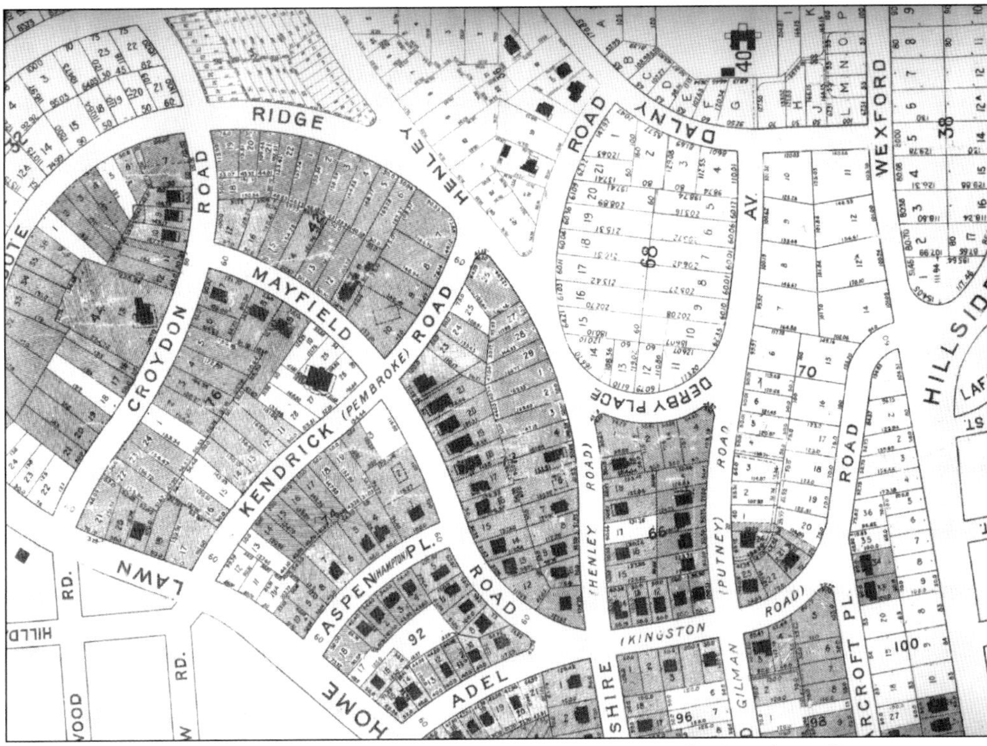

Shown in this 1928 map is the western part of Jamaica Estates with Homelawn Street serving as the border. Homelawn Street was also called Fresh Meadows Lane, which was named for the fresh water meadows through which it ran. On some maps it was also referred to as Black Stump Road because it led to the Black Stump Road of Colonial times, which is now Seventy-third Avenue.

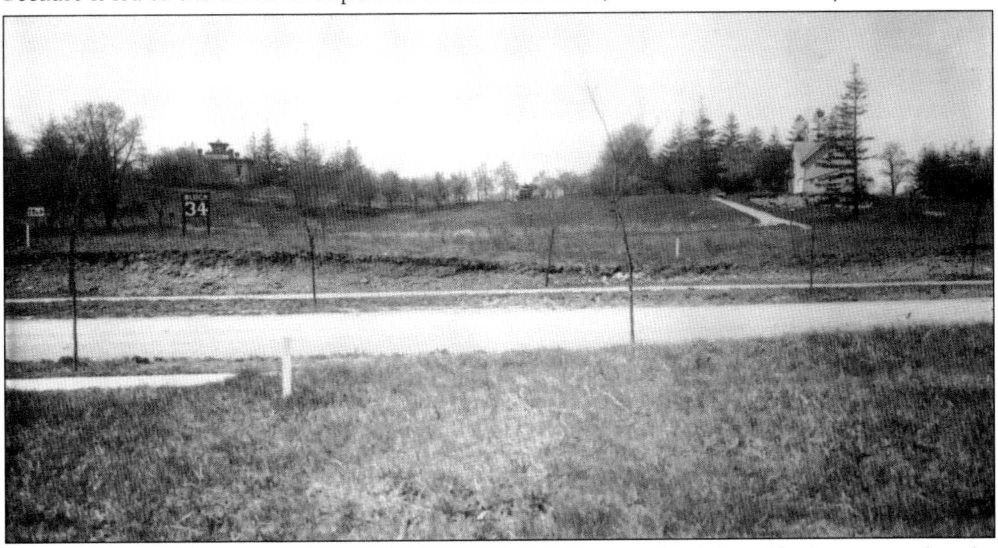

This 1910 photograph looks north and shows Jamaica Estates divided and laid out into plots for development. The same view is shown on the map at the top of the page. The house with the Victorian cupola in the distance is the Frost house. It can be located on the map at the southeast corner of Kendrick Road (Kendrick Place) and Mayfield Road. (Courtesy of the Queens Borough Public Library, Long Island Division, Frederick J. Weber Collection.)

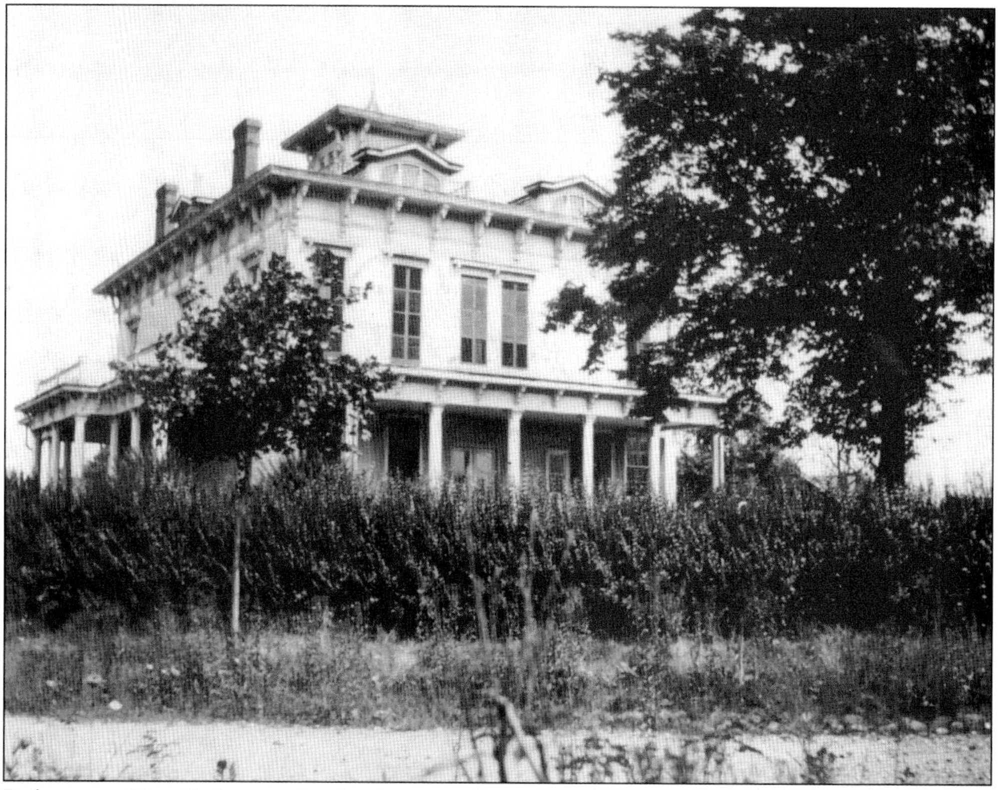

Before cars, New Yorkers maintained summer homes on Long Island, and the Frost house was a favorite boardinghouse. It is believed that it was erected around 1850 and is the oldest house in Jamaica Estates, located at the corner of Kendrick Road (Place) and Mayfield Road. (Courtesy of the Queens Borough Public Library, Long Island Division, Eugene L. Armbruster Collection.)

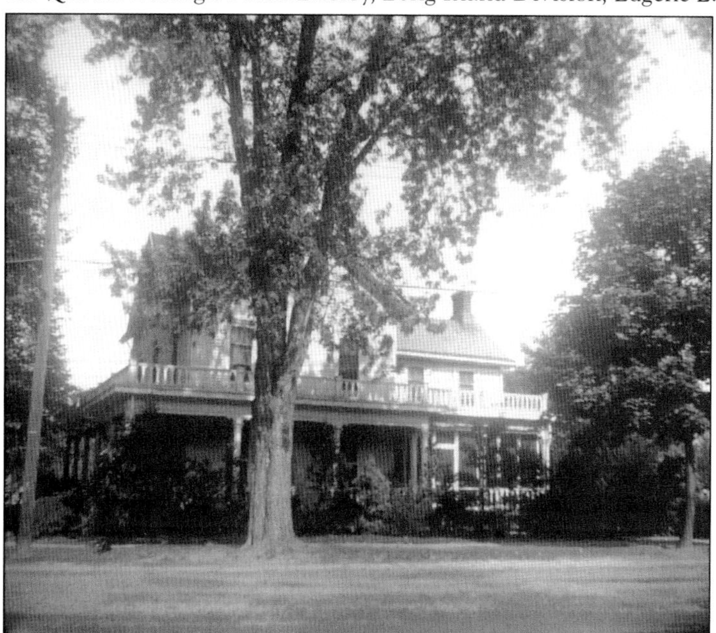

An early structure, the Croydon House stood on the north side of Croydon Road between Homelawn Street and Mayfield Road and can be seen on the 1928 map from the previous page. Today the United Nations School is located on this spot. (Courtesy of the Queens Borough Public Library, Long Island Division, Eugene L. Armbruster Collection.)

Three

The Passionist Parish
Immaculate Conception

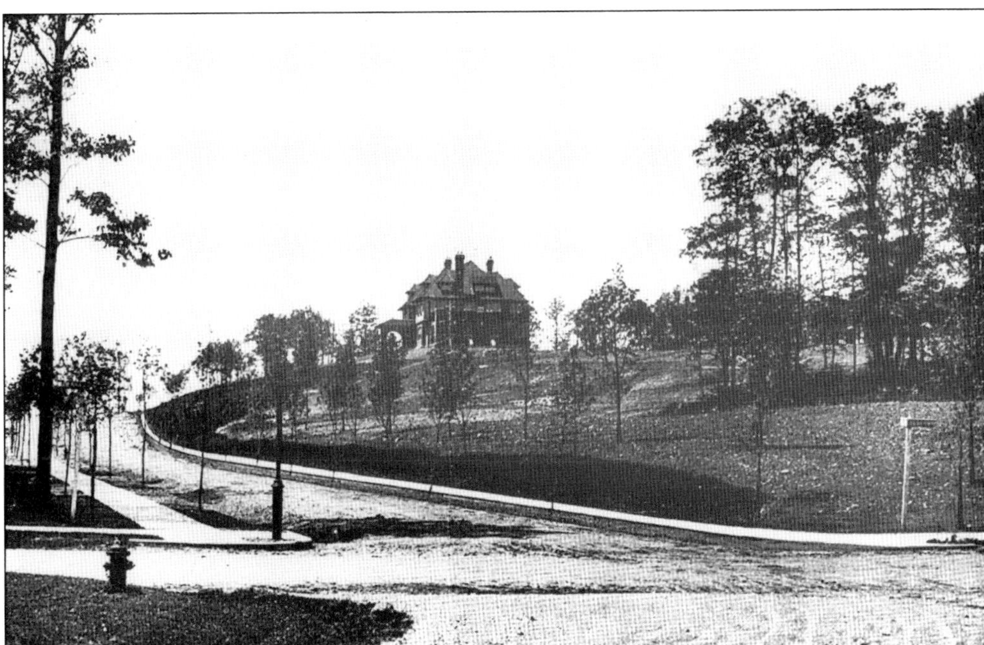

In 1923, Bishop Thomas Molloy of Brooklyn invited the Passionist Fathers to open a monastery and retreat house and to take care of a new parish to be established in Jamaica Estates. The Passionists were founded by St. Paul of the Cross in 1741, and the first group arrived in America in 1852. The mission of the Passionist Fathers is parish missions and retreats. Michael J. Degnon, a Catholic who had made a sizable donation to pay the debt for the building of St. Patrick's Cathedral in Manhattan, sold his 16-acre Jamaica Estates home and property to the Passionists, and thus began the history of the Immaculate Conception Parish. This photograph was taken from Midland Parkway looking west on Wexford Terrace with the Degnon house on the hill.

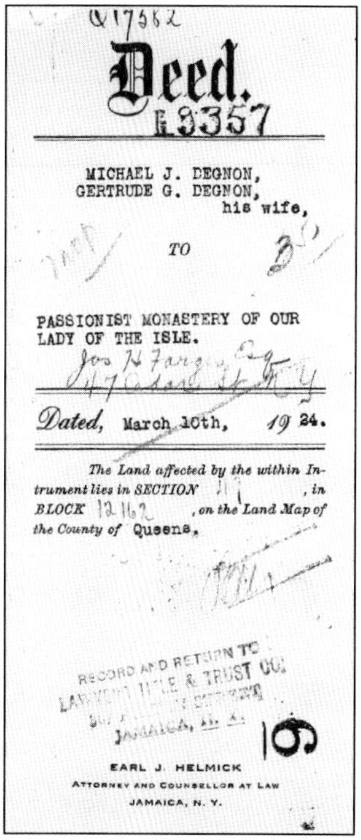

Deed.
L9357

MICHAEL J. DEGNON,
GERTRUDE G. DEGNON,
his wife,

TO

PASSIONIST MONASTERY OF OUR LADY OF THE ISLE.

Dated, March 10th, 1924.

The Land affected by the within Instrument lies in SECTION , in BLOCK , on the Land Map of the County of Queens.

RECORD AND RETURN TO

19

EARL J. HELMICK
ATTORNEY AND COUNSELLOR AT LAW
JAMAICA, N. Y.

On March 10, 1924, Michael Degnon and his wife, Gertrude, sold their 16-acre Jamaica Estates property to the Passionist Fathers. The Degnons moved to Kew Gardens, and in April 1925, Michael died at the age of 67. By July 1924, the Passionist Fathers had moved into the Degnon mansion and used it as a parish office, monastery, and retreat house.

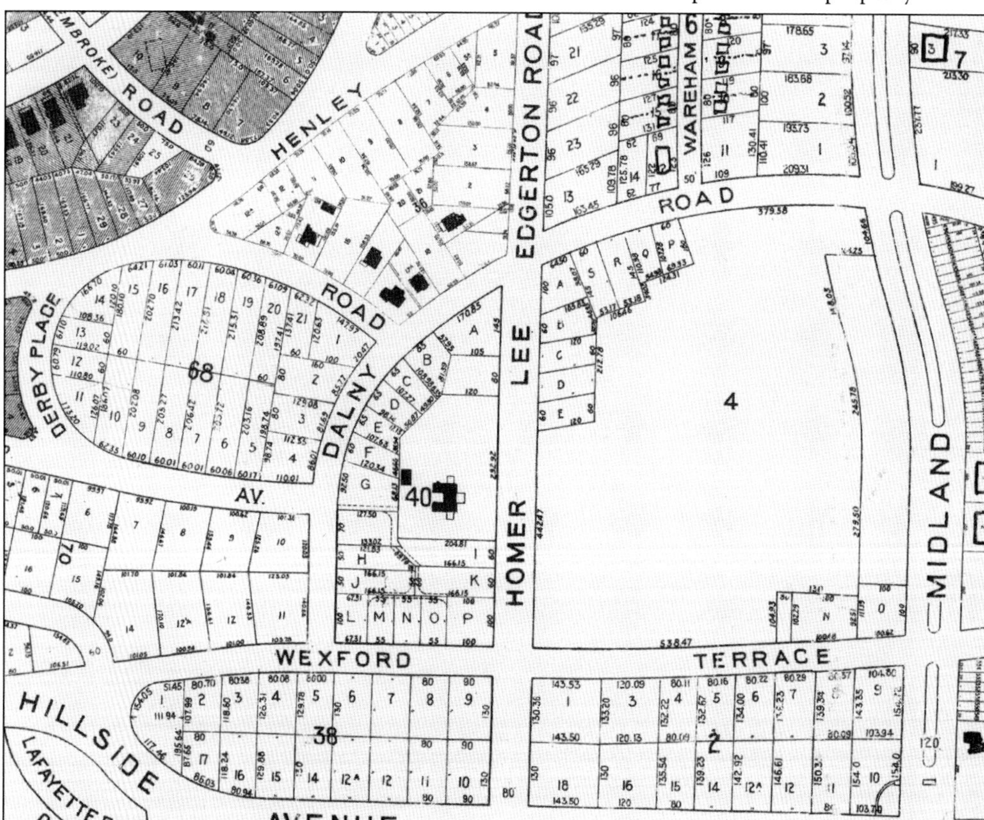

The Degnon property was located on a hill overlooking the town of Jamaica with stunning views of Jamaica Bay. It encompassed 16 acres and was bordered by Dalny Road on the north, Wexford Terrace on the south, Midland Parkway on the west, and Homer Lee Avenue (Edgerton Boulevard) on the east. In this 1928 map, No. 4 marks the location of the Immaculate Conception Parish property.

Fr. Chrysostom Smith, C. P., appointed first pastor, was born September 18, 1875, in New Jersey. He entered the Passionists and was ordained on January 18, 1903. The first Mass of the new parish was celebrated on July 5, 1924, in the library of the Degnon mansion. The parish was placed under the protection of the Immaculate Conception of the Blessed Mother.

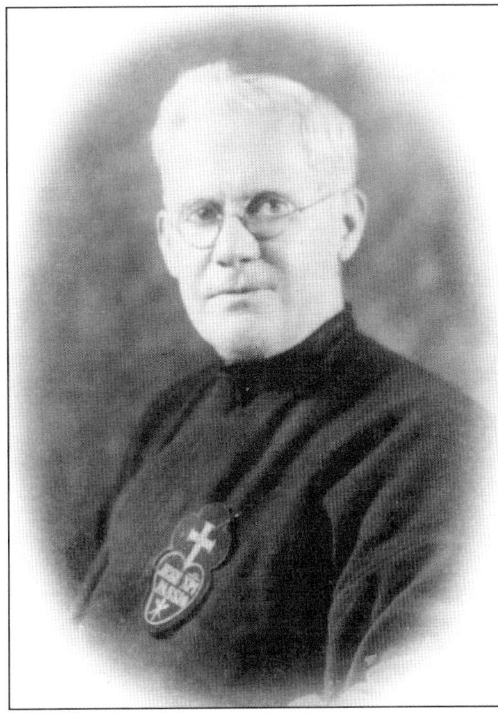

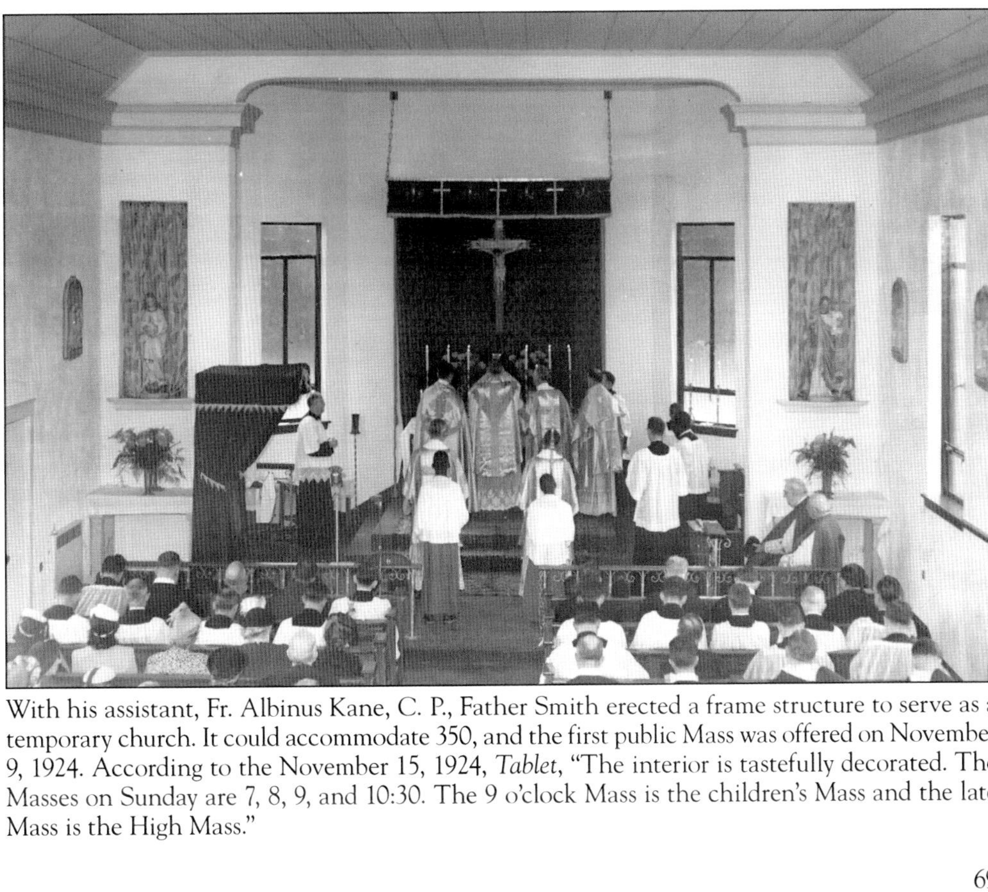

With his assistant, Fr. Albinus Kane, C. P., Father Smith erected a frame structure to serve as a temporary church. It could accommodate 350, and the first public Mass was offered on November 9, 1924. According to the November 15, 1924, *Tablet*, "The interior is tastefully decorated. The Masses on Sunday are 7, 8, 9, and 10:30. The 9 o'clock Mass is the children's Mass and the late Mass is the High Mass."

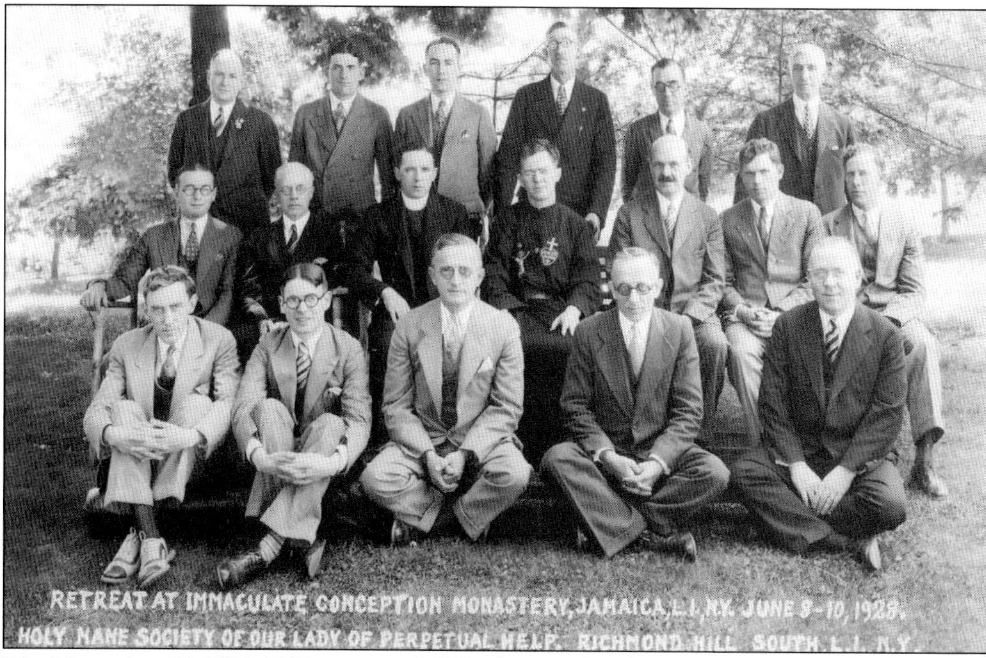

The November 15, 1924, *Tablet* reported, "The first weekend retreat for Laymen will be held at the Monastery of the Immaculate Conception from November 21 to November 23. It will begin on Friday night at 7:30 and end on Sunday night at 7:00." Nine men entered the retreat house, marking the first cloistered retreat in the Diocese of Brooklyn. By 1935, it was renamed the Bishop Molloy Retreat House. Pictured is the 1928 retreat.

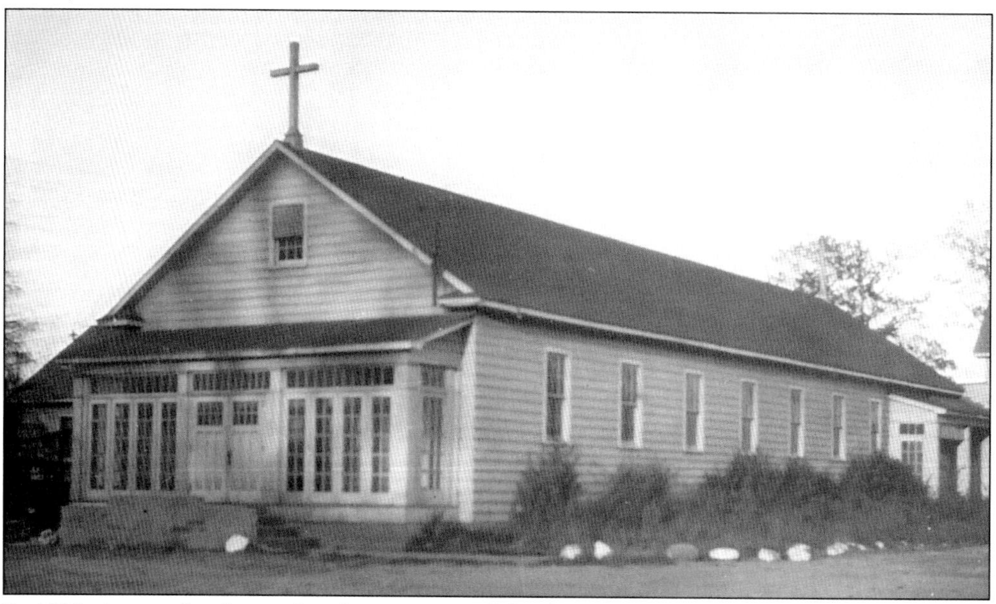

By 1926, the wooden frame church was too small for the growing congregation and was enlarged with an addition boasting the seating capacity to 800. After the permanent basement church was built, the goal was to use the first part of the old building as a temporary school, but this was not feasible, and it was demolished. The 1926 addition was moved to face Dalny Road and became the parish hall.

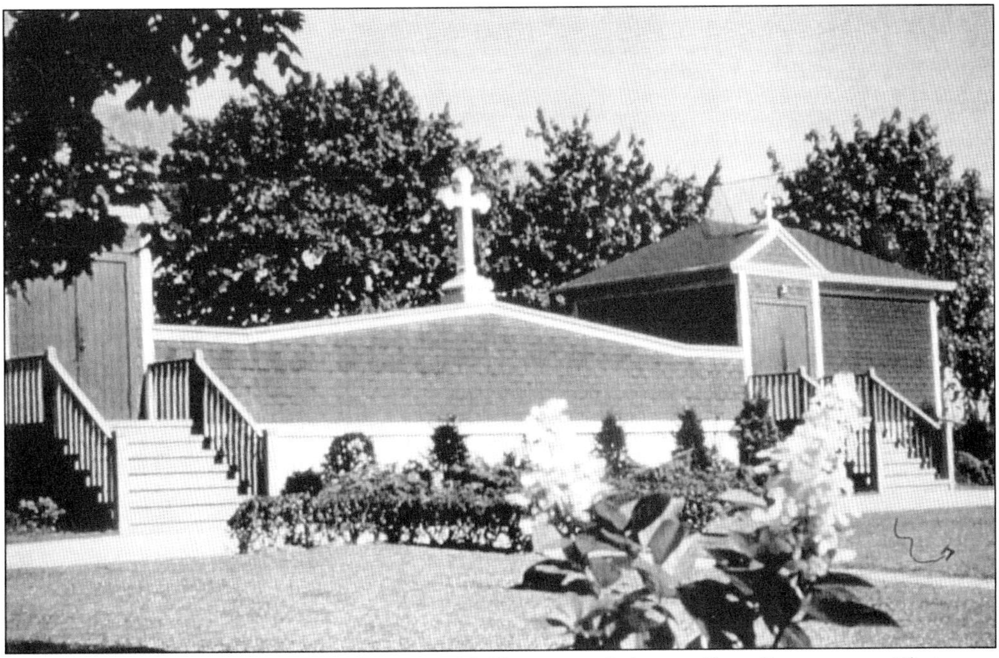

According to the *Tablet* on December 21, 1929, "Passionist fathers will say first mass on Christmas Day. Praises and glory will be sung for the first time in the new church of the Immaculate Conception, Jamaica in the care of the Passionist Fathers on Christmas at the Midnight Mass. The newly appointed pastor, Rev. Kevin Murray, C.P., extends a cordial invitation to all his people and their friends to attend the opening of this new temple."

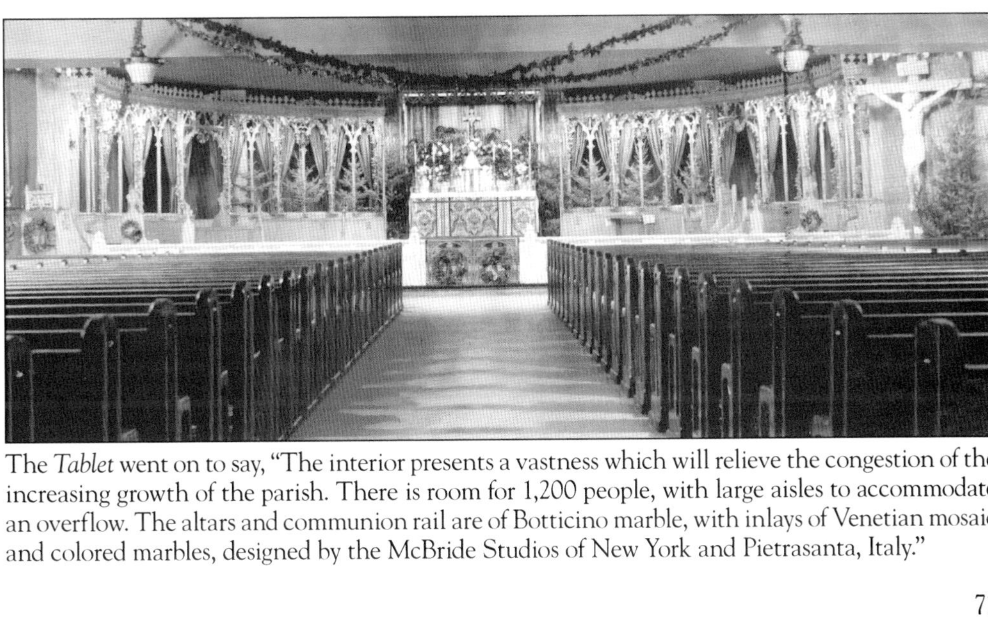

The *Tablet* went on to say, "The interior presents a vastness which will relieve the congestion of the increasing growth of the parish. There is room for 1,200 people, with large aisles to accommodate an overflow. The altars and communion rail are of Botticino marble, with inlays of Venetian mosaic and colored marbles, designed by the McBride Studios of New York and Pietrasanta, Italy."

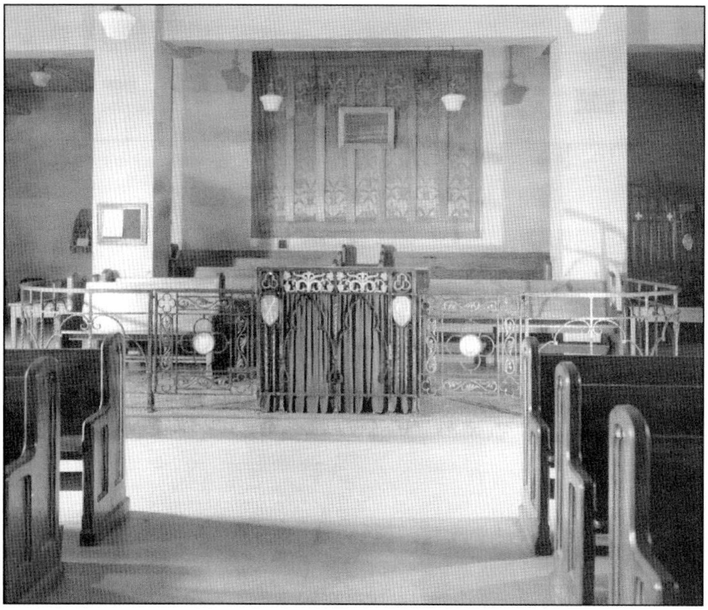

"A devotional atmosphere pervades throughout, which lends itself to reflection and prayer. The grand organ, with its resonant notes rebound to the glory of its maker and on Christmas night will re-echo that first message of Peace to men of Good Will," reported the *Tablet* on December 21, 1929. This elevated section was reserved for the choir. The organ is behind the pleated curtain, and the baptistery is located to the right.

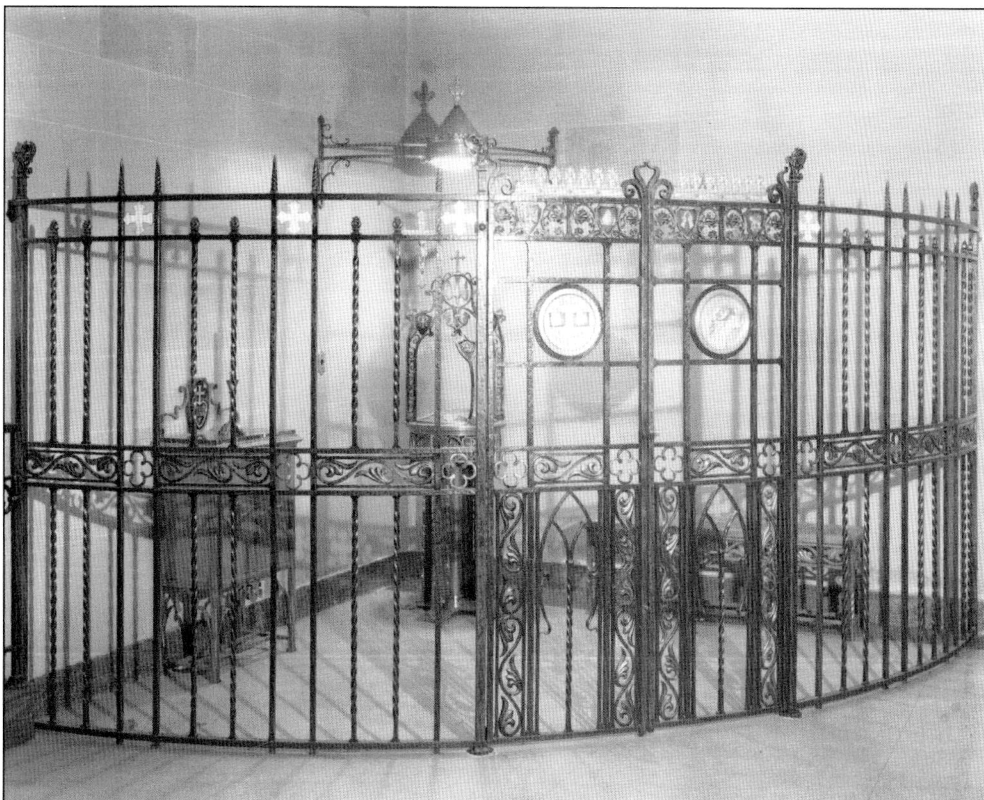

The ornate baptistery is encased by a gilded wrought iron enclosure. "The Passionist Fathers of the Immaculate Conception Monastery, Hillside Avenue and 178th street, Jamaica, celebrated a Solemn High Mass at midnight Christmas in their new church which faces 178th Street, just north of Hillside Avenue," reported the December 28, 1929, *Tablet*.

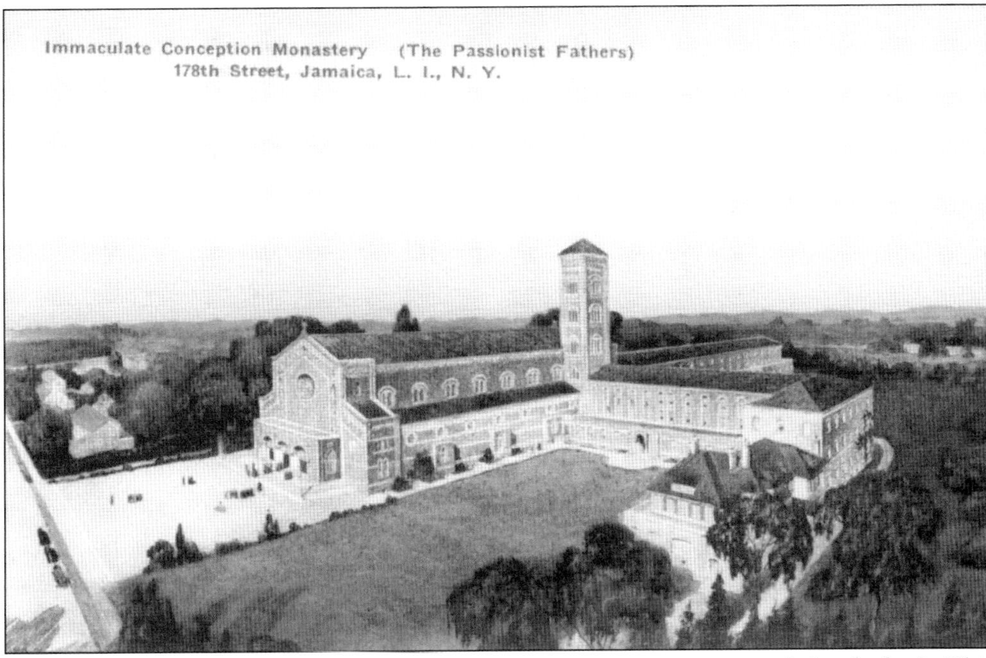

Building the lower church was a cost-cutting measure, as a monastery needed to be built. This 1927 postcard suggests what the upper church would look like. The Degnon mansion in the foreground is attached to the monastery. The 150-foot bell tower was never built. According to local folklore, residents did not want the sound of bells to disturb the community.

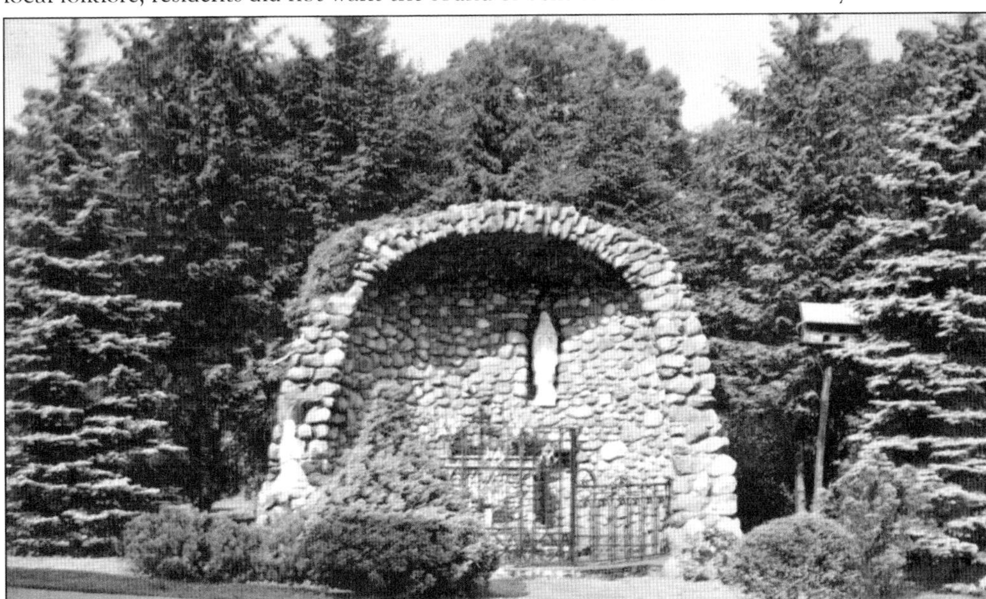

The gardens are noted for their beauty and serenity year-round. A Grotto similar to the one in Lourdes, France, was erected on the grounds, as well as a garden path for praying the Stations of the Cross. The Passionists also had a private cemetery erected on the property for its priests and brothers. The cemetery has memorials dedicated to the Passionist Missionaries of China, the Philippines, and the West Indies.

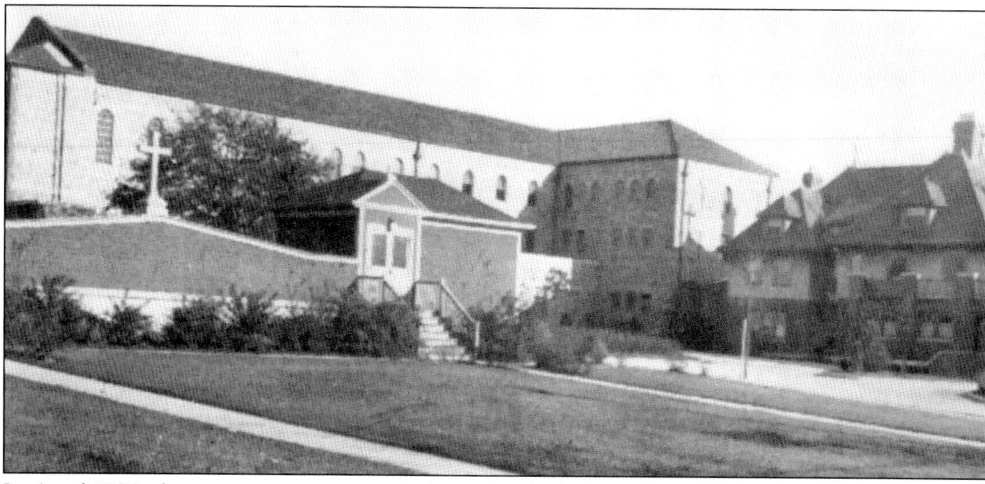

In April 1930, the new monastery was dedicated. The lower church is pictured in the foreground with the monastery behind it. The wing at the right and the old Degnon mansion served as the Retreat House. In 1934, the *Long Island Daily Press* reported, "The visitor rings the bell and a moment later a priest admits him. As he crosses the threshold he has stepped back centuries into a medieval atmosphere."

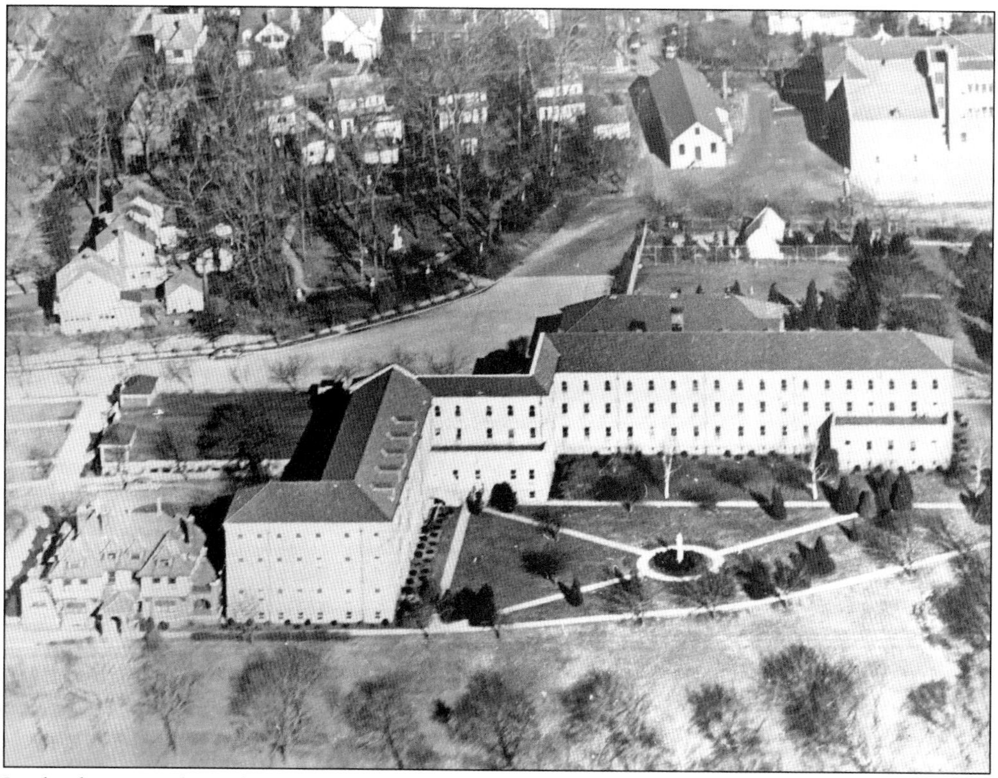

In the foreground are the monastery gardens; the Degnon mansion can be seen to the far left. Behind the monastery is the separate dining hall. In 1933, the *Long Island Daily Press* reported, "Quietly spoken men in black cassocks pass through the halls, holy images and paintings adorn the walls. From upstairs male voices are heard softly chanting an ancient office. There are 35 ordained priests and 20 theological students."

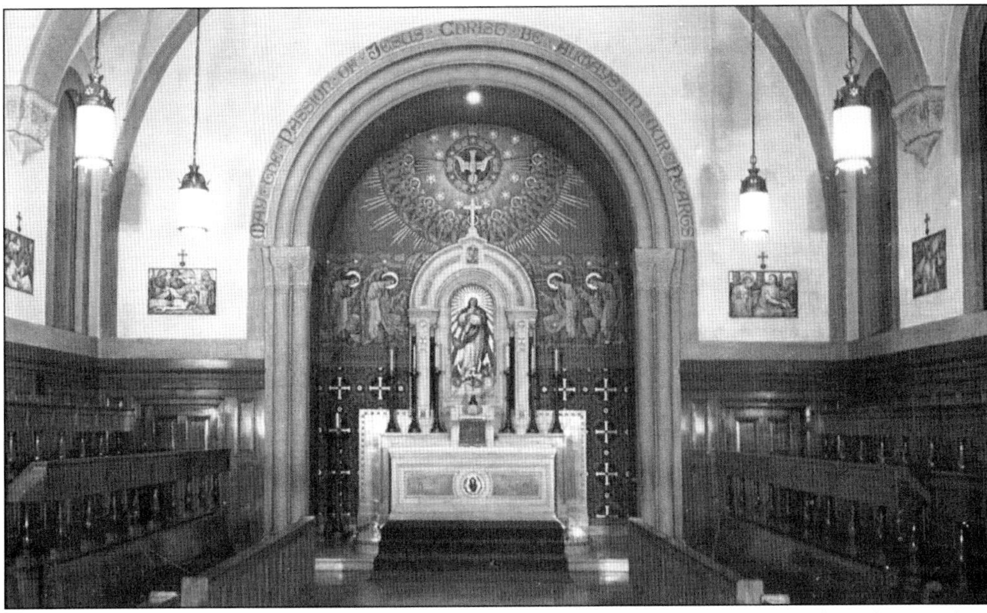

The Monastery Chapel of 1930, with a barrel-vaulted ceiling, was decorated in the art deco style. Above the main marble altar is a masterpiece in glass mosaic depicting the image of the Immaculate Conception. The wooden pews are arranged to face each other for prayer and chanting. "Each priest spends much time daily in solitude and meditation," reported the *Long Island Daily Press* in 1933.

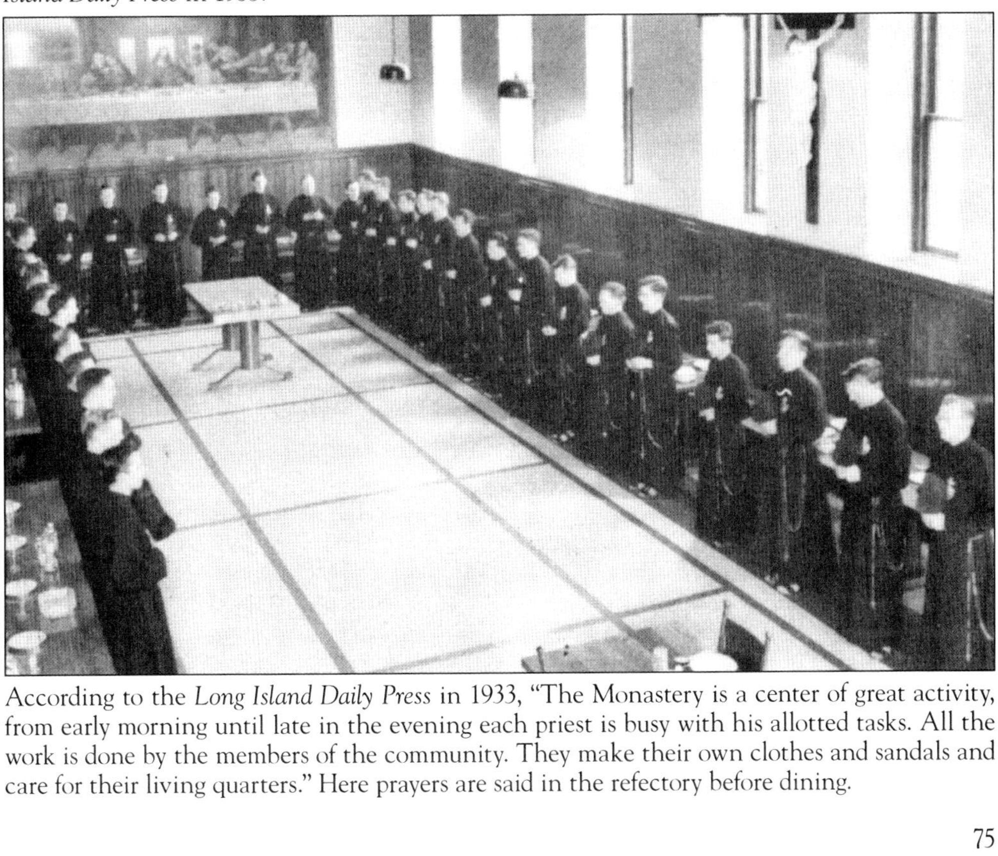

According to the *Long Island Daily Press* in 1933, "The Monastery is a center of great activity, from early morning until late in the evening each priest is busy with his allotted tasks. All the work is done by the members of the community. They make their own clothes and sandals and care for their living quarters." Here prayers are said in the refectory before dining.

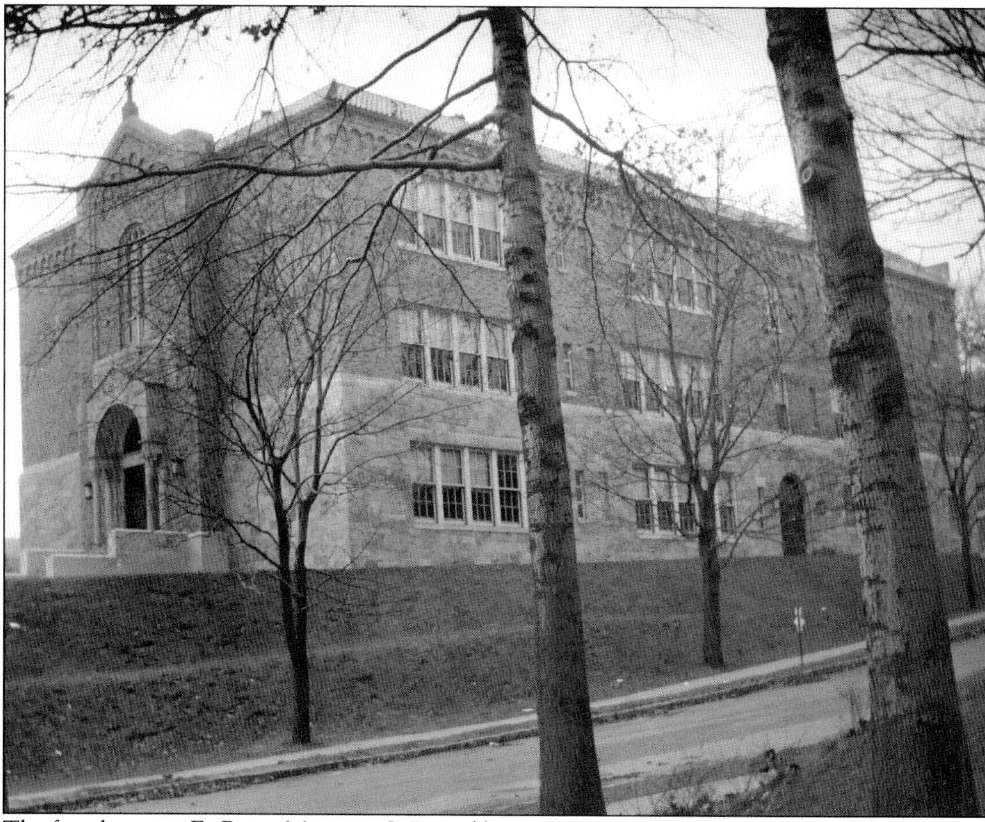

The fourth pastor, Fr. Roger Monson, C. P., and his assistant, Fr. Chrysostom Driscoll (1901–1950), were instrumental in opening the school. Father Monson was born in 1896 and died in 1969 and is buried in the Passionist cemetery behind the school he established. The cornerstone for the school was placed on February 2, 1937. The school was placed under the care of the Sisters of St. Joseph, Brentwood.

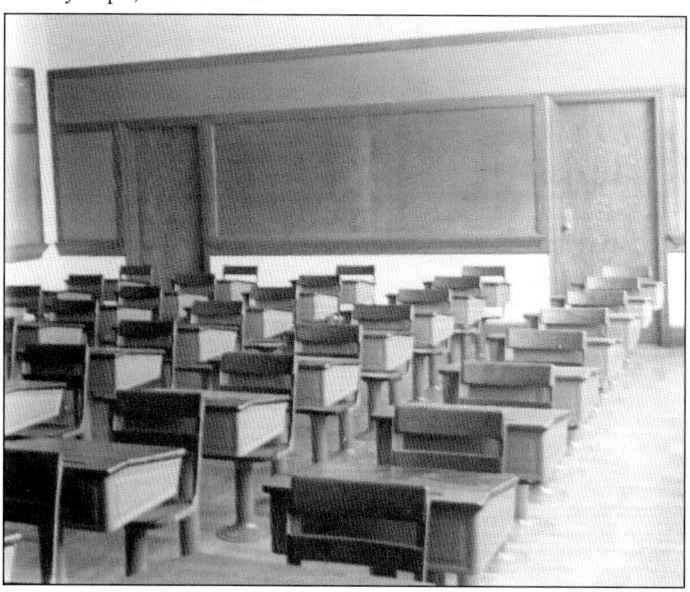

"On the feast of the Holy Name of Mary, September 12, 1938, five zealous pioneer Sisters and pupils began their first day in the Immaculate Conception School. For many years before this, Sisters had come weekly from Flushing to give instructions to the children of the parish for whom Father Chrysostom had conducted a well organized catechetical school," reported the *Flowering Staff* in 1956. The first graduation was held in June 1941.

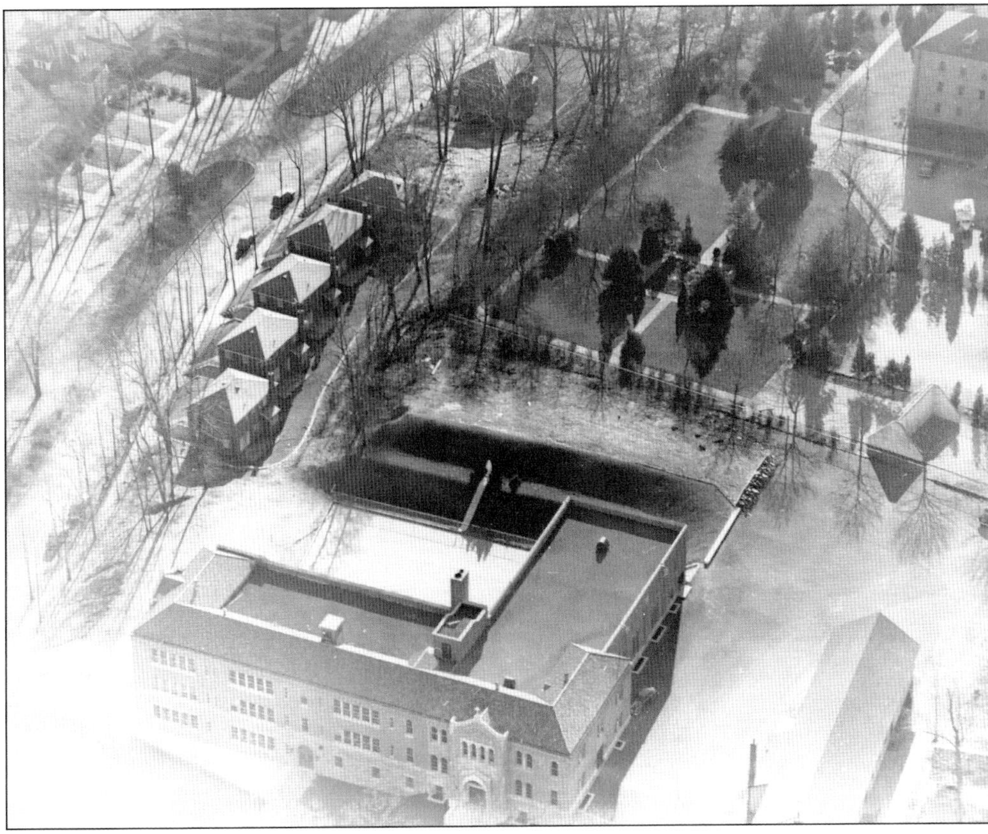

In 1950, a wing was added to the school on the right, creating more classrooms, a library, an auditorium, a gym, and a cafeteria. Behind the school, a grassy slope with staircase leads to a limestone statue of Mary and beyond the cemetery. Visible at the upper right are the handball and tennis courts once used by the priests and seminarians. The parish hall is seen on the lower right, and Midland Parkway is visible at the far left.

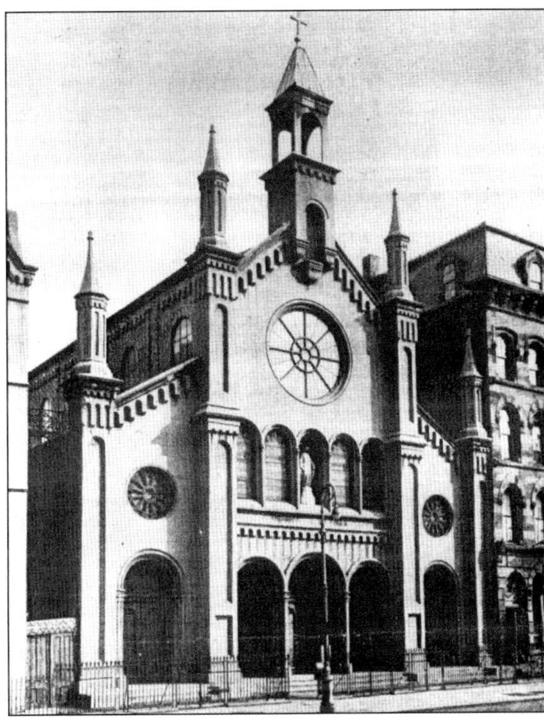

This church was the first dedicated to the Immaculate Conception in 1858. In 1945, it was demolished for the creation of Stuyvesant Town. Through the efforts of Thomas Campbell Sr., the limestone statue of Mary on the facade above the main door was saved and brought to the school yard of the Jamaica Estates Immaculate Conception School, seen in the photograph above.

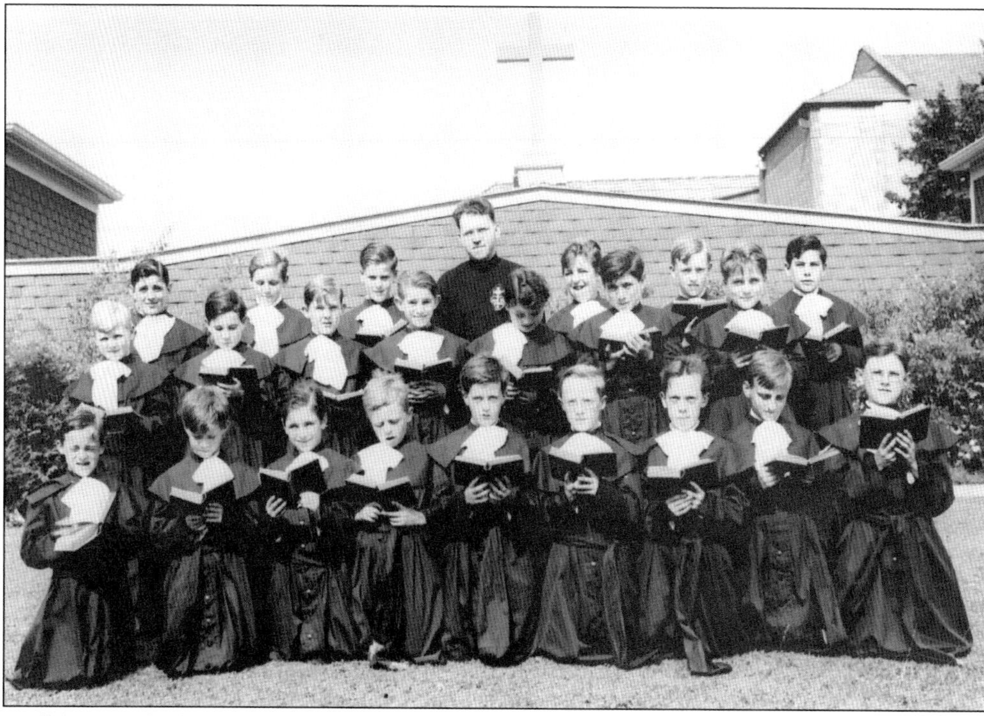

Well known for his work in Passionist Radio and Television ministry, Fr. Fidelis Rice, C.P., stated, "I received an incredible appointment, one never given to a Passionist before. I became the salaried Choirmaster and Organist at Immaculate Conception. Like any parish organist, I had to train the choir, play for all the Masses, weddings, and funerals, and all other choral needs of a growing parish."

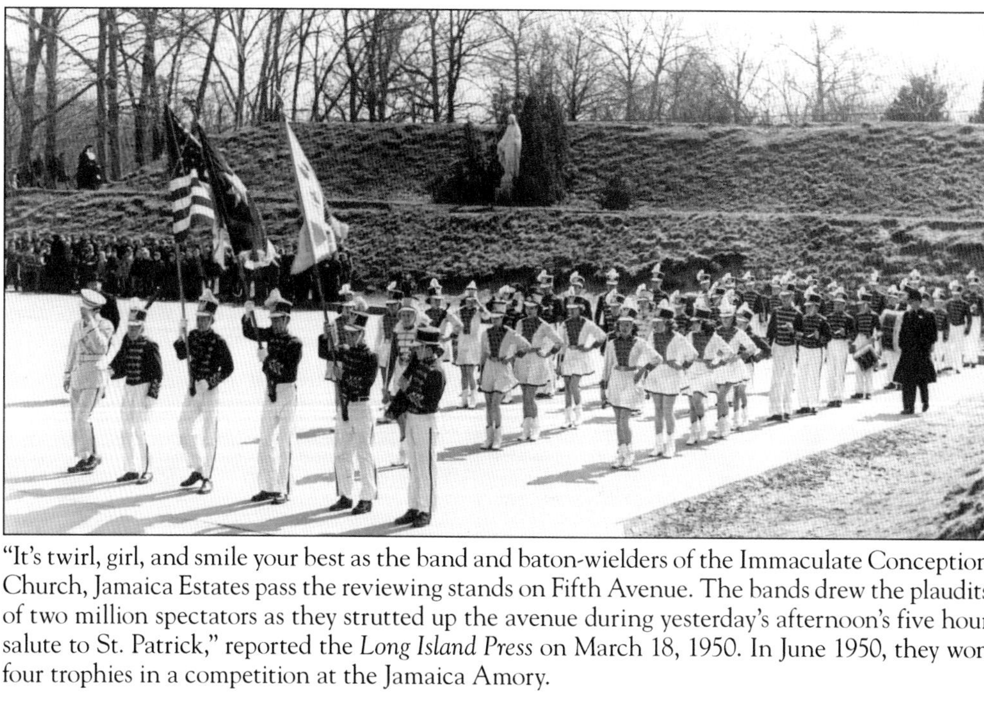

"It's twirl, girl, and smile your best as the band and baton-wielders of the Immaculate Conception Church, Jamaica Estates pass the reviewing stands on Fifth Avenue. The bands drew the plaudits of two million spectators as they strutted up the avenue during yesterday's afternoon's five hour salute to St. Patrick," reported the *Long Island Press* on March 18, 1950. In June 1950, they won four trophies in a competition at the Jamaica Amory.

It was decided that the old Degnon mansion of 1910 should be torn down for a new Retreat House wing. It had been parish folklore that parts of the mansion were preserved and that the new wing was built around it, but in this 1952 photograph, it is clearly visible that nothing is left of the old stately home. Louis E. Jallade, the famed architect, designed the new Retreat House addition.

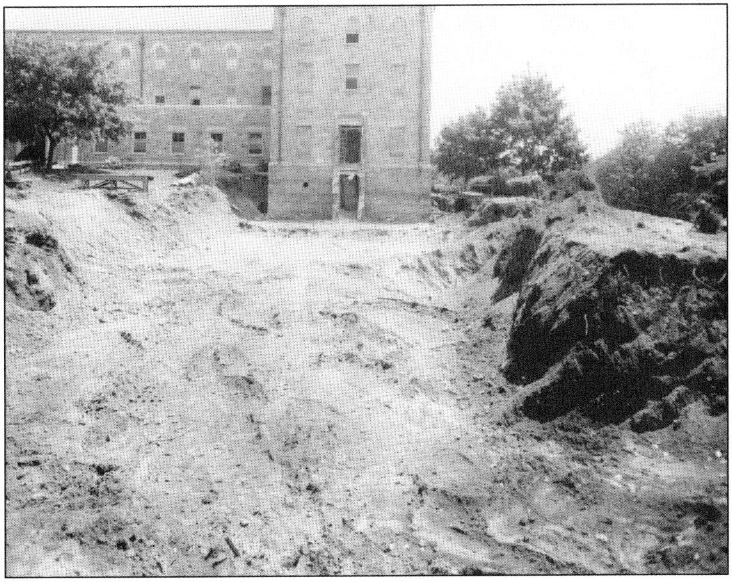

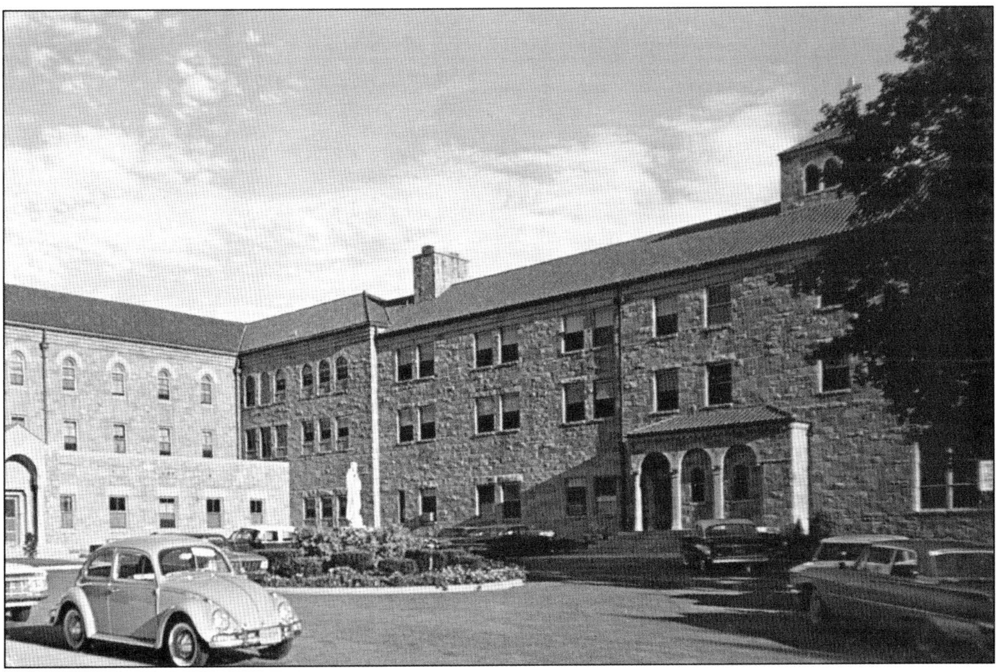

According to the July 5, 1952, *Tablet*, "The new building is built in the form of a 'T.' The new kitchen and dining room will have light and ventilation on three sides with a recreation and study room. There will be 75 bedrooms in addition to the 50 rooms in the old building. It will be connected to the existing Monastery and Chapel by means of a direct corridor."

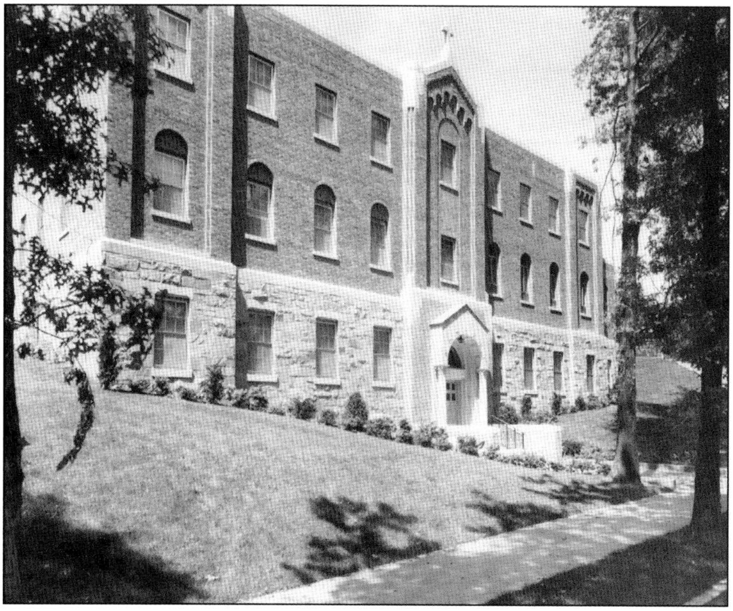

Under the direction of the fifth pastor, Fr. Owen Doyle, C.P., a new convent was erected. Father Doyle (1898–1971) served as pastor from 1942 to 1966. "On July 1, 1954 the Sisters moved to the beautiful new convent erected for them and was voted in the Queens architectural competition for 1954, the outstanding structure erected in the borough," reported the *Flowering Staff* in 1956.

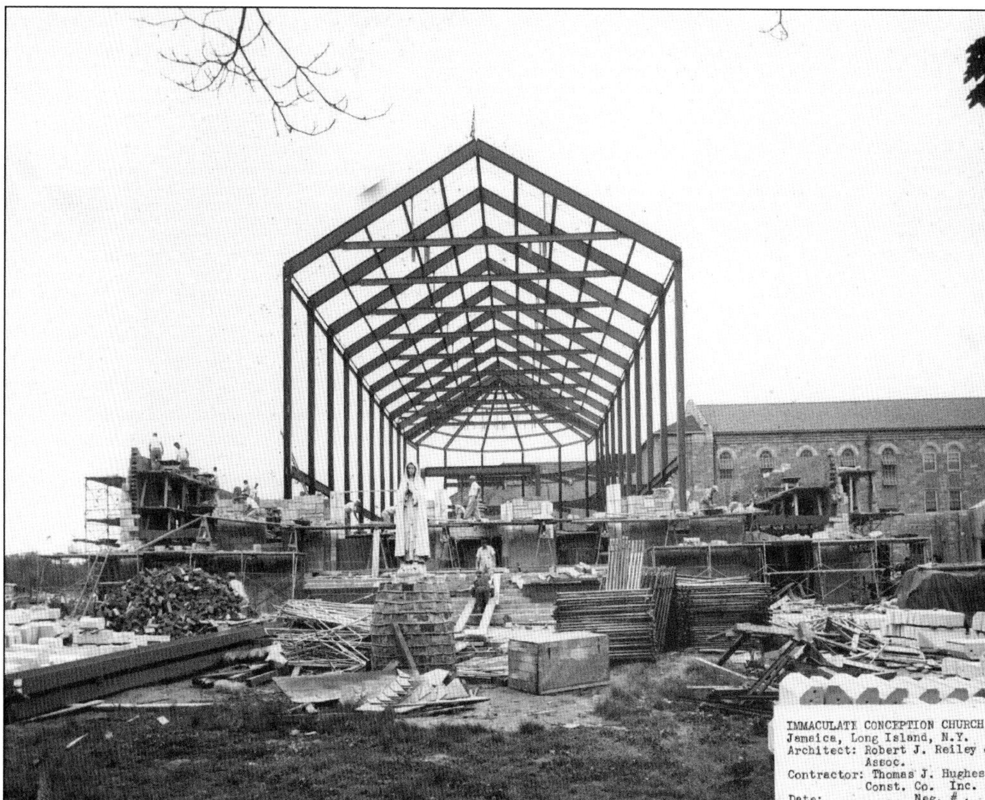

After decades of planning, contracts were signed in 1958 to construct the long-awaited Upper Church. Construction was well under way in this June 1960 photograph. Noted church architect Robert J. Reilly designed the building in the Romanesque style to seat 1,350 people. The construction of the building took three years to complete.

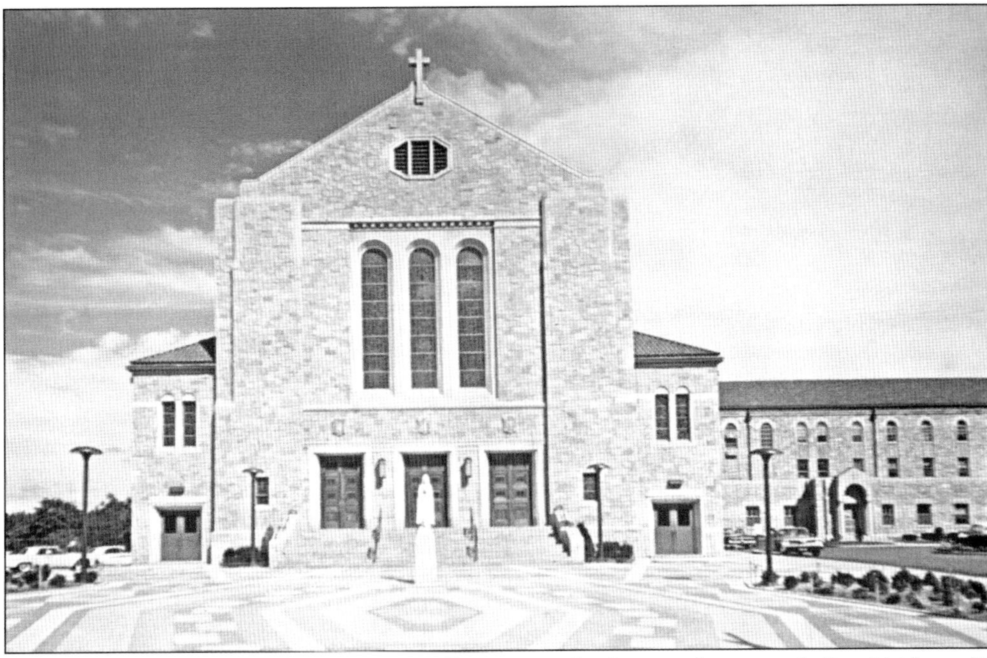

On September 22, 1962, Bishop Bryan J. McEntegart, with a large gathering including 3 bishops, 30 monsignori, 80 priests, and over 150 sisters, dedicated the completed church. "Bishop McEntegart officiated at the blessing and also spoke, citing the Blessed Mother, Patroness of the parish, Diocese and Country, as a model for the people," reported the *Tablet* on September 30, 1962.

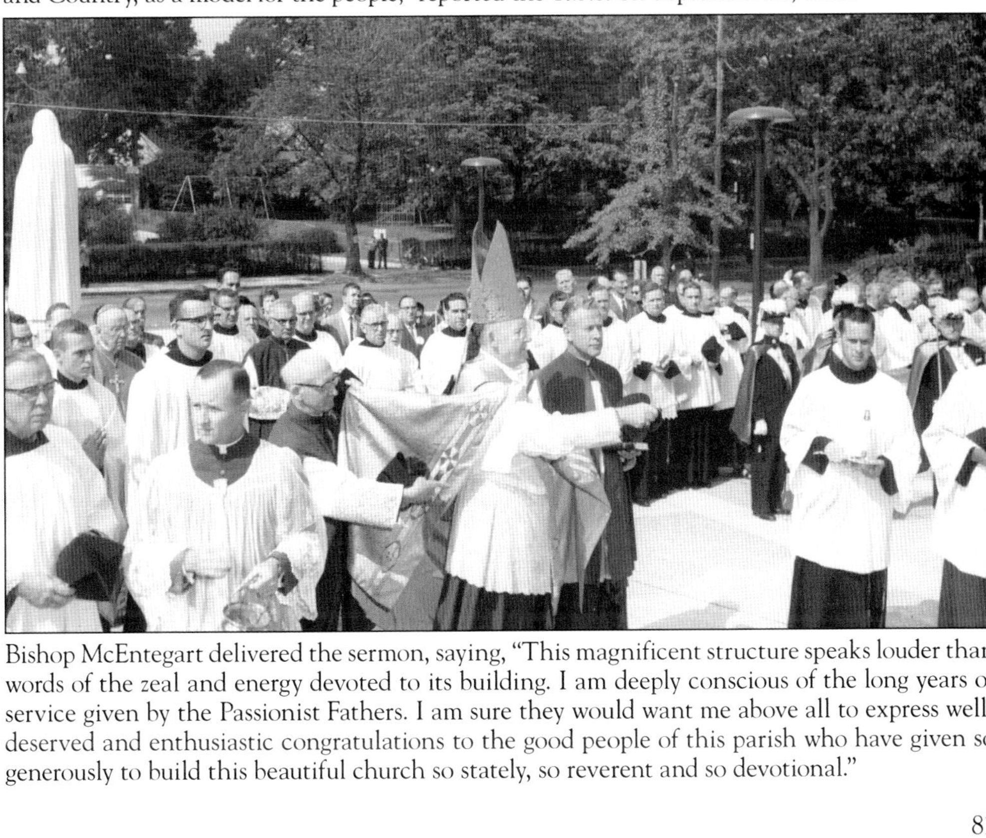

Bishop McEntegart delivered the sermon, saying, "This magnificent structure speaks louder than words of the zeal and energy devoted to its building. I am deeply conscious of the long years of service given by the Passionist Fathers. I am sure they would want me above all to express well-deserved and enthusiastic congratulations to the good people of this parish who have given so generously to build this beautiful church so stately, so reverent and so devotional."

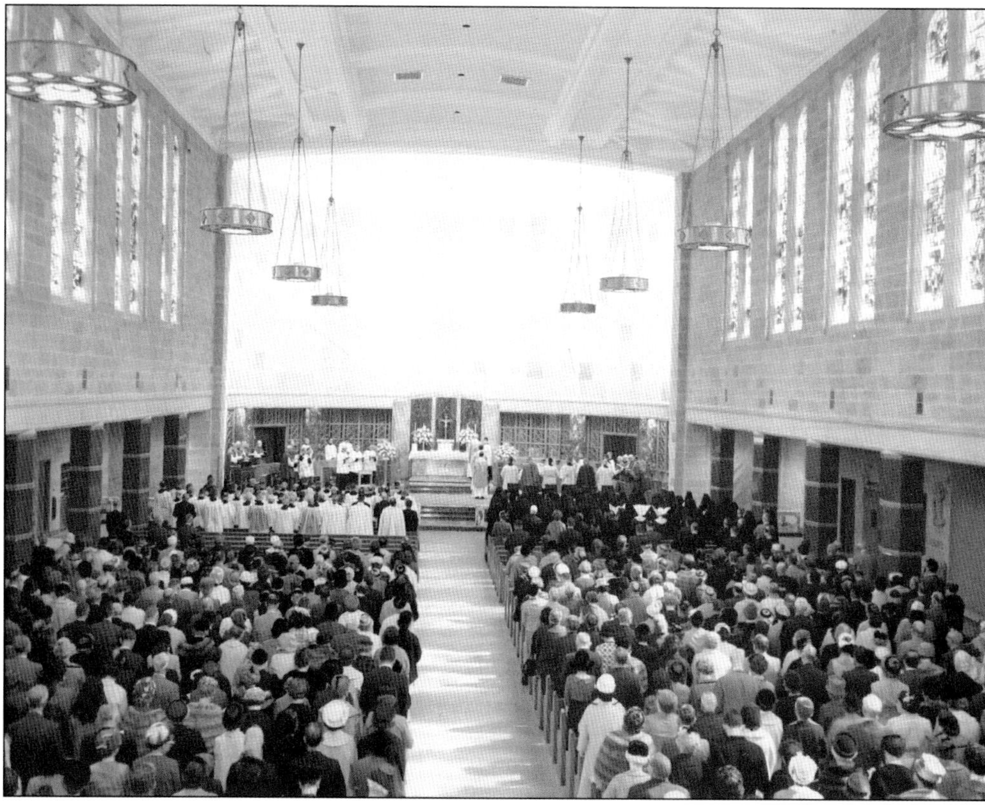

There are 35 windows that measure 17 feet by 3 feet. The story of the Immaculate Conception is told in the three windows over the choir loft. On the right side is a complete Rosary in symbols. The picture on the left depicts the seven Sacraments and the gift of the Holy Spirit that goes with each Sacrament. There is a 14-foot bronze crucifixion group above the main altar.

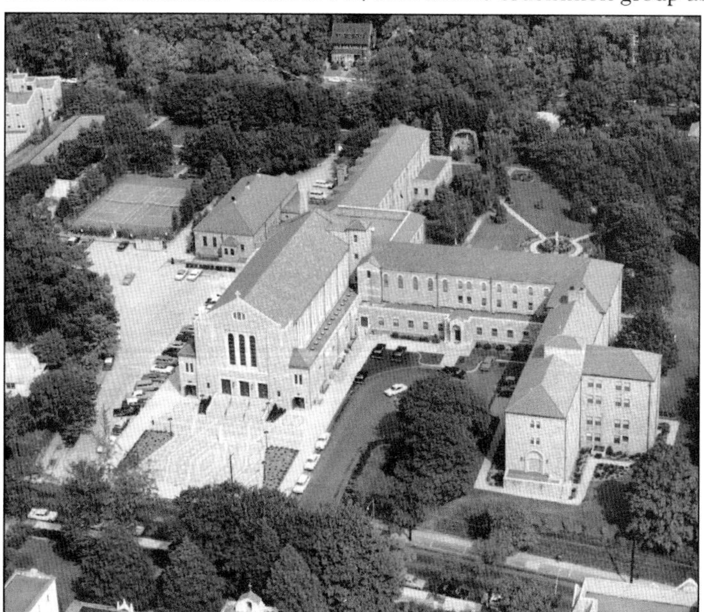

This 1962 aerial view shows the school and convent in the upper left. Next are the monastery and separate refectory, then the Upper Church and the Bishop Molloy Retreat House. Passionist Fathers who also served as pastors included Fr. Kevin Murray (1929–1931), Fr. Theodore Noonan (1931–1935), Fr. Hurbert Arliss (1966–1969), Fr. Peter Quinn (1969–1976), Fr. Alexis Paul (1976–1982), Fr. Thomas Joyce (1982–2007), and Fr. Jed Sumampong (2007 to present).

Four

People, Places, and Events

Making Jamaica Estates Unique

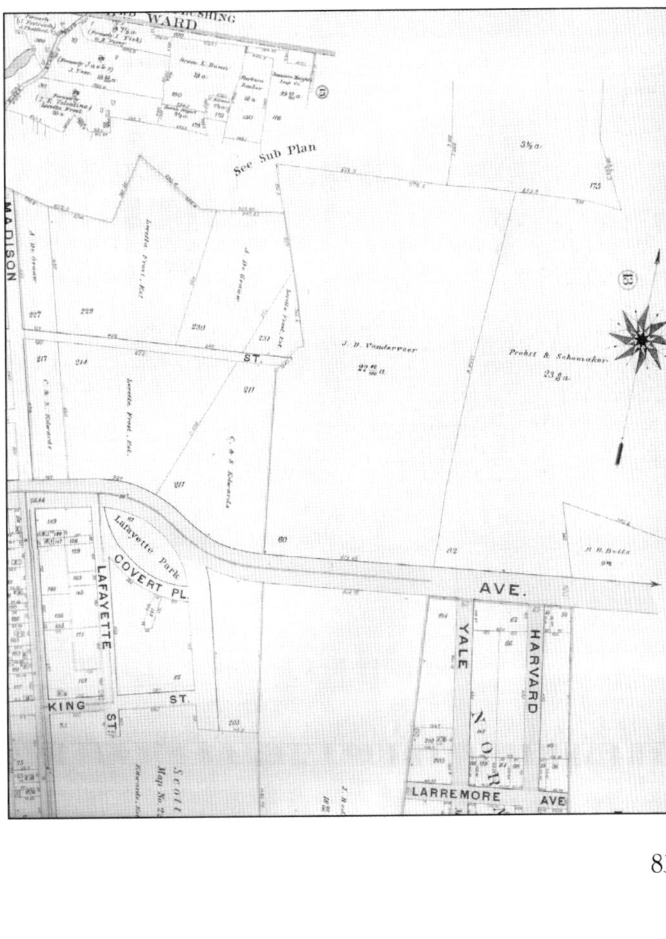

Michael Bookbinder, former president of the Jamaica Estates Association explains, "This 1891 map was created before the development of Jamaica Estates. The land once owned by Vandeveer, Schomaker, Betts, Frost, DeGrauw and Edwards. Since 1929, The Jamaica Estates Association has actively served this community to maintain and promote the civic and social welfare and interest of all residents and property owners."

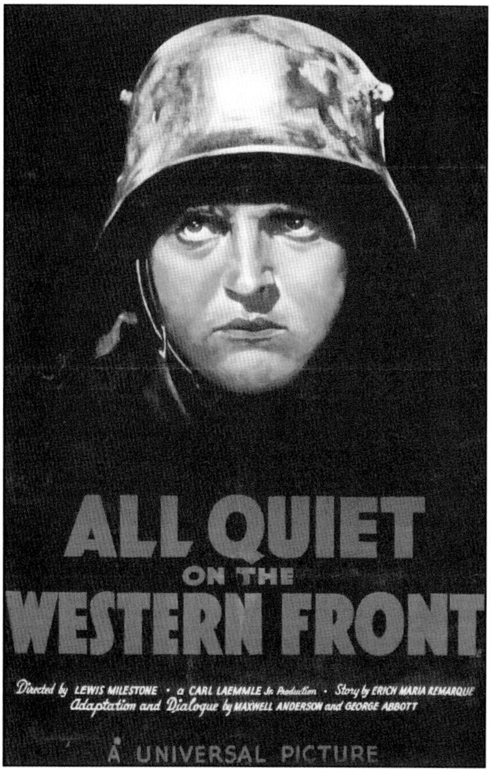

"Edmund Breese, the actor, bought an acre plot at Avon Road and Lancaster Boulevard. Plans for a white concrete house with red tile roof," reported the *New York Times* on January 3, 1908. Born 1871, he enjoyed a long pre-film career as a vaudevillian, touring actor, monologist, dialectician, and playwright. Breese made his talking-picture debut in Al Jolson's *Sonny Boy* and went on to play Herr Meyer in *All Quiet on the Western Front* (1933) and Prime Minister Zander in the Marx Brothers' *Duck Soup* (1933).

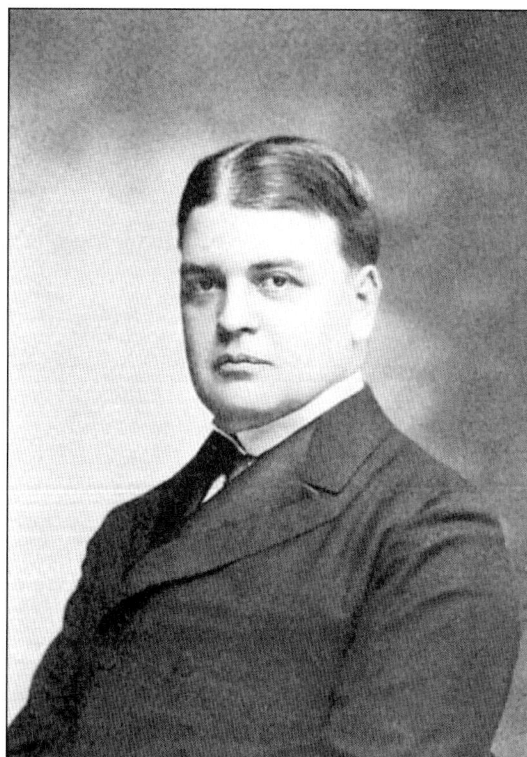

"Mr. Woodruff is the newly elected President of Jamaica Estates," the *New York Times* reported on January 30, 1910. Orphaned as a boy, Timothy Lester Woodruff was an enterprising and self-made man. In 1896, he was appointed Brooklyn Park Commissioner and later elected lieutenant governor of New York. In 1900, he had been promised the vice presidential nomination, but the William McKinley campaign preferred Theodore Roosevelt. Had he been chosen, he would have succeeded to the presidency upon McKinley's assassination in 1901.

According to the *New York Times* on May 24, 1908, "The Ernestus Gulick Company has sold at Jamaica Estates the corner of Doncaster Boulevard and Midland Parkway, a plot to Francis H. Kimball. He is drawing the plans for a home." Architect Francis Hatch Kimball (1845–1919) was best known for his work on skyscrapers in Manhattan and a pioneer in the use of ornamental terra-cotta. He designed the Adams Building, pictured here in 1916.

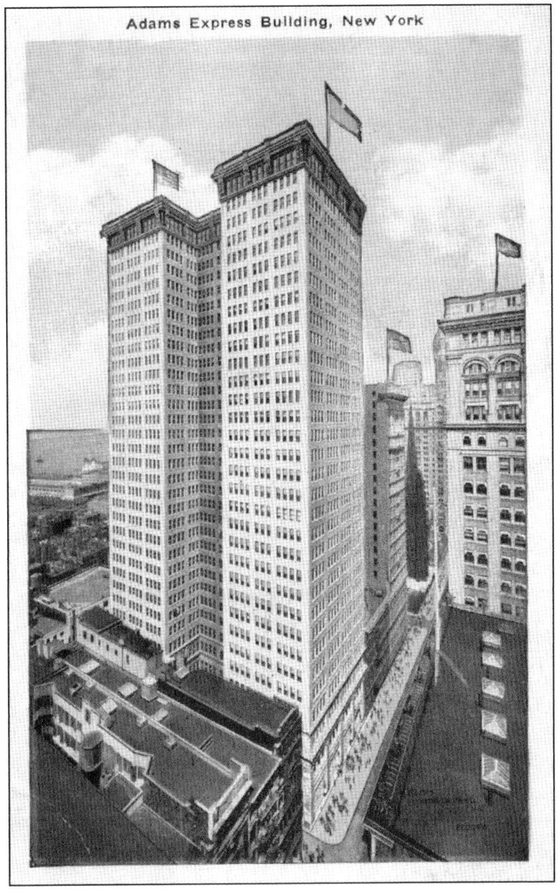

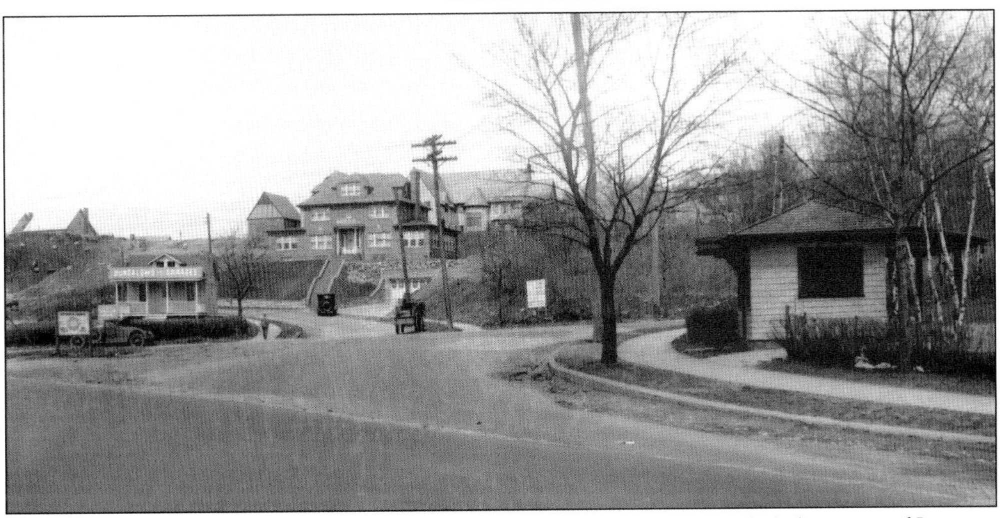

According to the *New York Times* on June 26, 1910, "The rolling, wooded character of Jamaica Estates has given some difficult problems to its engineering force, especially as every effort is made to preserve the heavy timber lands while installing the permanent underground work. Splendid progress has been made. Six more houses are to be started this coming week." This photograph shows Hillside Avenue north of 173rd Street in 1931. (Courtesy of Q Gardens Gallery.)

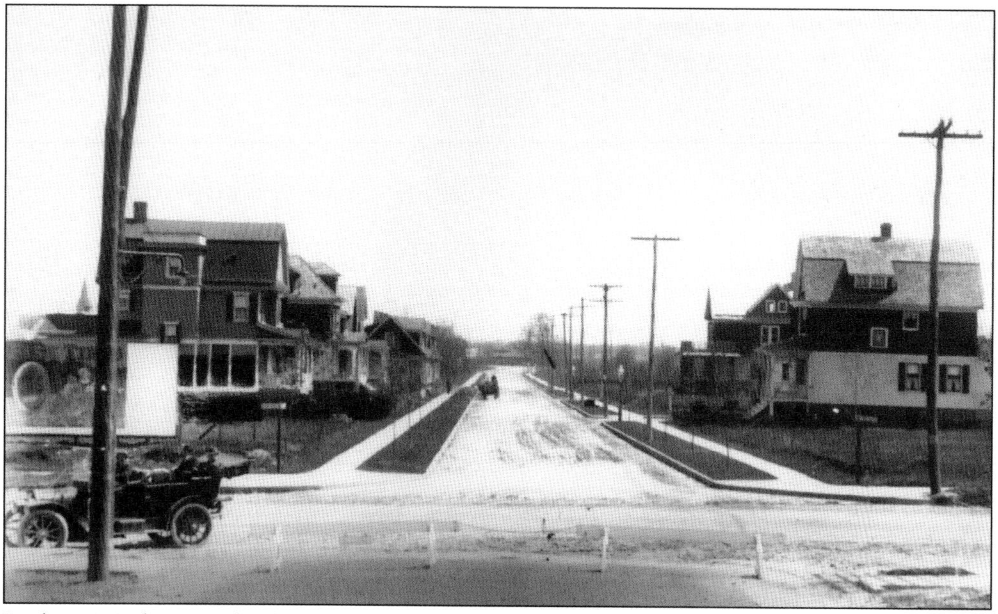

In this 1910 photograph of Hillside Avenue looking south on Homer Lee Avenue (178th Street), old gaslights line the street in the distance. On the pole in the foreground is a newly installed electric light. The Jamaica Estates Corporation bought property along this block to their Hillside Station on the Long Island Railroad, which can be seen in the distance. (Courtesy of the Queens Borough Public Library, Long Island Division, Frederick J. Weber Collection.)

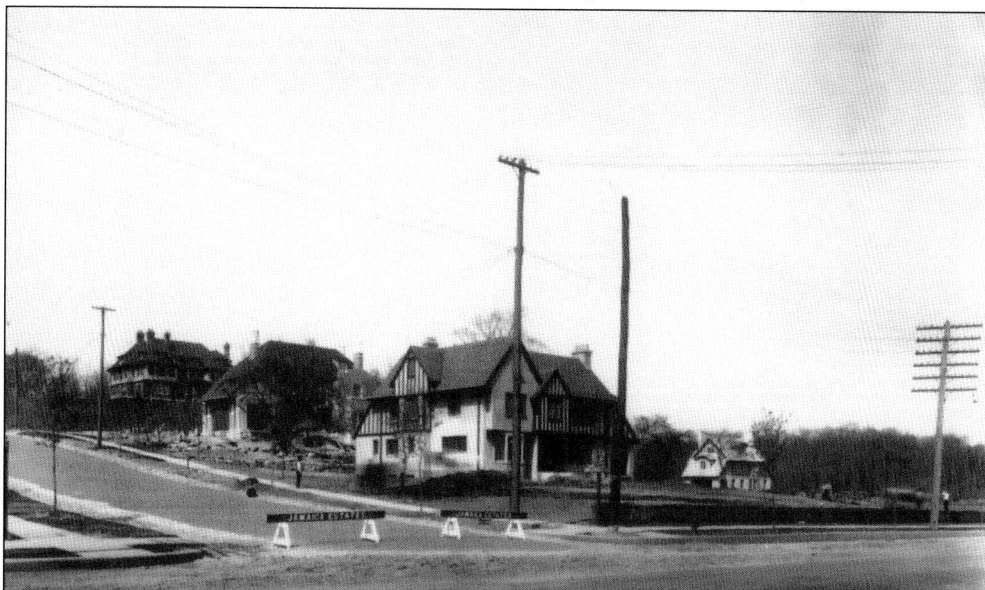

Here is the same intersection looking north from Hillside Avenue to Edgerton Boulevard. The Degnon mansion is visible at the top. "Major Gulick has contracted for a number of gasoline automobile omnibuses for Jamaica Estates, that were first popular in London and Paris. The big buses have a seating capacity of forty-eight and have two decks," reported the *New York Times* on August 27, 1907. (Courtesy of the Queens Borough Public Library, Long Island Division, Frederick J. Weber Collection.)

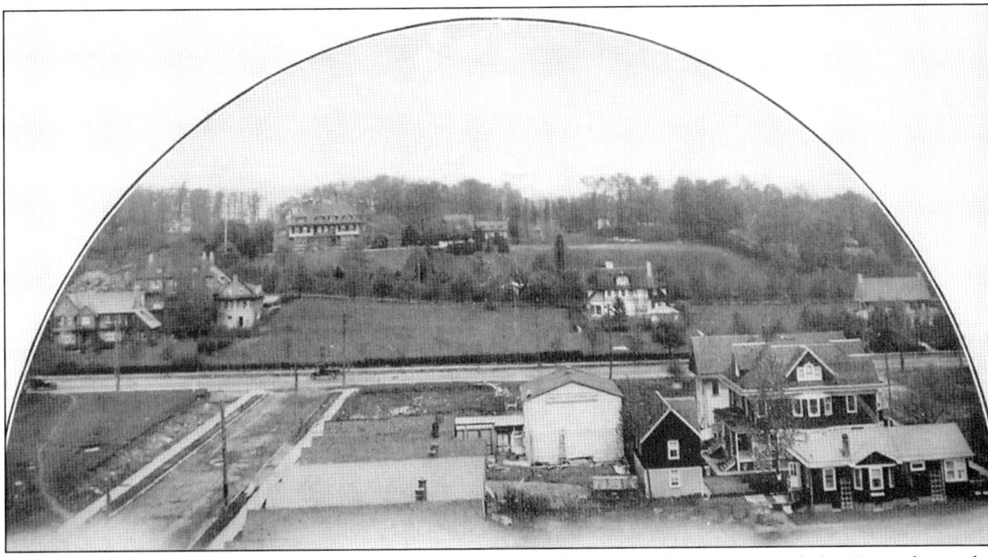

"The property is well wooded and is located half way between the ocean and the Sound, on the high ridge equal in altitude to Washington Heights on New York City. All improvements have been installed, including sewers, water, gas, electricity, and telephones," reported the *New York Times* on June 30, 1912. Looking north, 179th Street is seen at the left and Hillside Avenue is in the center. The Degnon house and stables are on the hill.

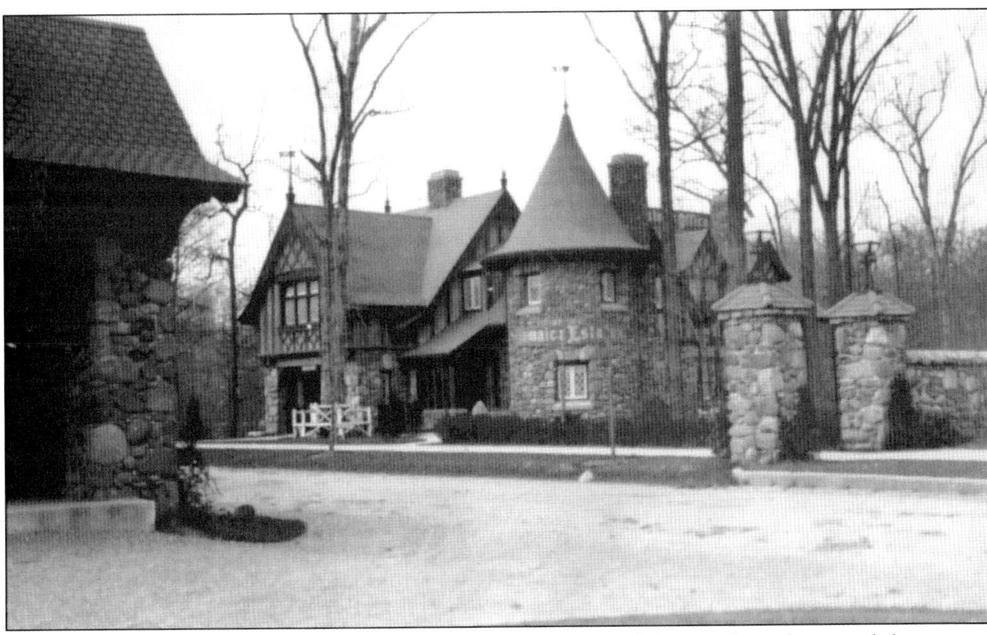

The September 8, 1912, *New York Times* reported, "A count of the number of automobiles passing the entrance lodge in fifteen minutes were 560 cars; in one hour, 1,664, and in four hours, 3,845 cars. The owners of the Estates are considering operating a bus line from New York City to Jamaica. Each bus will make the trip in little over half an hour." (Courtesy of the Queens Borough Public Library, Long Island Division, Post Card Collection.)

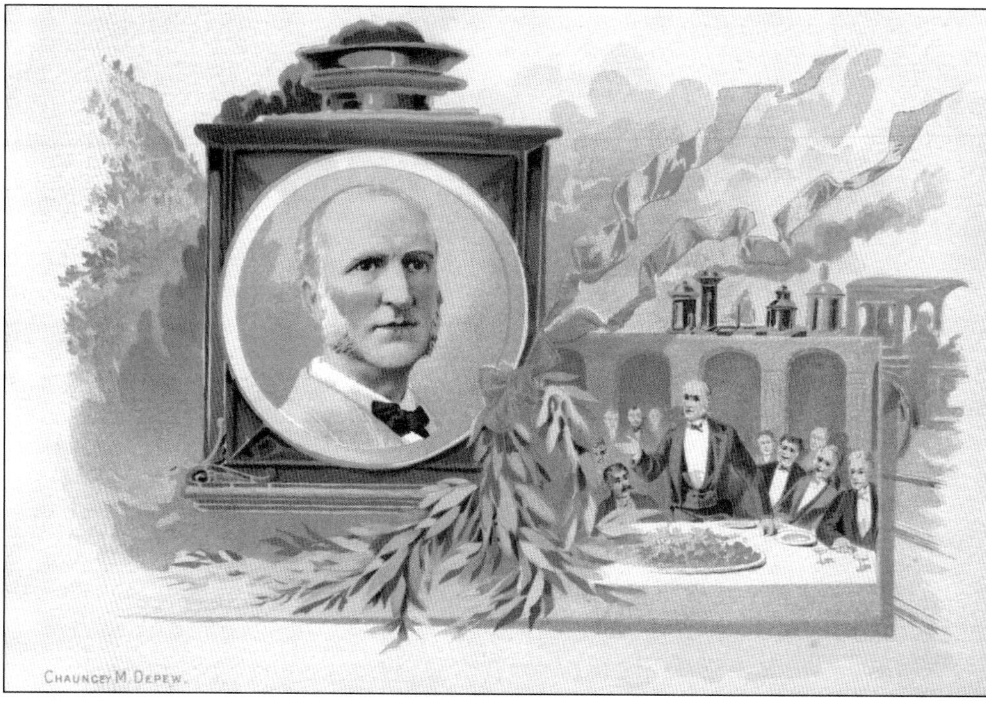

"Midland Parkway house for Chauncey Depew at Jamaica Estates by Mann and MacNeille Architects," reported the *New York Times* on August 24, 1913. Chauncey Depew (1834–1928) was a lawyer, politician, and railroad man. He also served as New York secretary of state (1863–1865) and New York senator (1899–1911). He escorted Pres. Abraham Lincoln's body from the New York State border to Buffalo. A friend of Lincoln, his house was a brick replica of Lincoln's Springfield home.

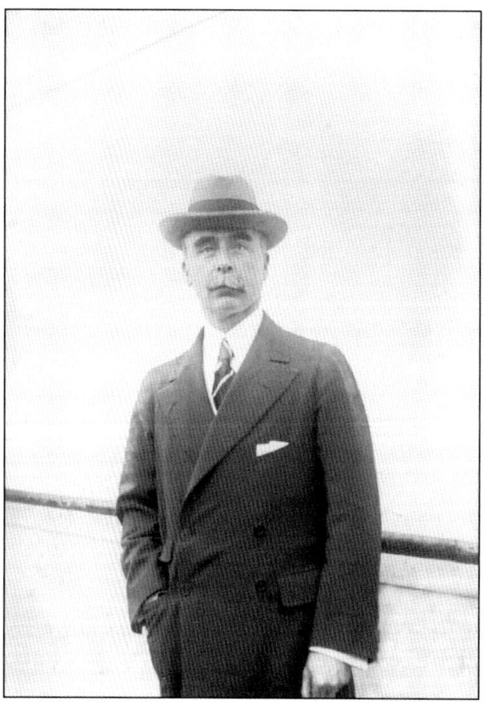

The March 5, 1914, *New York Times* reported, "Clarence H. MacKay has purchased eight plots in Jamaica Estates. The property is on Radnor Road and is one of the most desirable." Son of "Silver King" John W. Mackay, he inherited his father's fortune. When his daughter married composer Irving Berlin against his wishes, he disinherited her, but they later reconciled. He invested but did not live in Jamaica Estates. Other investors were William K. Vanderbilt and Harry Payne Whitney.

J. Wilbur Chapman (1859–1918) was an evangelist, revivalist, and pastor. Chapman took on several pastorates before shifting to the evangelistic circuit. He began preaching with the legendary D. L. Moody in 1893, as well as leading many evangelistic events of his own. Among Chapman's disciples on the evangelistic circuit was William "Billy" Sunday. He wrote the words to the hymns "One Day," "Jesus! What a Friend for Sinners" ("Our Great Saviour"), and " 'Tis Jesus."

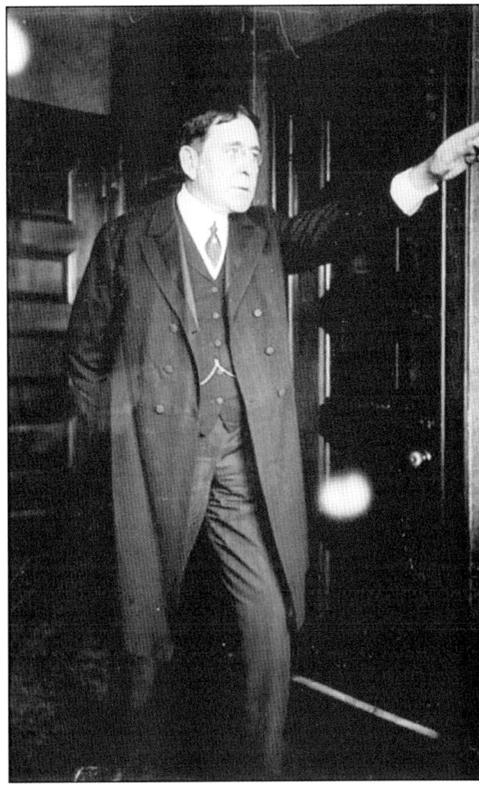

On January 29, 1911, the *New York Times* reported, "Rapid progress has a been made on the new residence being built in Jamaica Estates for Dr. J. Chapman." Another article on January 16, 1915, stated, "Evangelist's daughter is to wed. Agnes Chapman and Frederick Linder engagement announced. The wedding is to take place in the early spring at the Chapman home at Jamaica Estates, L. I." (Illustration by Ken Boatwright.)

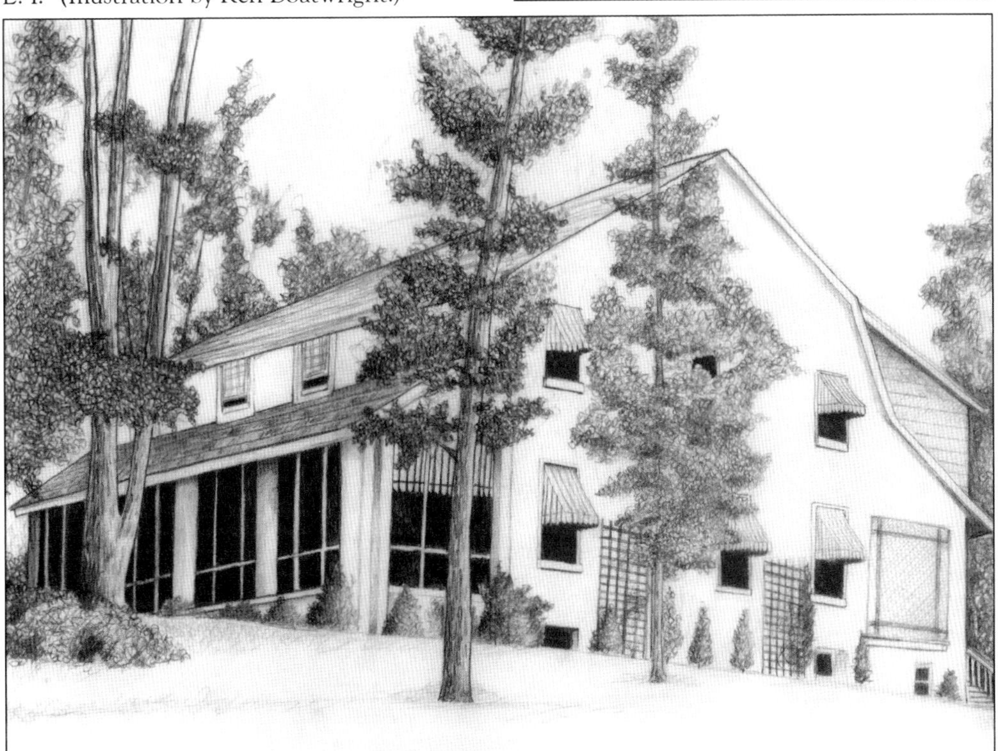

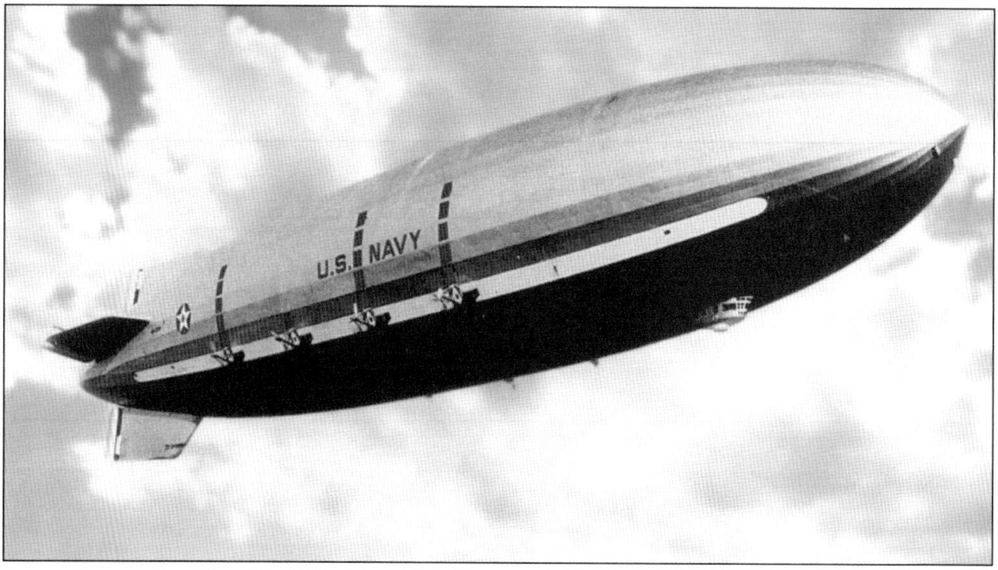

According to the May 12, 1918, *New York Times*, "A US Navy dirigible floating over the city aiding in the Liberty Loan war campaign was forced to land. While the balloon was drifting over Jamaica Estates it took a sudden dip over the property of Michael Degnon. Part of the rigging was torn by a limb of a high tree. The escaping gas caused it to tilt downward going down slowly. Three men in the car were not injured."

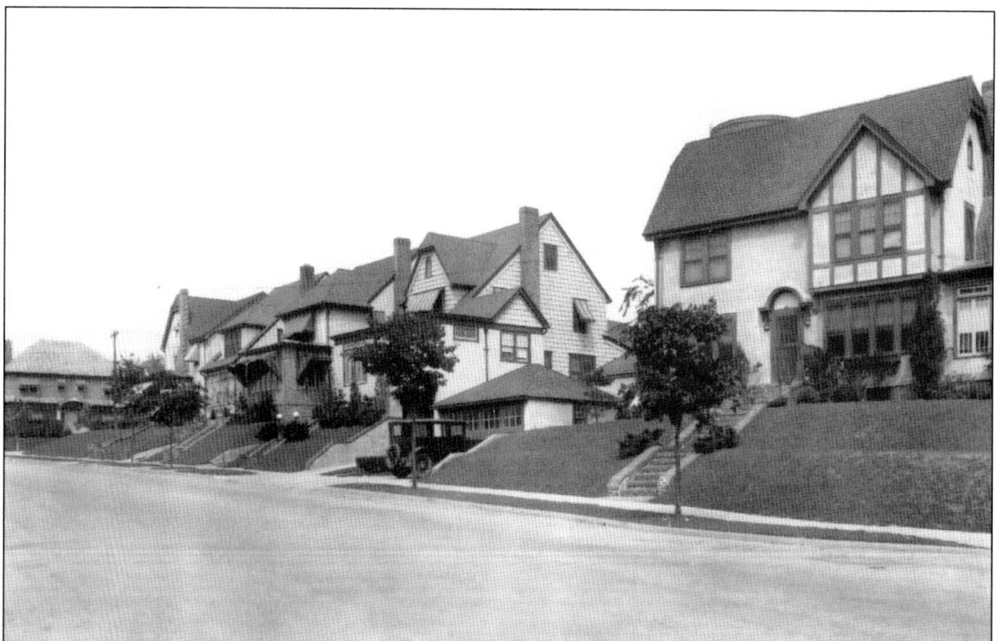

"A meeting of 2,500 owners of property at Jamaica Estates has formed the Jamaica Estates Property Owners' Association, James Murphy as President," reported the *New York Times* on June 19, 1921. Another article on October 2 reported, "At a meeting the numerous good points of Jamaica Estates were explained and sanctioned the plan for regulating and grading, installation of sewers and other city improvements by private contract." Homelawn Street (Avenue) is pictured here in 1930. (Courtesy of Q Gardens Gallery.)

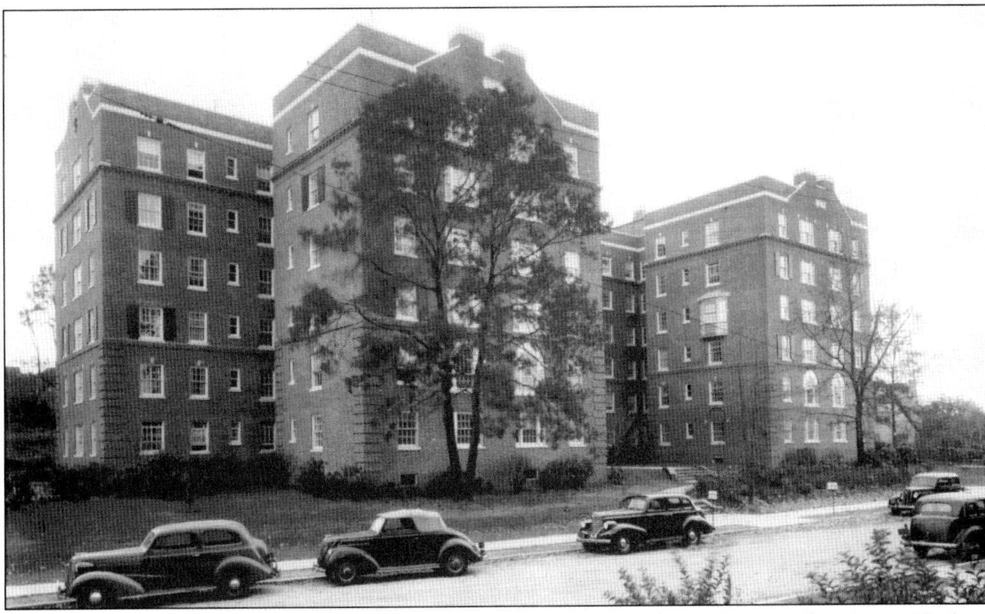

This 1927 photograph shows the apartment on Devonshire Road (Henley Road). "Harry Clark an actor residing at Henley Hall plays the part of Harry Kaye in 'Will Success Spoil Rock Hunter?'. A school teacher before appearing in Broadway Shows like 'Kiss Me Kate' singing and dancing in many of his roles, he had many appearances on television, including 'No Time For Sergeant,'" reported the February 29, 1956, *New York Times*. (Courtesy of the Queens Borough Public Library, Long Island Division, Frederick J. Weber Collection.)

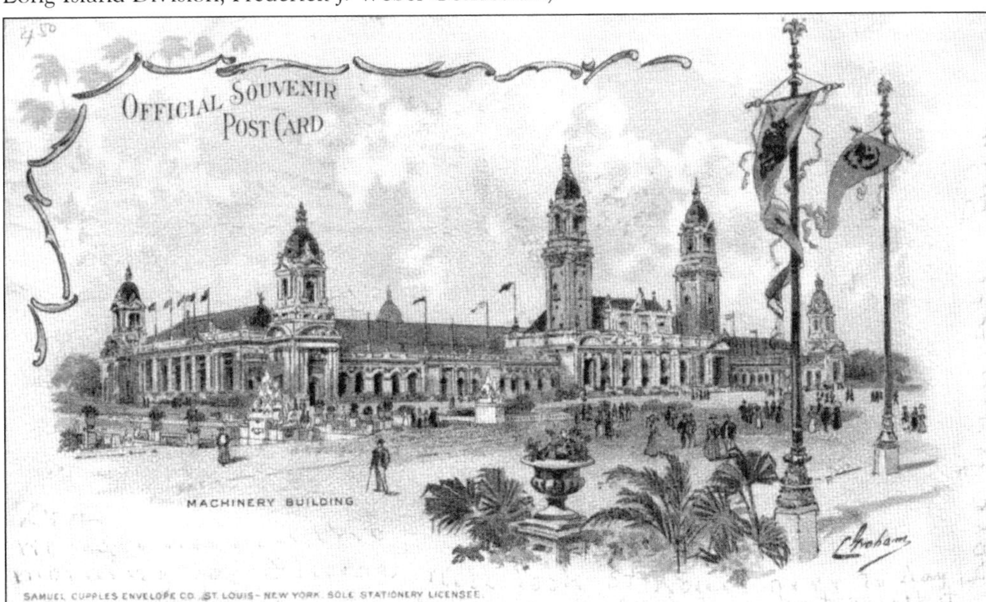

The following was reported in the January 21, 1933, *New York Times*: "Augustine Davis, inventor and manufacturer of acetylene lighting and welding apparatus of Wexford Terrace, Jamaica Estates. Born in 1852 in Iowa he moved to Lewiston, N. Y. and took a leading part in the construction of the Niagara Power Canal. In 1904 he received a gold medal for his exhibition of acetylene apparatus at the Louisiana Purchase Exposition at St. Louis."

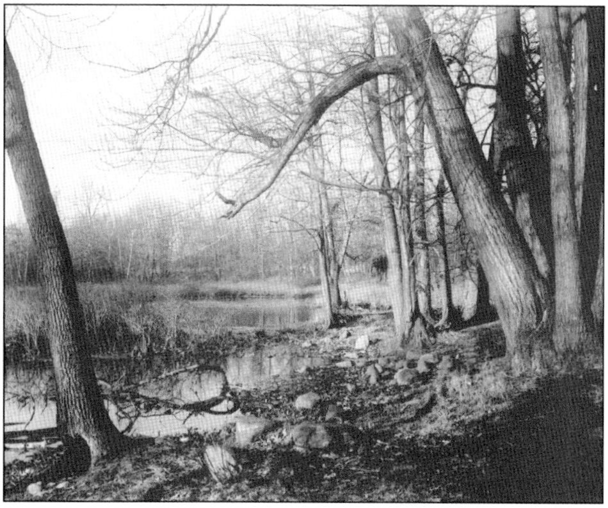

"Vicki Baum, author of 'Grand Hotel', was riding in the woods north of Jamaica Estates, north of Midland Parkway and 188th Street, when a squirrel darted out. Her horse galloped away. Falling she suffered a lacerated head and fractures of at least two ribs," reported the *New York Times* on May 23, 1932. Her novel became the 1932 Best Picture movie starring Greta Garbo, John Barrymore, and Joan Crawford. (Courtesy of the Queens Borough Public Library, Long Island Division, George Winans Collection.)

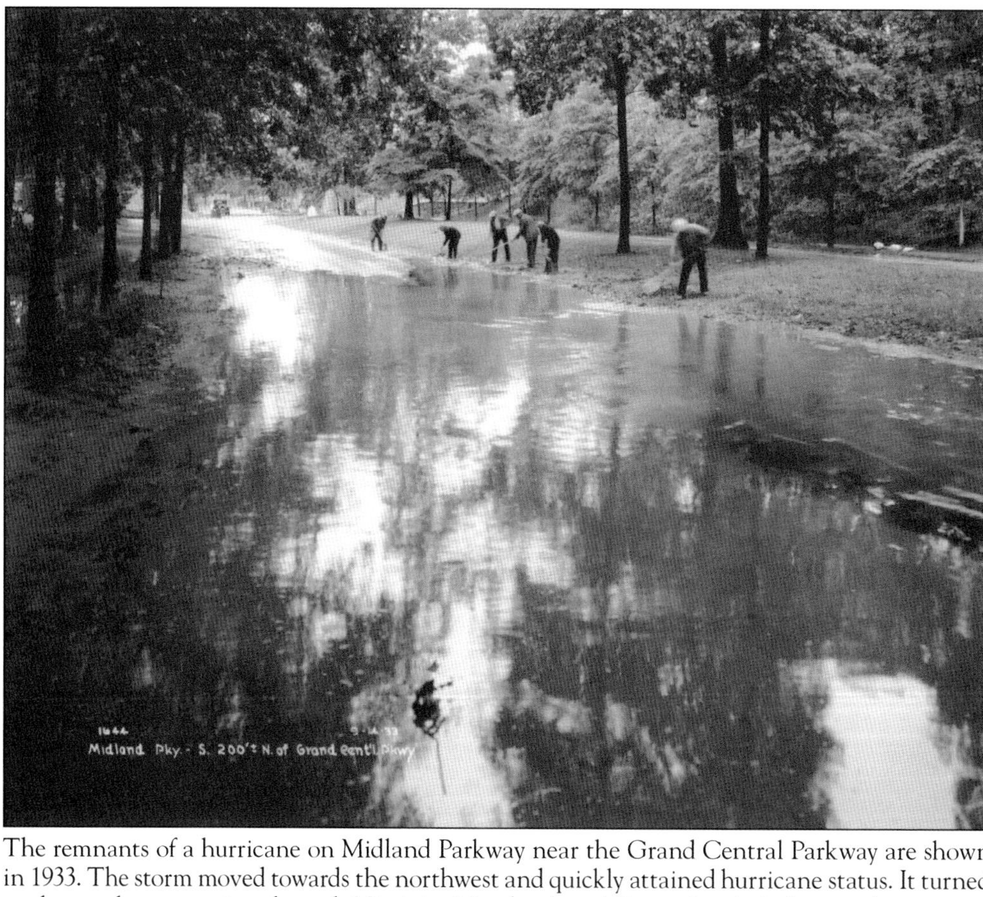

The remnants of a hurricane on Midland Parkway near the Grand Central Parkway are shown in 1933. The storm moved towards the northwest and quickly attained hurricane status. It turned to the northeast, passing through Virginia, Maryland, and Pennsylvania before weakening to a tropical depression over New York. (Courtesy of the Queens Borough Public Library, Long Island Division, Borough President of Queens Collection.)

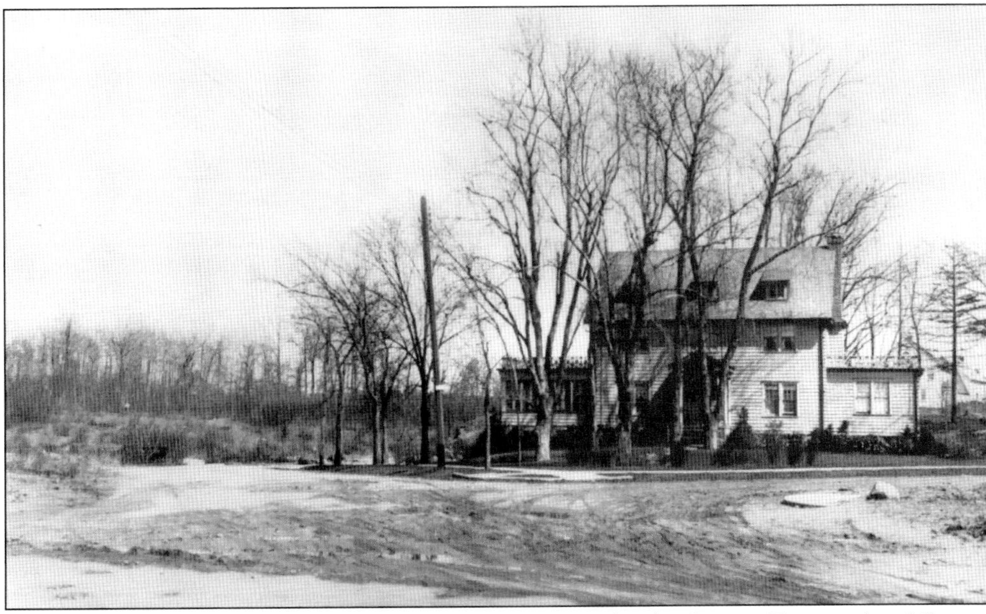

The parkway had been planned as early as 1913. Engineers for the Queens Topographical Society proposed a limited-access parkway connecting Queens Boulevard in Kew Gardens with Nassau County. This April 6, 1927, photograph looks east from Homelawn Street with Charlecote Ridge to the right of the house. The forest to the left is now the six-lane Grand Central Parkway. (Courtesy of the Queens Borough Public Library, Long Island Division, Eugene L. Armbruster Collection.)

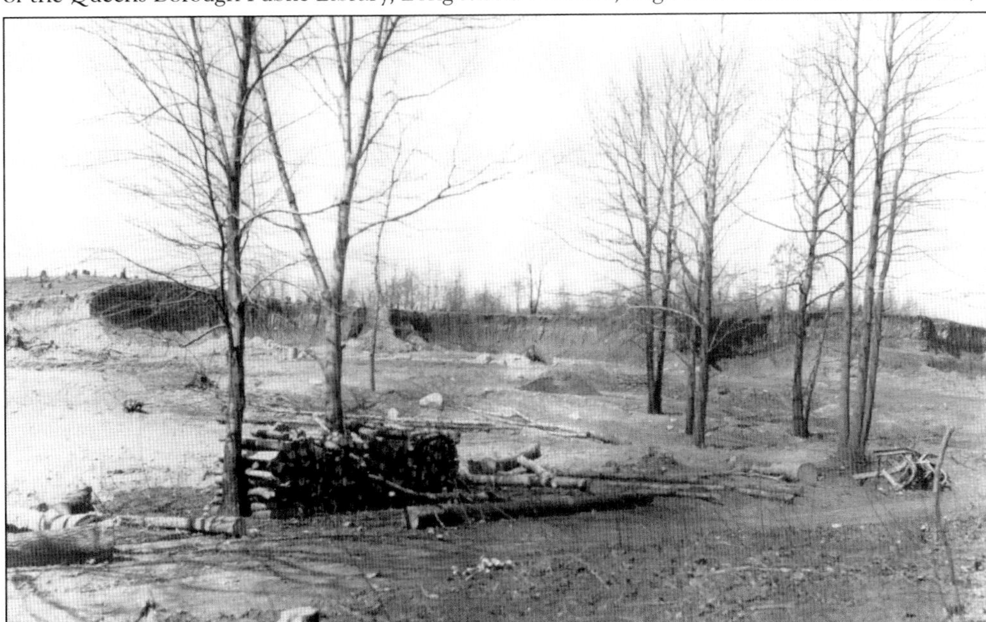

Begun in July 1931 at a ceremony held at the Queens-Nassau border attended by Robert Moses and Gov. Franklin D. Roosevelt, the initial section of the parkway, a 9-mile-long, four-lane section between Kew Gardens and Glen Oaks, opened in July 1933. This April 6, 1927, photograph shows the land north of Jamaica Estates cleared for the proposed Grand Central Parkway. (Courtesy of the Queens Borough Public Library, Long Island Division, Eugene L. Armbruster Collection.)

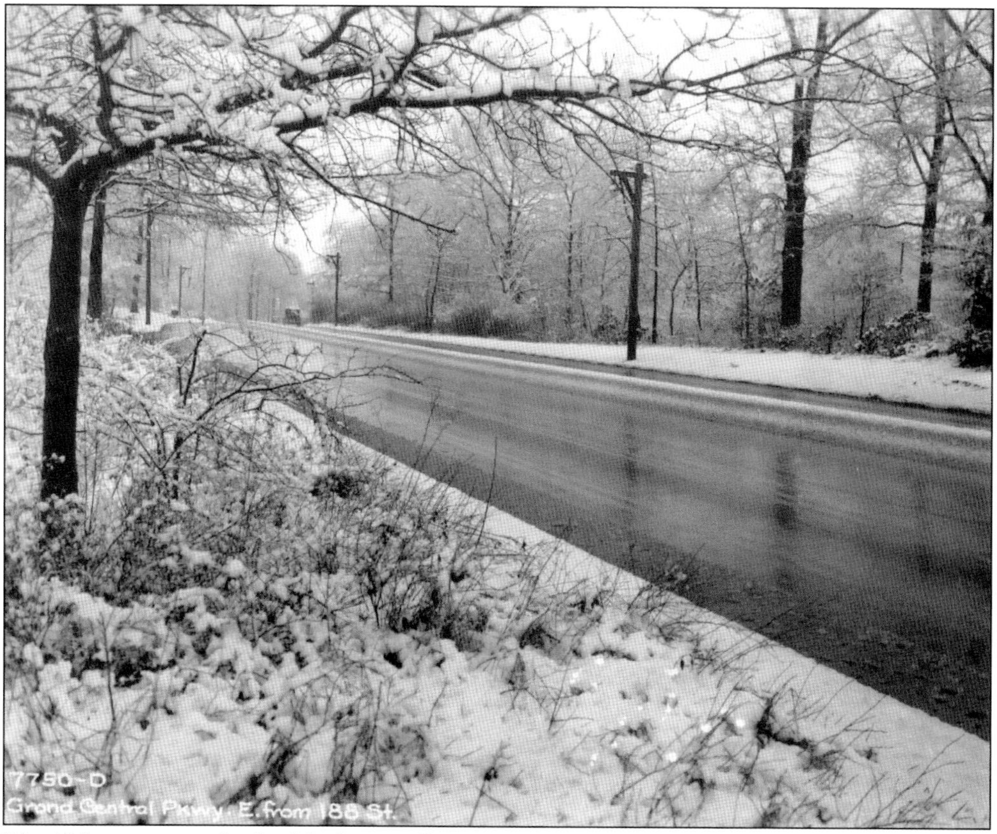

The 40th anniversary book of the Jamaica Estates Association reports: "The Grand Central Parkway opened in 1933. When the state decided to widen the Parkway to six lanes it caused the condemnation of 10 houses by the Midland Parkway. The city took title to these condemned houses in November 1961 and the residents were ordered to vacate by July 1, 1962." (Courtesy of the Queens Borough Public Library, Long Island Division, Borough President of Queens Collection.)

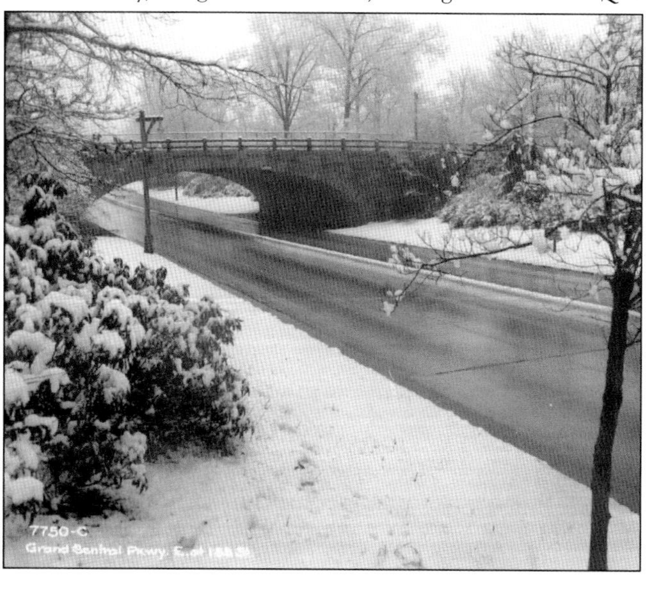

"They began their celebrations at a fifty foot Christmas tree on Midland and the Grand Central Parkway with Santa Claus on a white horse, preceded by two trumpeters on white horses and followed by an Old English tally-ho, of people in Old English costumes, a truck with forty carolers and thirty automobiles," reported the *New York Times* on December 25, 1935. (Courtesy of the Queens Borough Public Library, Long Island Division, Borough President of Queens Collection.)

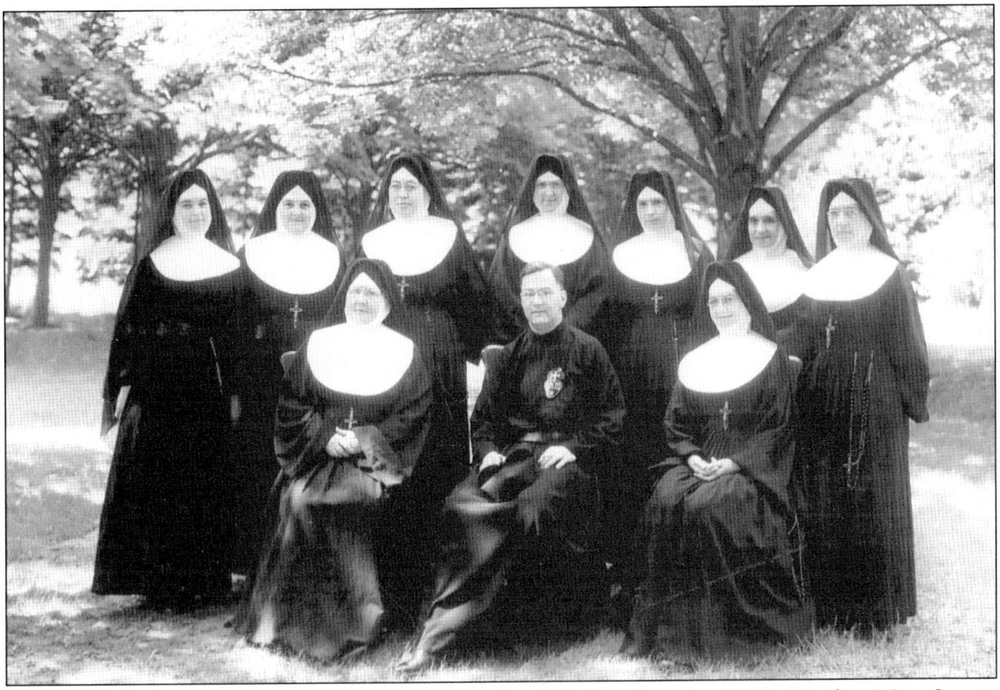

Tradition states that while traveling the Long Island Railroad in the 1930s, Mother Mary Louis, General Superior of the Sisters of St. Joseph, gazed upon the hilltops of Jamaica and selected it as the site for a school. Although she passed away in 1932, her dream of establishing an academy for young women in Jamaica Estates lived on. Fr. Roger Monson of Immaculate Conception Parish poses with the founding sisters of Mary Louis Academy. (Courtesy of the Mary Louis Academy.)

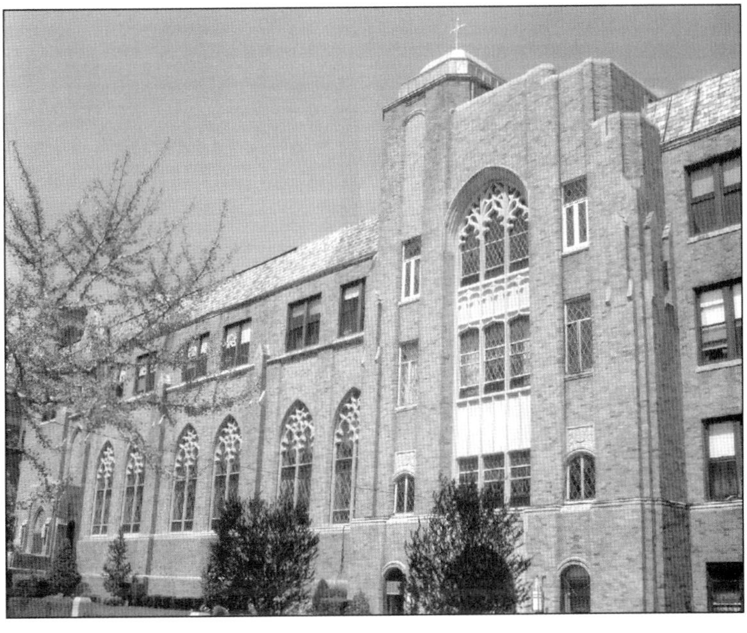

The sisters purchased the Adikes property and used the old mansion as their convent. On September 14, 1936, the Mary Louis Academy opened with 57 young women and a faculty of eight sisters. Classes were held in the convent until the main building opened on October 16, 1938. Henry V. Murphy, the noted architect of St. John University, designed the building.

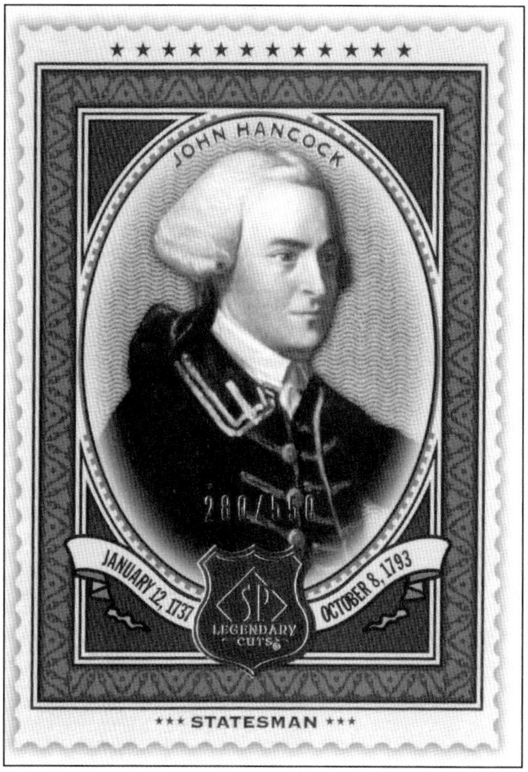

On May 10, 1934, the *New York Times* reported, "Isabella L. King, descendant through her father of John Hancock died at her home, on Kendrick Road, Jamaica Estates. She was born on September 28, 1854. She was married in 1878 to Albert M. King of Jamaica, a descendant of Rufus King, one of the framers of our Constitution and United States and minister to England in 1796."

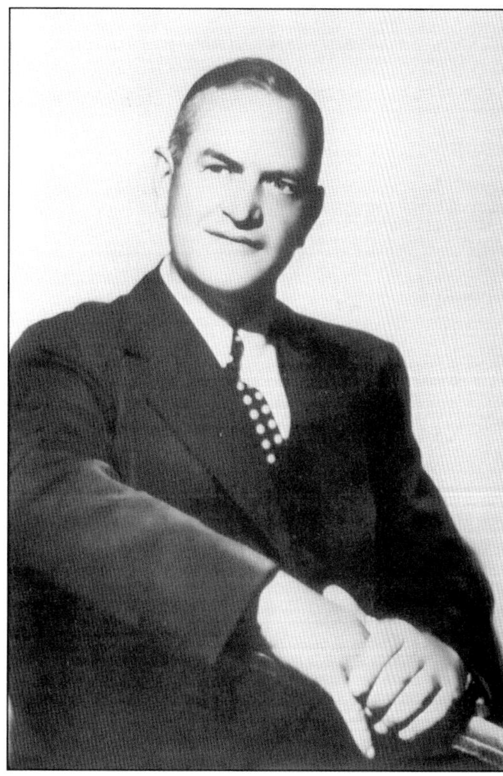

"Michael J. Cullen, known as 'King Kullen,' of Jamaica Estates. The founder and head of the King Kullen markets of Queens and Nassau," reported the *New York Times* on April 26, 1936. King Kullen is recognized by the Smithsonian Institution as America's first supermarket, and the first location was opened by Michael J. Cullen on August 4, 1930, in Jamaica. (Courtesy of the King Kullen Grocery Company, Inc.)

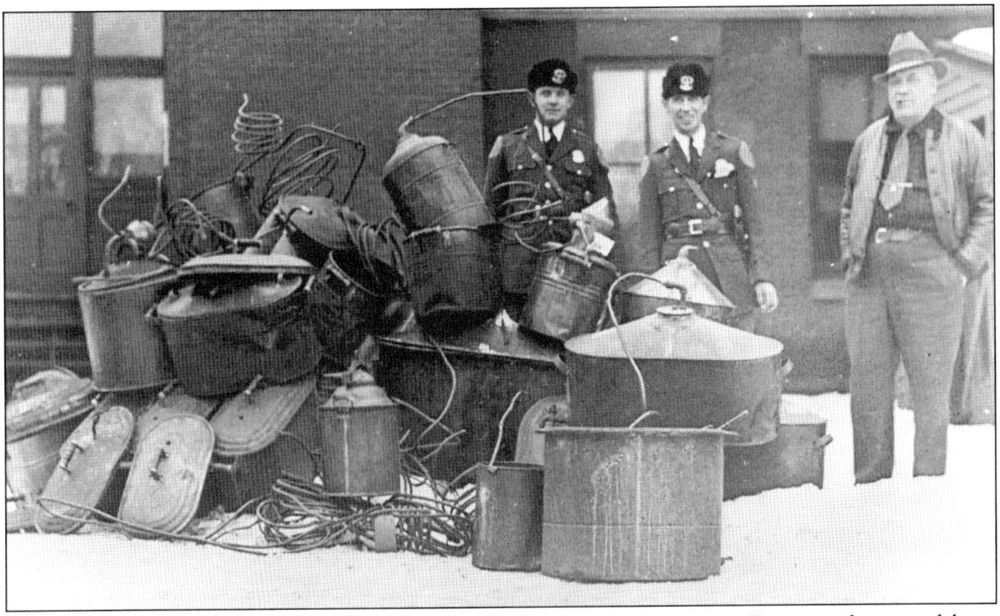

"Police raided a dwelling on Tudor Road in the exclusive Jamaica Estates after neighbors communicated their suspicions. Walls and floors had been cut for pipes and a motor had been attached to the oil burner in the cellar, and upper floors used to house the still. There was evidence of at least four 1,000 gallon stills," reported the *New York Times* on September 7, 1936. This photograph is from the post-Prohibition era.

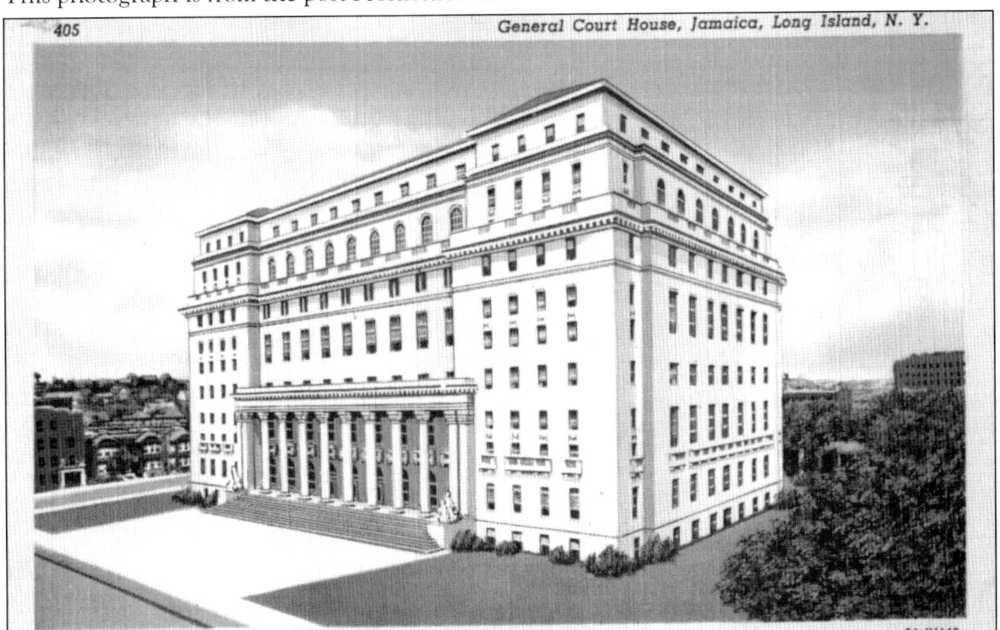

On December 14, 1940, the *New York Times* reported, "A funeral service for Burt Jay Humphrey, retired Supreme Court Justice who died at his home in Jamaica Estates was held yesterday afternoon in the First Presbyterian Church of Jamaica." New York State Supreme Court Justice Burt Jay Humphrey worked with the architects on plans for the General Court House of Jamaica, dedicated on March 1, 1939, by Mayor Fiorello La Guardia.

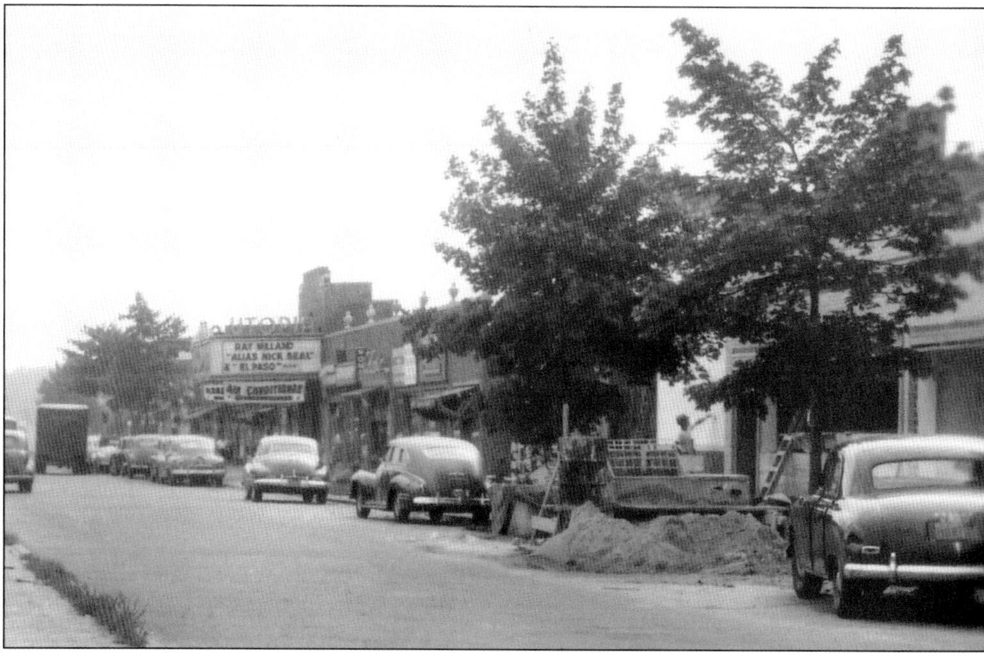

In December 1941, Paul Raisler and Ruth Wright wrote the following: "Dear Friends. We announce the opening of our new theatre, The Utopia, Union Turnpike and 188th Street on January 1, 1942. In selecting a name for our theatre, we symbolized what we have endeavored to do. To build a theatre that embodies every comfort . . . deeply cushioned spring seats . . . air conditioning . . . a beautifully cozy lounge . . . and the latest in sound equipment and projection. Truly a moviegoer's UTOPIA. Paul Raisler and Ruth Wright." (Courtesy Q Gardens Gallery.)

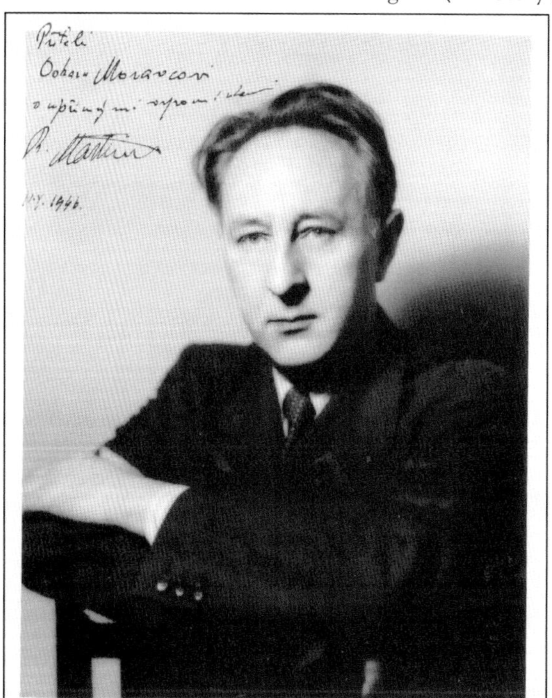

According to the January 31, 1942, *New York Times*, "If you are strolling late some night in Jamaica Estates and you should meet a tall, slim man with gray eyes, sandy grey hair and a shy smile—don't stop to talk for he wants to be alone." He was classical composer Bohuslav Martinu. "Walking alone helps me relax. Sometimes it is possible for me to work out the difficulties in a composition that may have been troubling me."

Boshuslav Martinu (1890–1959) was a prolific Bohemian Czech composer who wrote 6 symphonies, 15 operas, 14 ballet scores, and a large body of orchestral, chamber, vocal, and instrumental works. He fled Europe during World War II and stayed at the home of the Castagnolia family on Croydon Road, composing his Symphony No. 1, a violin concerto and a cello sonata, while staying in Jamaica Estates.

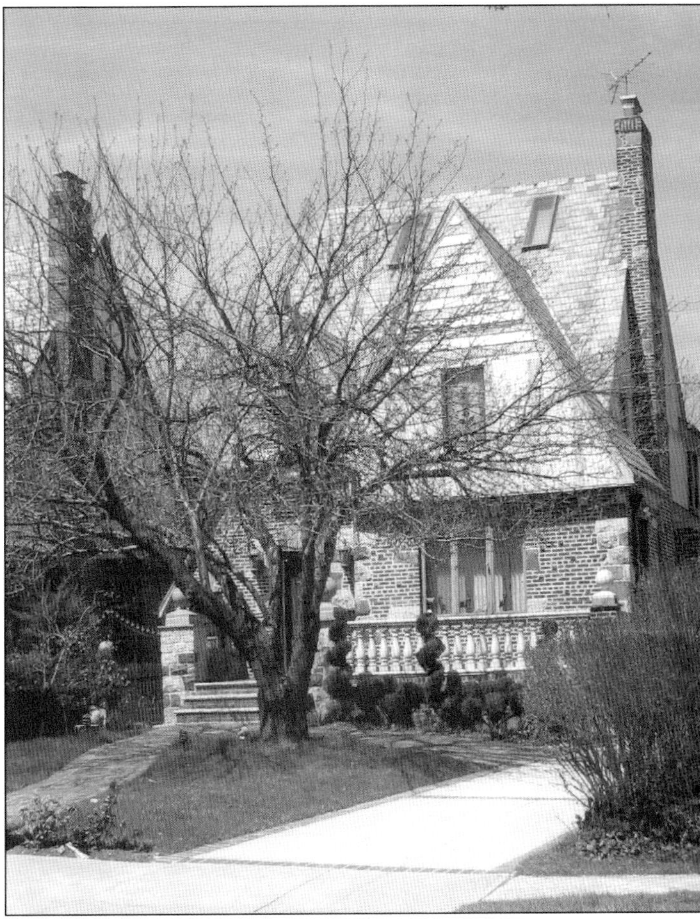

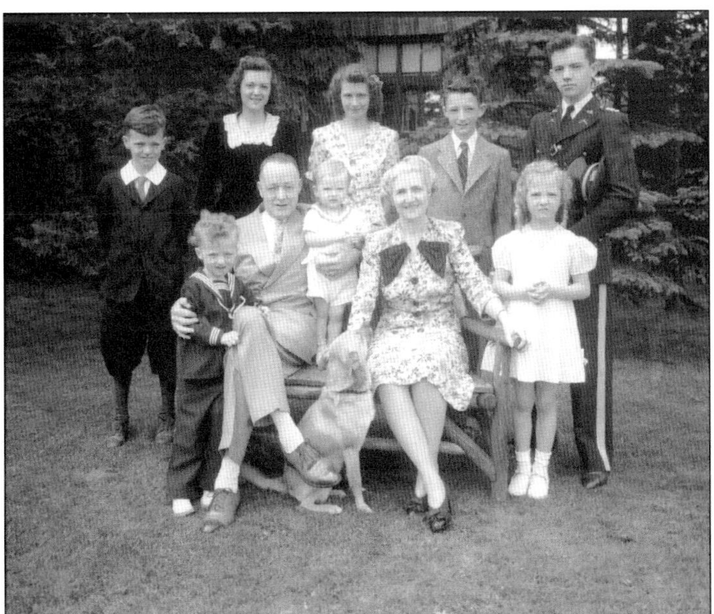

Living at 181–34 Grand Central Parkway, the Drapers took this family photograph on June 4, 1944, at the Draper family home. Pictured are, from left to right, (first row) Robert, Dr. Thomas Sr., Michael, Ann, and Jacqueline; (second row) Edward Raymond, Barbara, Patricia, David, and Thomas Jr. Dr. Draper was a family practitioner in Queens Village for 50 years. Their home was razed due to the expansion of the Grand Central Parkway in 1964.

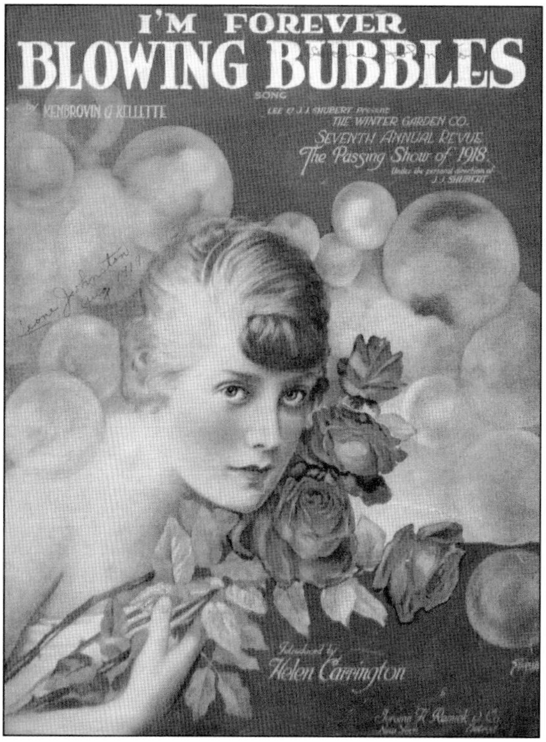

"James Kendris, who wrote 'I'm Forever Blowing Bubbles' and many other song hits, has hummed his last tune. He passed away at his home on Cedarcroft Avenue, Jamaica Estates, where he lived for 25 years," reported the *Long Island Daily Press* on November 16, 1946. The lyrics are credited to "Jaan Kenbrovin," actually a collective pseudonym for the writers James Kendis, James Brockman, and Nat Vincent. He was a composer and songwriter.

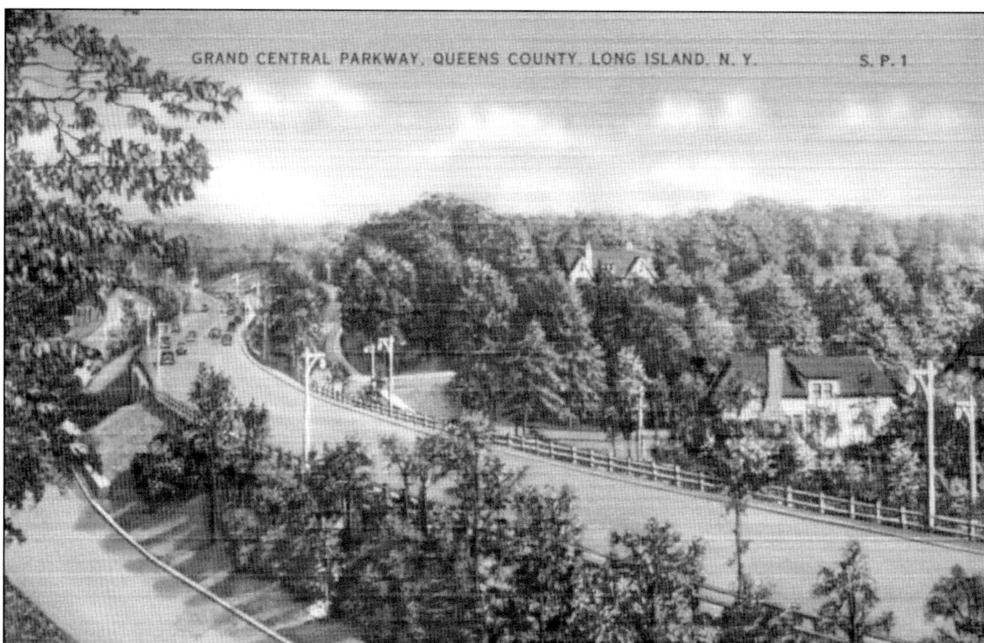

"Wilfred Andrew Surber of Grand Central Parkway, Jamaica Estates was an aviator in the first World War. Commissioned a first lieutenant with one of the first air units to go to France during the war, he was shot down in combat in 1918, suffering injuries from which he had never completely recovered," reported the *New York Times* on June 11, 1948. The Grand Central Parkway at Midland Parkway is pictured in 1938.

"Richard Gerard Husch resided at Kingston Place, Jamaica Estates. Sweet Adeline written in 1903, the most famous of his compositions made millions for music publishers, netted him $3,000," reported the *New York Times* on July 3, 1948. "Sweet Adeline," written by Richard H. Gerard, the pseudonym of Richard Gerard Husch (1879–1948), is perhaps the ultimate barbershop quartet number. Adeline refers to the famous Italian opera star Adelina Patti.

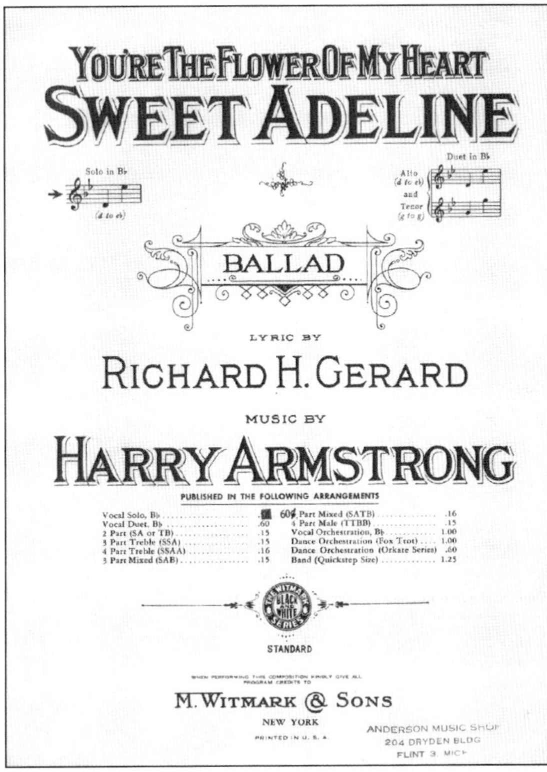

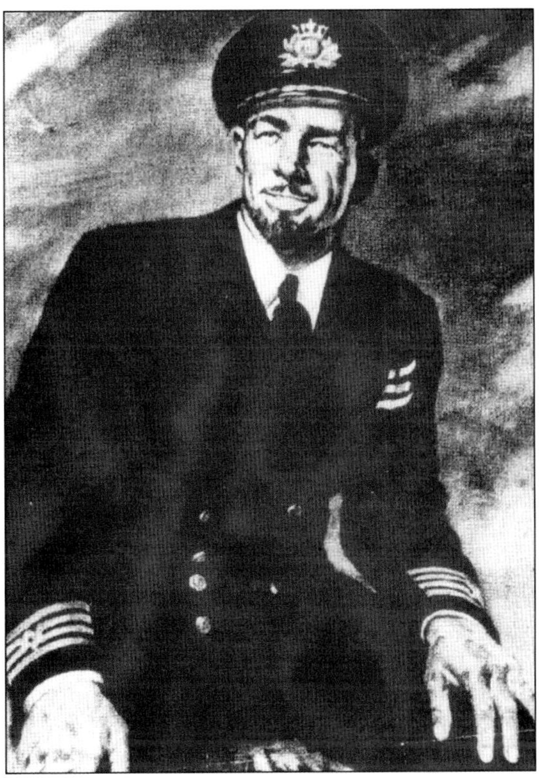

"Captain Dod Orsborne sailed a 35 foot ketch from Spain to the Sagasso Sea near the Bahamas. His autobiography, written in a basement room in Jamaica Estates is a best seller," reported the *Long Island Sunday Press* on March 6, 1949. His novel *Master of the Girl Pat* was named for the trawler he sailed on. He was described as a sea captain, whaler, big game hunter, secret agent, and "Commando Beachmaster."

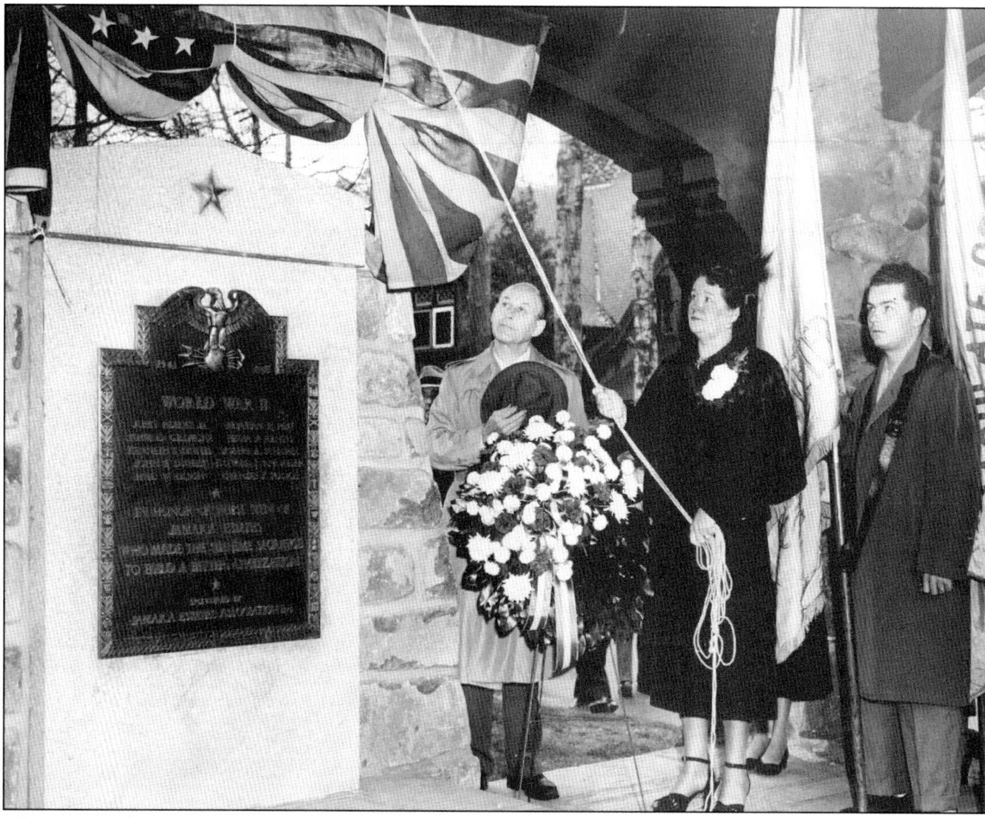

The November 10, 1950, *New York Times* reported, "In Queens the permanent War Memorial of the Jamaica Estates Association at Midland Parkway and Hillside Avenue will be dedicated at 11:15 A.M." The memorial is located inside the gatehouse with a bronze plaque and inscription. It was designed by William Leppinwith with stonework by Etienne Gueniz, an early settler of Jamaica Estates.

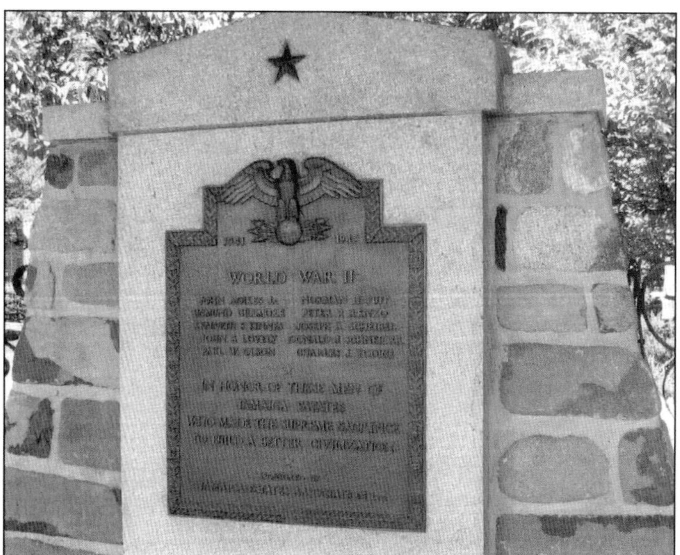

The memorial was unveiled by Margaret Lovely, the Gold Star Mother of John Lovely, one of the 10 on the plaque. The inscription reads, "1941–1945 World War II—In Honor of These Men of Jamaica Estates Who Made the Supreme Sacrifice to Build a Better Civilization.— John Adikes, Jr., Sigmond Gilmore, Kenneth Skene Kinnis, John Browne Lovely, Paul W. Olson, Norman H. Puff, Peter Renzo, Joseph A. Schiebel, Donald Schneider, and Charles J. Yodice."

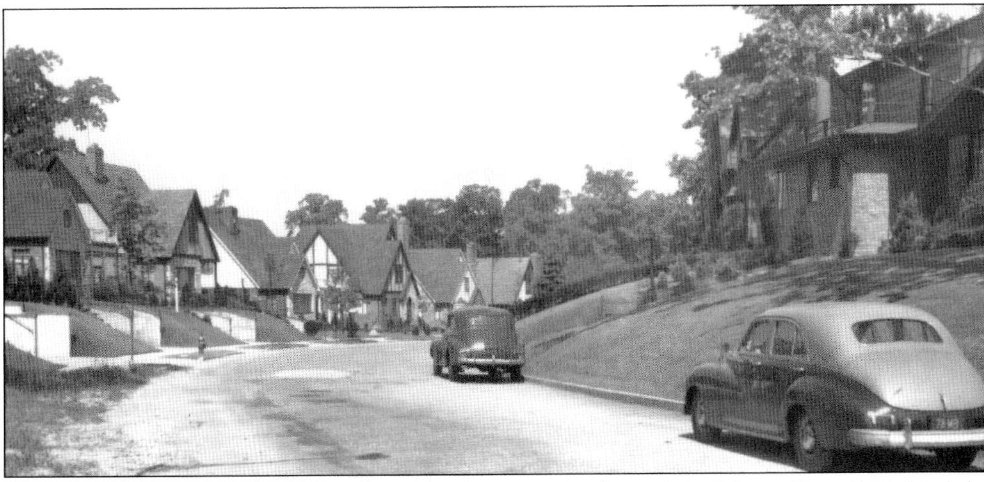

"Antonina Cicio, remembers when Brooklyn 'was mostly all woods,' celebrated her 100th birthday at her Jamaica Estates home. Affectionately called 'Grandma' she came to America in 1884. She thinks children are most disobedient today than they used to be and stay up too late for good health. She attributes her long life to hard work, plenty of rest and a careful diet," reported the *New York Times* on April 10, 1950. This photograph of Wicklow Place was taken in July 1950. (Courtesy of the Q Gardens Gallery.)

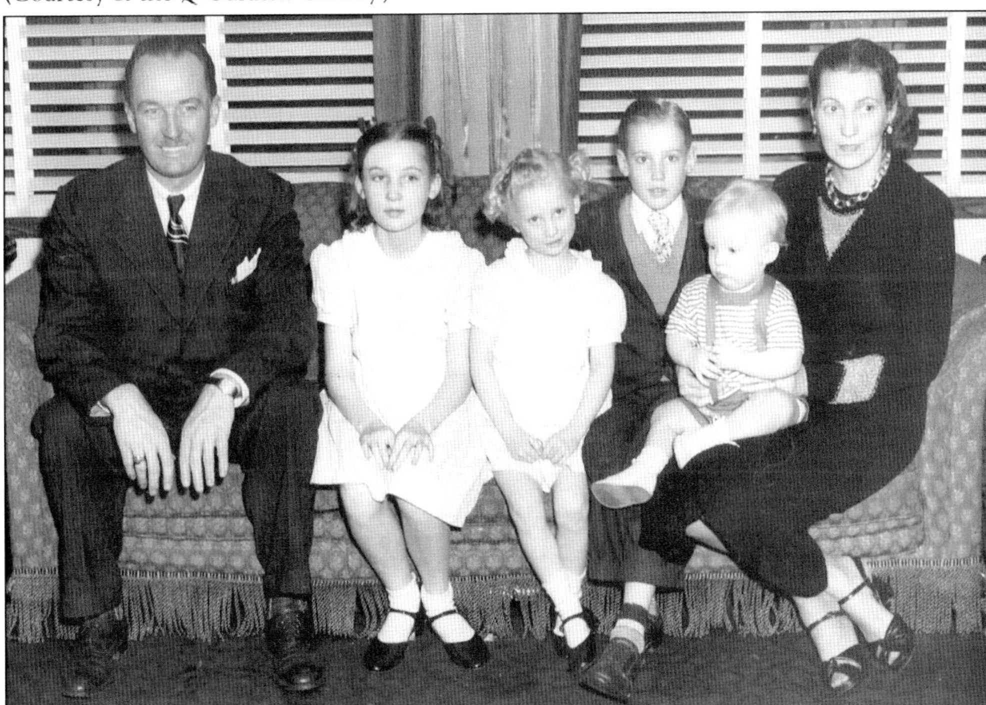

Frederick Christ Trump of Jamaica Estates was a major postwar builder of housing. A self-made man, he built more than 27,000 apartments and row houses in the neighborhoods of Coney Island, Bensonhurst, Sheepshead Bay, Flatbush, and Brighton Beach in Brooklyn and Flushing and Jamaica Estates in Queens. This 1947 photograph pictures Frederick Trump, with children Maryanne, Elizabeth, Fred Jr., Donald, and wife Mary Macleod. Their youngest son Robert was born after the photograph was taken. (Courtesy of the Judge Maryanne Trump Barry.)

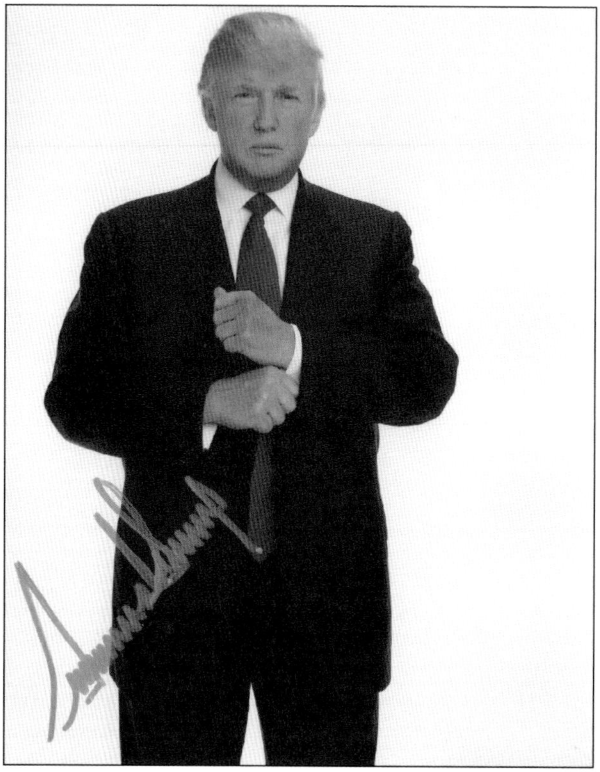

Born in 1946, Donald Trump is an American business magnate, socialite, television personality, and author. He is the chairman and CEO of the Trump Organization, a U.S.–based real estate developer. Trump is also the founder of Trump Entertainment Resorts, which operates numerous casinos and hotels across the world. On the NBC reality show *The Apprentice* he serves as host and executive producer.

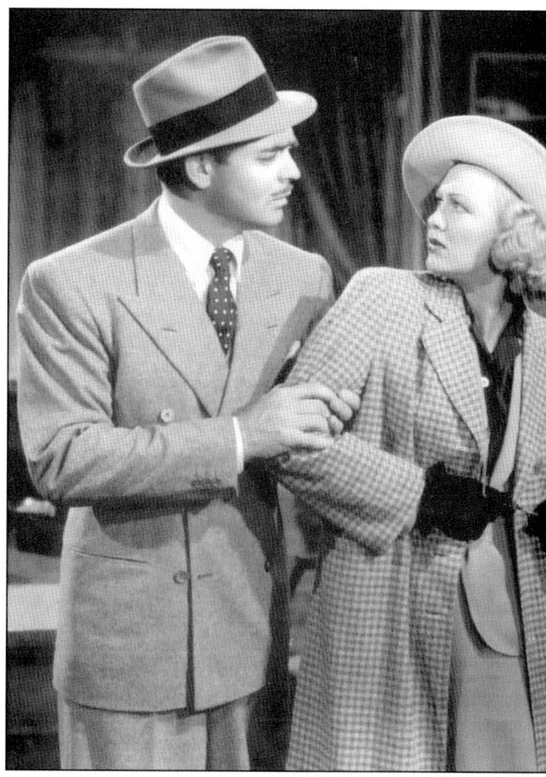

The following was reported in the January 19, 1954, *New York Times*, "William A. Fitzgerald, president of A. Sulka & Company, men's haberdashery lives on Dalny Road, Jamaica Estates. He entered the business as a stock clerk at the age of 11. Joining A. Sulka as a salesman, he rose to the position of president and caters to members of royalty and sartorially discriminating commoners. Clients include Winston Churchill, Harry Truman, the Duke of Windsor, Clark Cable and Bing Crosby."

Sidney "Sid" Gordon (1917–1975) lived in Jamaica Estates and was a powerfully built right-handed Major League Baseball (MLB) outfielder, third baseman, and first baseman. He had a 13-year career in MLB for the New York Giants (1941–1943, 1946–1949, and 1955), Boston Braves (1950–1952), Milwaukee Braves (1953), and Pittsburgh Pirates (1954–1955) batting .283, hitting 202 home runs, and batting in 805 runs. A slugger, he also had a great eye—he drew 731 walks against only 356 strikeouts. He was a two-time All-Star.

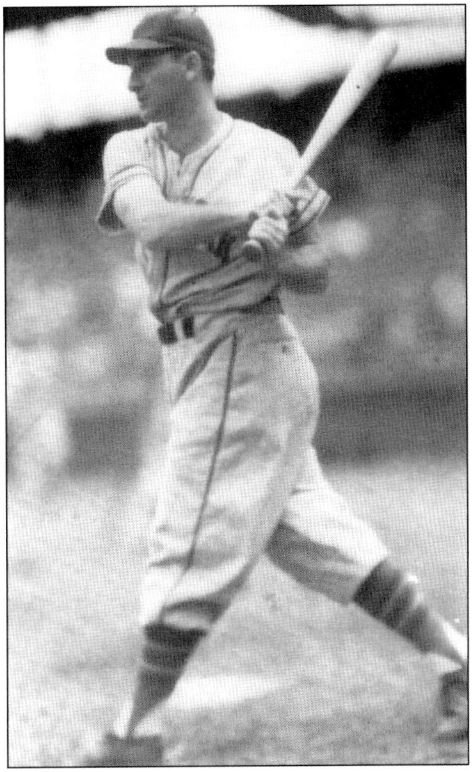

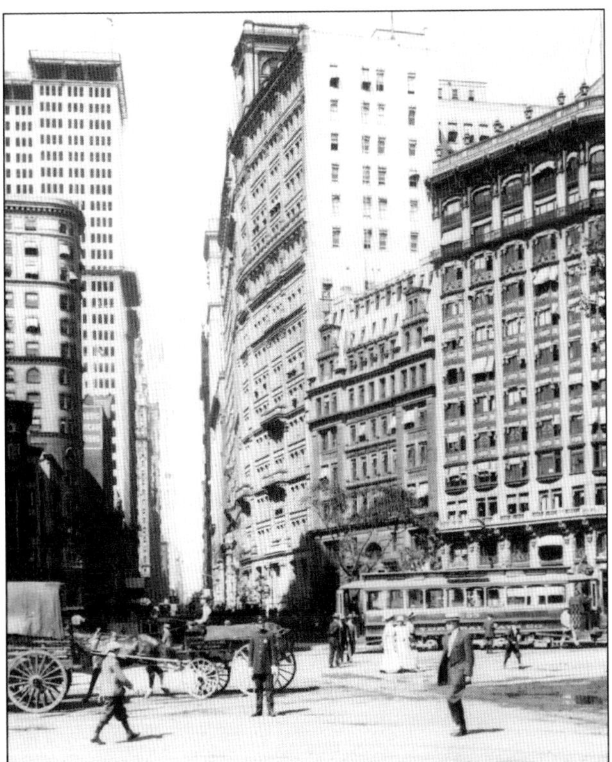

"In 1956, George J. Schmidt of Midland Drive, Jamaica Estates directed The Daily News' photographic staff that won a Pulitzer Prize for 'consistently excellent news picture coverage.' He served as a photographer for Underwood & Underwood and International News Pictures before joining The Daily News on May 22, 1920," reported the *New York Times* on January 20, 1959. This is a 1915 Underwood and Underwood photograph of Lower Broadway.

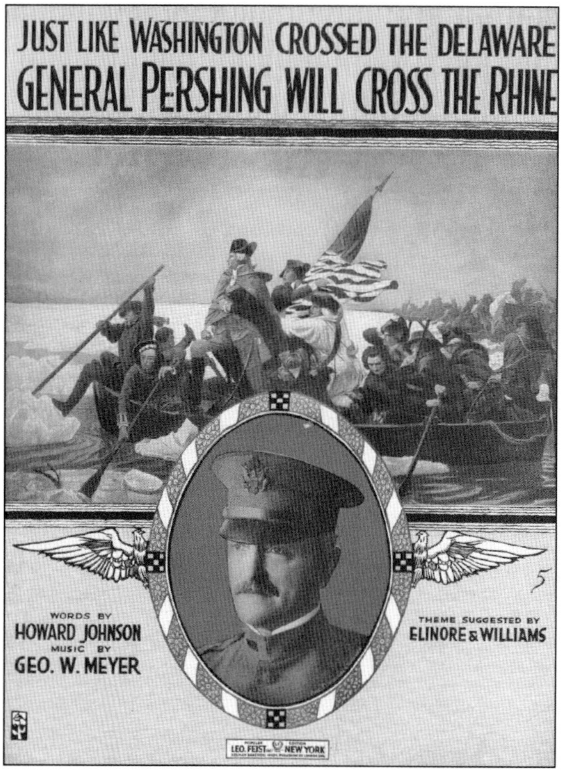

"Dr. David Warshaw of Croydon Road, Jamaica Estates had a distinguished record as an infantry officer in World War I, when he was on the staff of General of the Armies John J. Pershing. Dr. Warshaw is a pioneer in the use of electro-surgery. . . . Executive director at Doctor's Hospital of Queens and served on the surgical staffs at Mount Sinai and Memorial Hospitals," reported the *New York Times* on May 28, 1960.

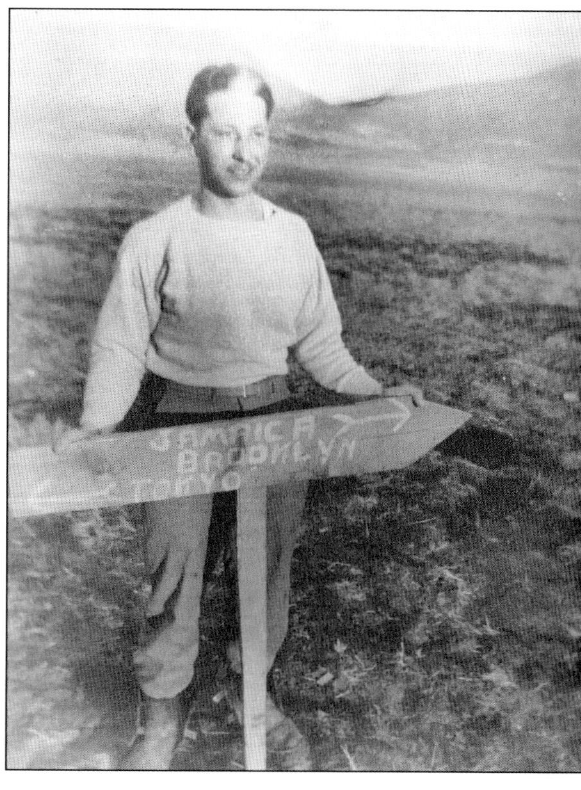

The April 16, 1964, *New York Times* reported, "Colonel John Rachek of Radnor Road, Jamaica Estates enlisted in the Army in 1904, and served in World War I as a captain. He was injured and won the Distinguished Service Cross, the Silver Star and the Purple Heart. In World War II, he was involved with the training of National and State Guard units of the Second State Guard." Rachek is pictured in this World War II–era photograph.

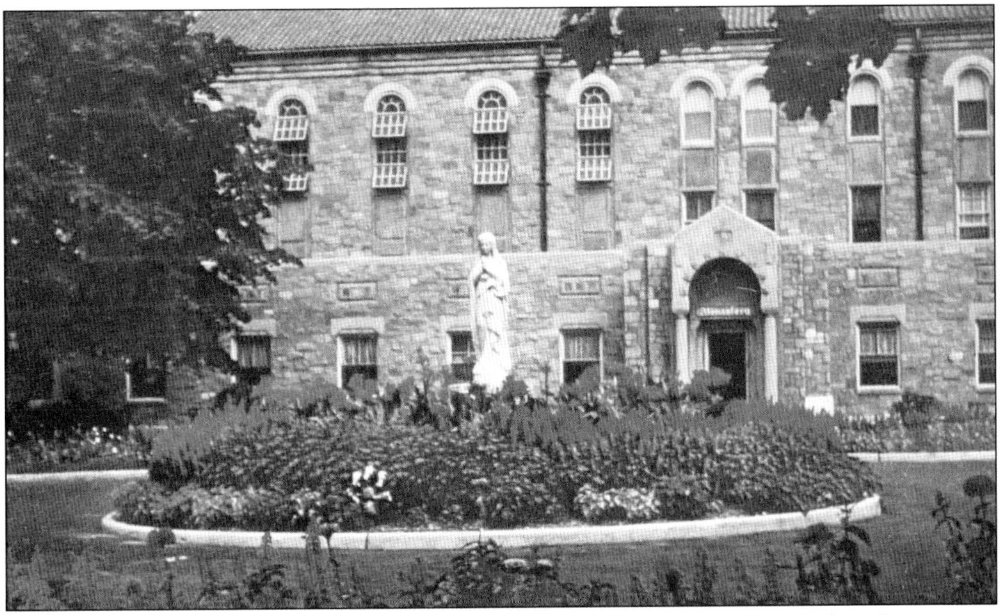

"For the first time since it was opened 37 years ago, the doors of the Immaculate Conception Monastery were flung open and tours of the grounds were conducted. This was the first time women were allowed into the monastery. The basement is the heart of the monastery. Here, one can find a barber, cook, tailor, launderer, recreation room and a color television set," reported the *Long Island Press* on December 4, 1967.

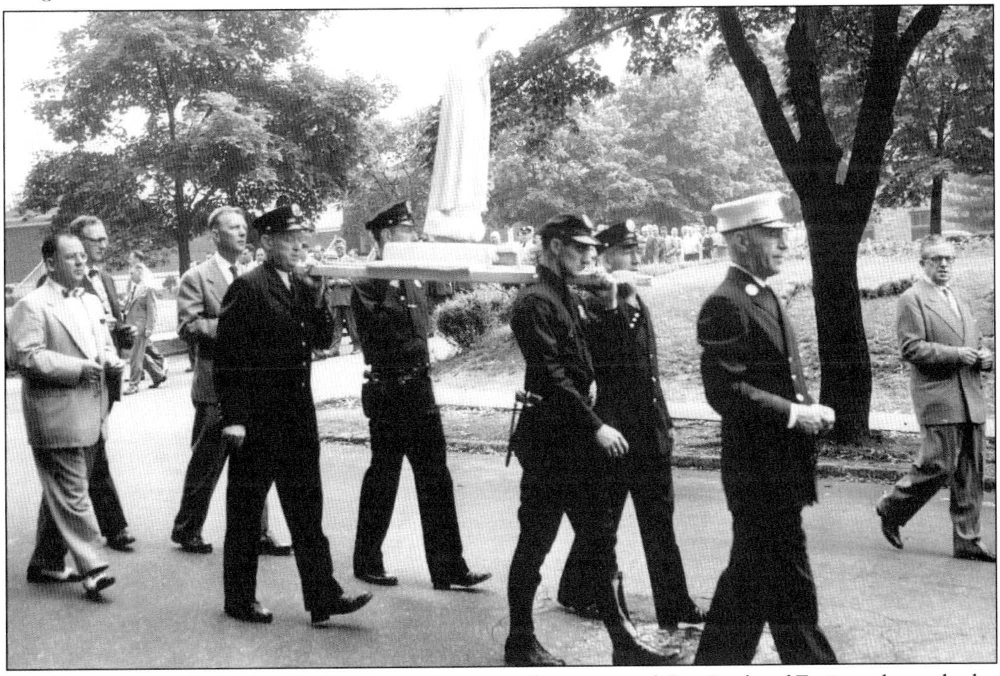

Members of the police and fire department carry the statue of Our Lady of Fatima through the streets of Jamaica Estates. Another procession well remembered by many residents was the annual Rosary Rallies when a sea of people would fill Midland Parkway from one end to the other holding candles and chanting prayers during the month of October.

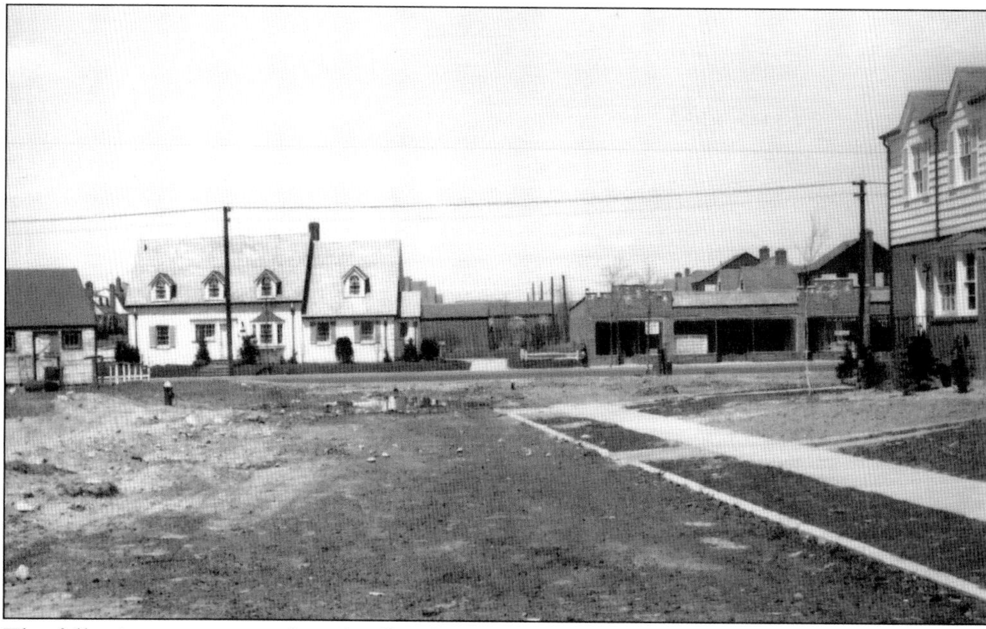

The following was reported in the October 29, 1968, *New York Times*, "Cyril I. Crowther of Tudor Road, Jamaica Estates, president of the Leonard Wood Memorial for the Eradication of Leprosy from 1958 to 1966. An economist and accountant he had been executive director of the Near East Foundation, set up to extend direct relief to property-stricken in the Near East." This photograph of Chevy Chase Street looks north at Eightieth Road to Union Turnpike. (Courtesy of Q Gardens Gallery.)

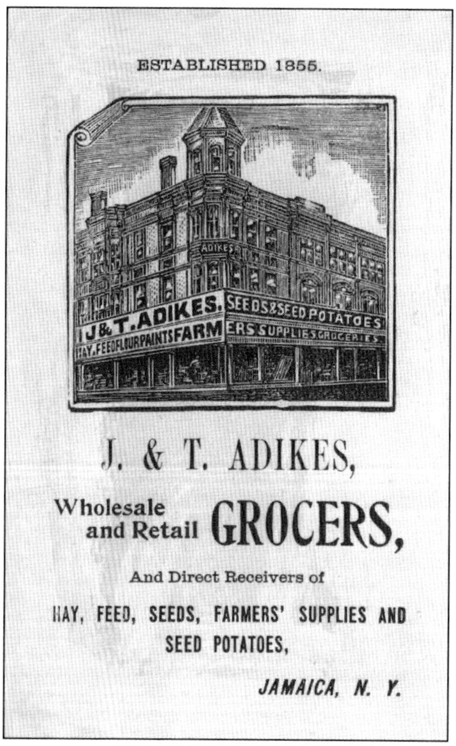

"John Adikes, chairman of the Board of the Jamaica Savings Bank lived at Wareham Road, Jamaica Estates. He trained as a lawyer, entered the savings banking field in 1926 as a trustee of the Jamaica bank. His son John was killed in action in World War II. (His name is on the Jamaica Estates Memorial)," reported the *New York Times* on July 3, 1970. In 1855, ancestors of the Adikes family established a grocery in Jamaica.

"Estella Fisher King of Highland Avenue, Jamaica Estates was one of the first women to become a Fellow of The Actuarial Society of America," reported the *New York Times* on December 28, 1970. An actuary is a business professional who deals with the financial impact of risk and uncertainty. Putney Road (Highland Avenue) is pictured in 1910. The cylinder-shaped structure is the water tower. (Courtesy of the Queens Borough Public Library, Long Island Division, Frederick J. Weber Collection.)

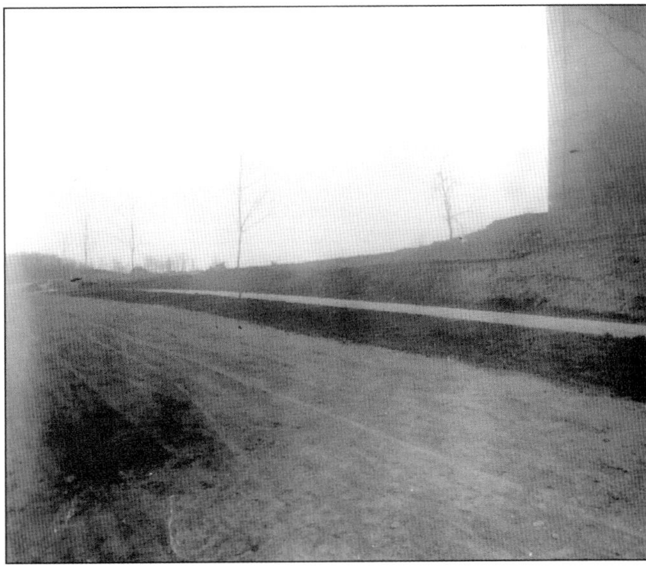

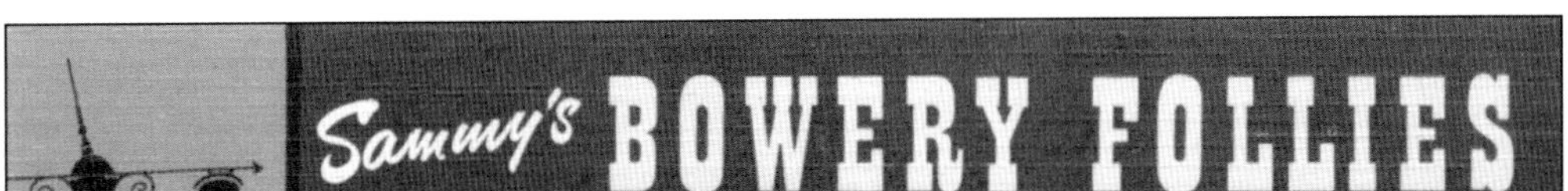

"Jamaica Estates—Sammy Fuchs, the rudy-faced, portly, honorary 'mayor of the Bowery' and friend to the down and out, died yesterday in his home," reported *Newsday* on April 5, 1969. Sammy's Bowery Follies, the nationally known nightspot where drifters and celebrities and the rich and the forgotten mingled for 35 years in rowdy laughter and melancholy song, was started by Sammy Fuchs at 267 Bowery Street, between Houston and Stanton Streets.

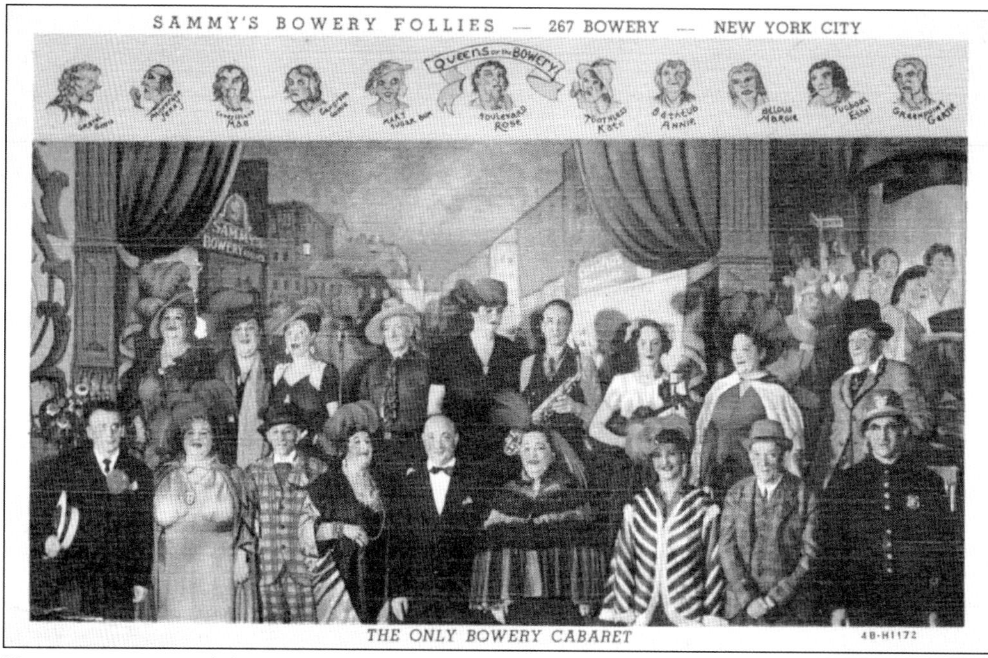

Honorary "Mayor of the Bowery" Sammy Fuchs was known for his generosity to the needy. He would hand out money freely and on Thanksgiving Day provided free turkey dinners. He sponsored a "Bum of the Month," selecting a "deserving bum," one considered worth rehabilitating, and gave him new set of clothes, a room in a decent hotel, and job leads. Sammy's Follies, featured in a 1944 issue of *Life* magazine, closed their doors in 1970.

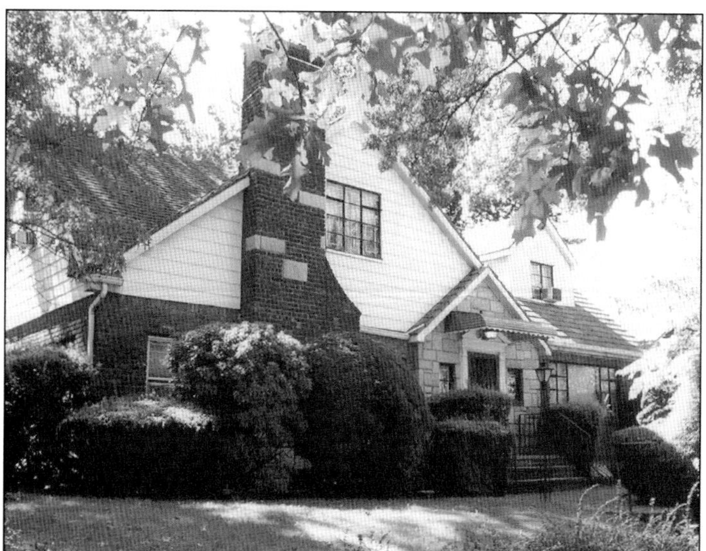

Fuchs died at his Jamaica Estates home on 188th Street in 1969. Sammy's daughter, Arlene Fuchs Katz, was a community leader, longtime member of Community Board No. 8, and teacher at PS No. 131 for 25 years. When Arlene was born in 1935, the first person to visit her mother in the hospital was New York City mayor Jimmy Walker. Sammy instilled in her very strong principles—loyalty, devotion, passion, and compassion.

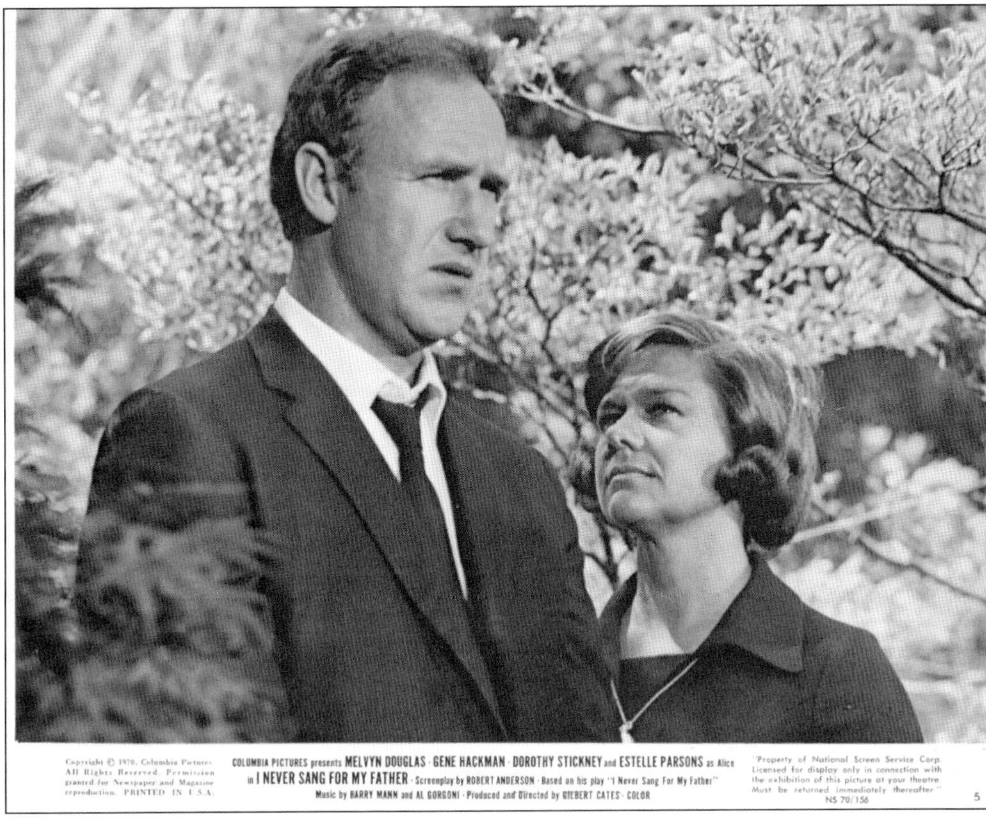

According to the *New York Times* on May 4, 1972, "Samuel Dinin motion picture photographer lives on Kingston Place, Jamaica Estates. He did the still photography for some major motion pictures, among them, 'Goodbye Columbus,' 'The Incident' and 'I Never Sang for My Father'. During World War II, as a motion picture cameraman with the Army Signal Corps with Sir Hubert Wilkins, the Arctic explorer shot an Army training film in Alaska on Arctic survival."

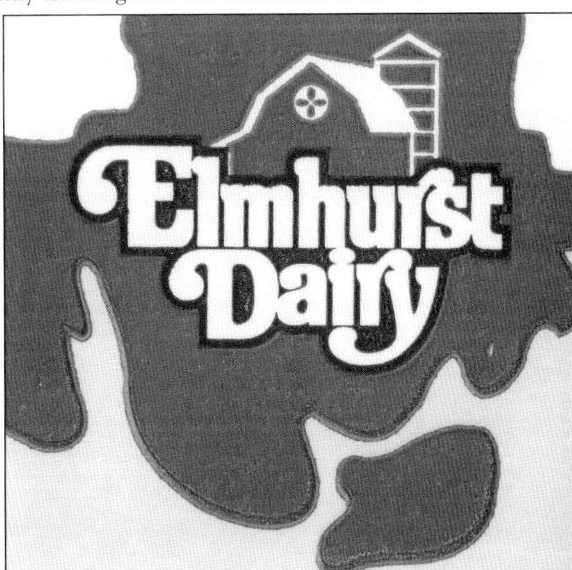

"Max Schwartz, founder and president of the 50 year old Elmhurst Milk and Cream Company in Jamaica, lived on Surrey Place, Jamaica Estates. The son of a dairy farmer, Max started his delivery business driving a horse and wagon to costumers," reported the *New York Times* on December 28, 1977. Today Elmhurst Dairy still produces milk and dairy products. It was founded in 1919 and based in Jamaica.

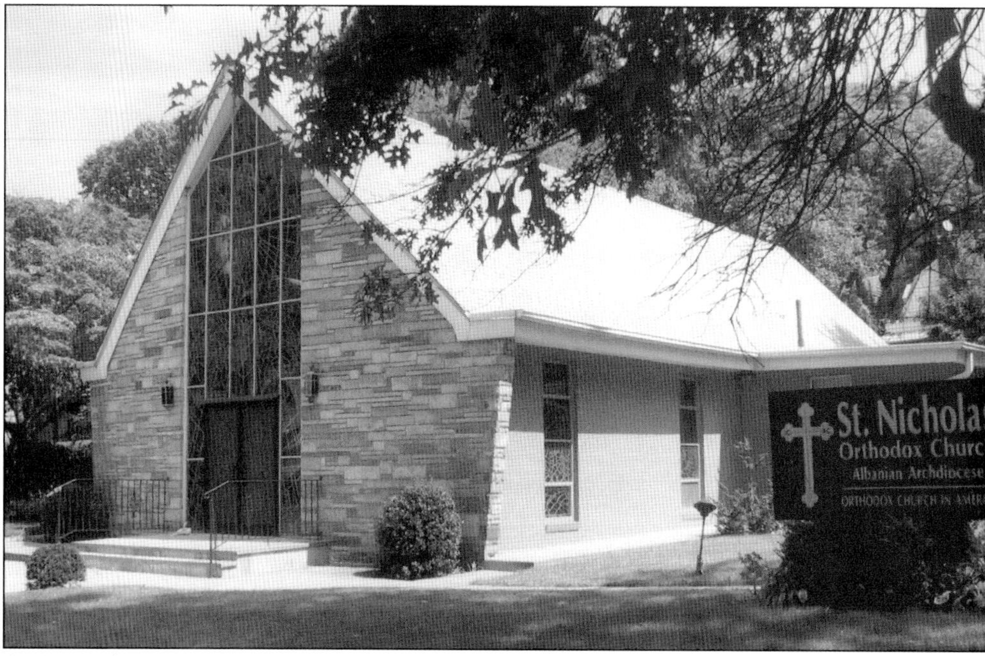

On December 21, 1941, a group of Albanian Americans met at the Diplomat Hotel. With a treasury of $11 and faith in God, they succeeded in building a church. In 1943, Rev. Pandeli Checho was appointed first pastor and the Presbyterian Church at West Forty-eighth Street was purchased. Members chose the name of St. Nicholas for the church. On May 22, 1976, the new St. Nicholas Orthodox Church was consecration in Jamaica Estates.

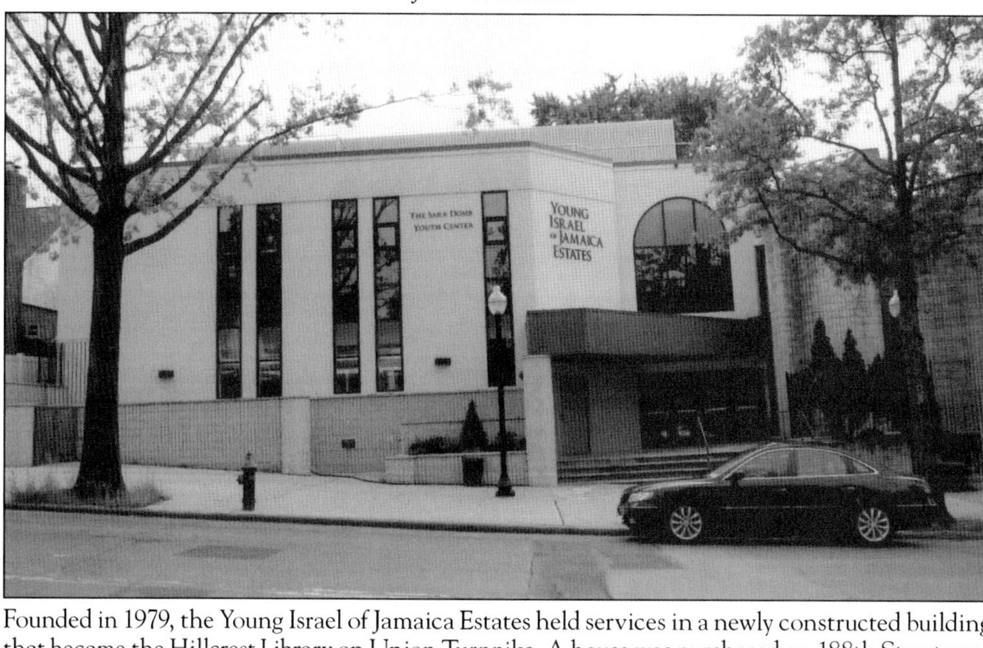

Founded in 1979, the Young Israel of Jamaica Estates held services in a newly constructed building that became the Hillcrest Library on Union Turnpike. A house was purchased on 188th Street near Midland Parkway but was razed in 1985 when a larger building was needed. Rabbi Yitzchak Adler was appointed first Rabbi in 1982. In 2008, it was expanded with a new addition. A noteworthy event is the annual L'Chaim 5K Walk/Run for Israel.

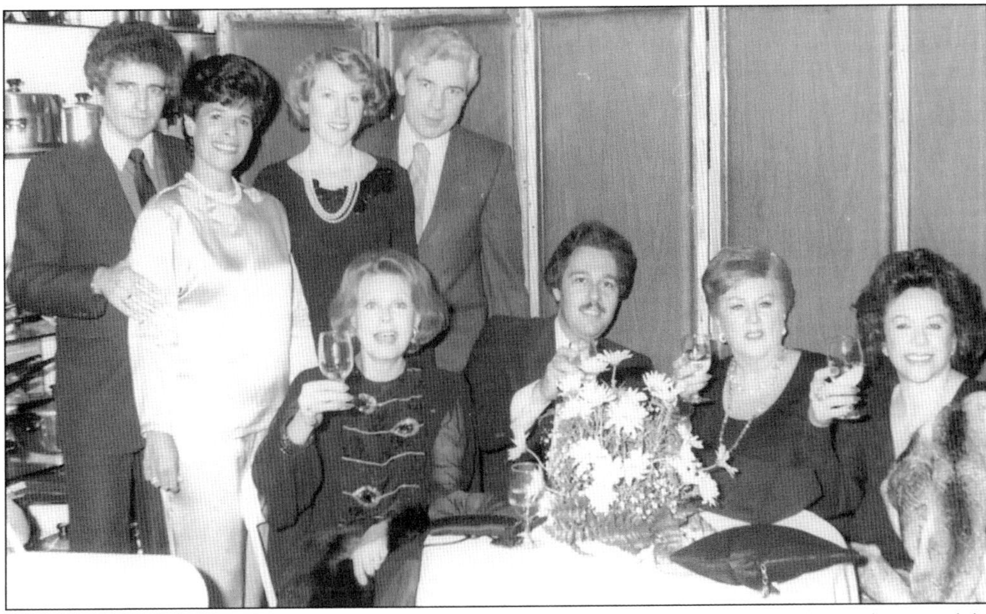

A grand celebration of the 55th anniversary of the Jamaica Estates Association was held at Bloomingdales Department store in 1984, which was once located at 188th Street and Long Island Expressway. Pictured are, from left to right, (seated) actress Arlene Dahl, Marty Rosen, and singers Margaret Whiting and Fran Warren; (standing) Michael Bookbinder, Janet Kramer, Laureen Stanton Knutsen, and Dr. Barry Weinberg.

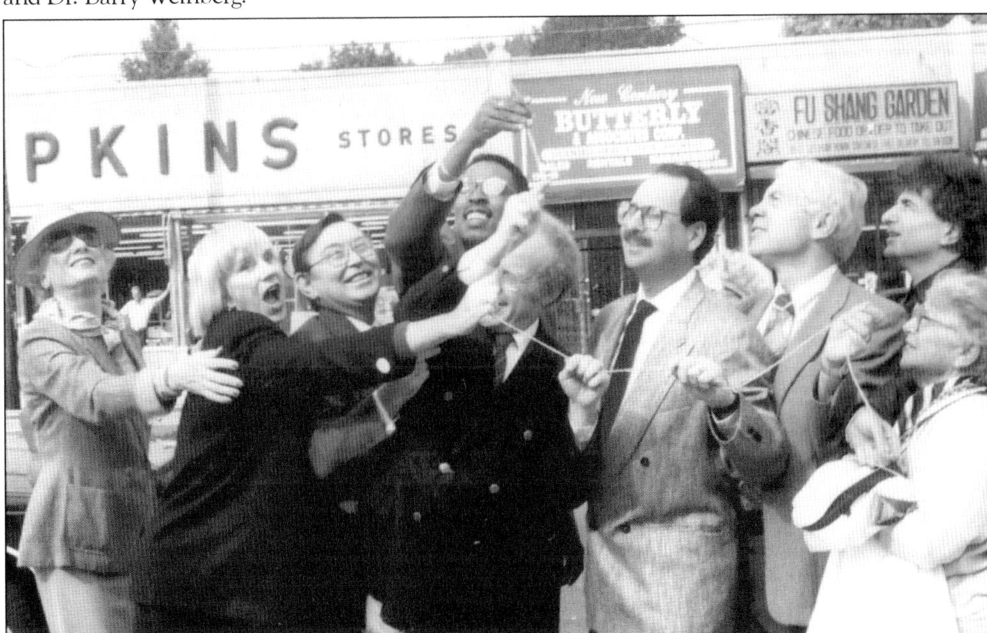

Jenkin Hockert (1894–1990) of Jamaica Estates was Queens county clerk, New York City magistrate, municipal court judge, city court judge, and acting justice of the State Supreme Court. In World War I, he was an aviator serving under the command of Fiorello H. LaGuardia, who later, as mayor of New York City, appointed him to the bench. This 1991 photograph shows residents and friends unveiling a sign at Surrey Place and Union Turnpike placed in his honor.

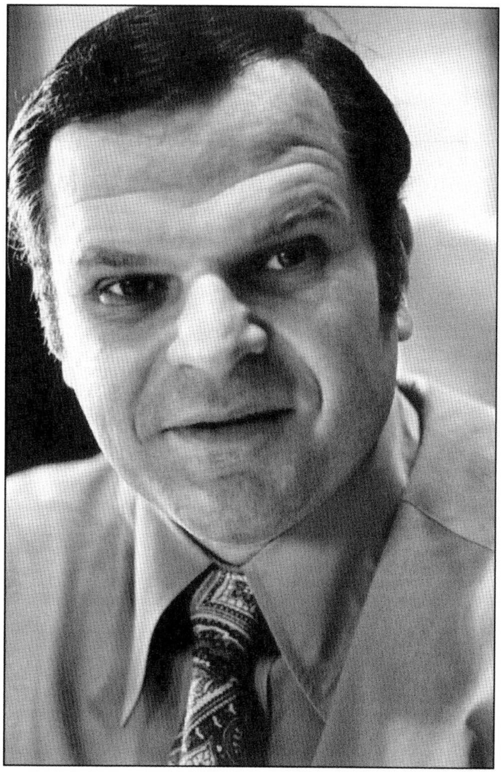

As Queens Democratic leader and borough president, Donald Manes was one of New York City's most powerful political figures. He stabbed himself in the heart on March 13, 1986, in the kitchen of his Jamaica Estates home as reports came out pointing to him as a central figure in a municipal corruption scandal. (Courtesy of the Queens Borough Public Library, Long Island Division, Portraits Collection.)

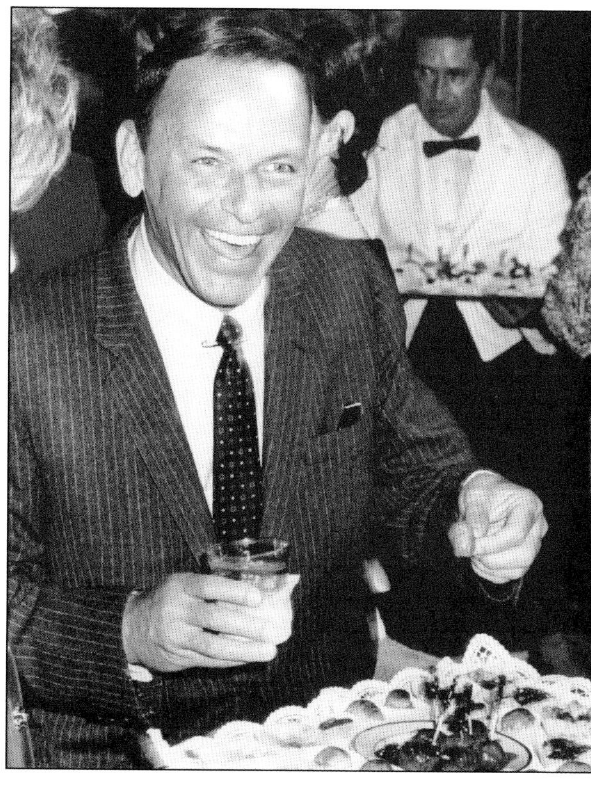

According to the *New York Times* on June 7, 1999, "Bruno Caravaggi of Jamaica Estates was the suave co-owner of Quo Vadis, one of New York's most fashionable restaurants for almost four decades. He opened this plush restaurant on East Sixty-third Street between Madison and Park Avenue in 1946. Immediately it became a fashionable destination for celebrities like Princess Grace, Jacqueline Kennedy, Frank Sinatra, Truman Capote, Nat (King) Cole and Diane Vreeland."

According to the *New York Times* on June 18, 1996, "The envelope was postmarked Frankfurt, Germany. It was delivered last month to an elderly, white Jewish woman living in a two–story brick house in Jamaica Estates. 'Margaret Bergmann Lambert, it is my honor and pleasure to inform you that the National Olympic Committee for Germany has decided to invite you to be our guest of honor during the Olympic Centennial Games in Atlanta.'"

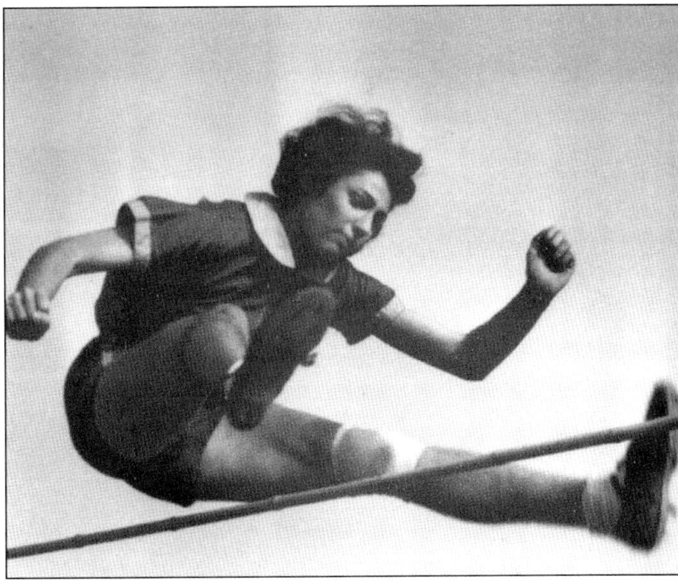

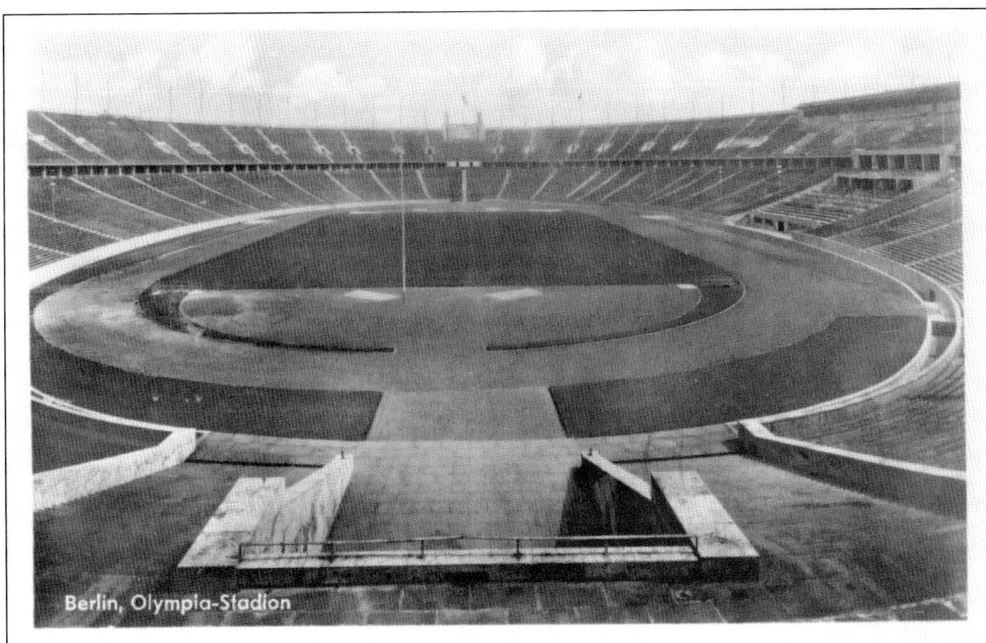

One of Germany's top female athletes preparing for the 1936 Berlin Olympics, the Nazis expelled Margaret Bergmann for being Jewish. At the British Championships, she won the high jump by crossing 1.55 meters. Germany wanted her back to portray Germany as liberal-minded and tolerant. Her family threatened, she returned there, tying the German record by crossing 1.60 meters but was forced to withdraw. In 1999, in Laupheim, her birthplace, a stadium was named in her honor.

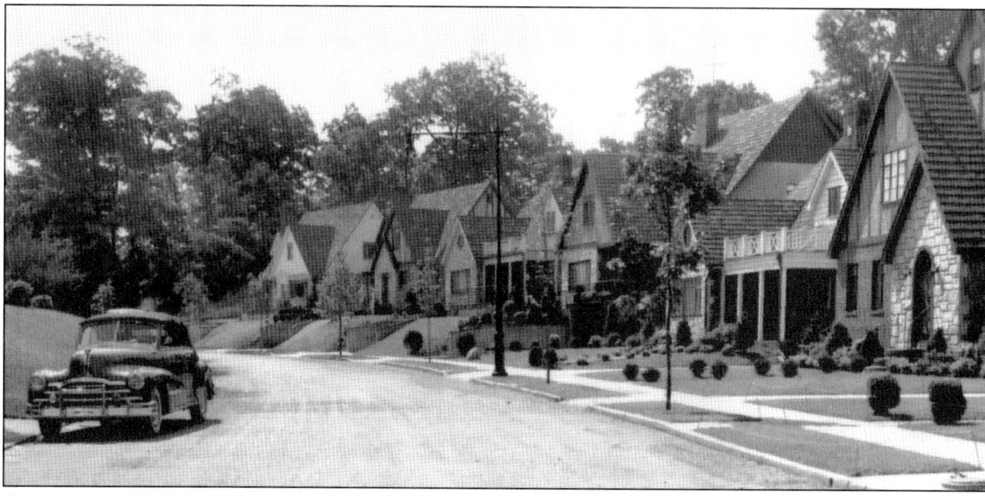

Some streets have not changed over time: Tudor Road, Aberdeen Road, Midland Parkway, Radnor Road, Avon Road, Doncaster Place, Wicklow Place, Cambridge Road, Henley Road, Dalny Road, Charlecote Ridge, Croydon Road, Hillside Avenue and Union Turnpike. Others have only had the last part of their name changed: Homelawn Street (Avenue), Kildare Street (Avenue), Somerset Street (Road), Chevy Chase Street (Road), Troon Road (Place), Perth Road (Place), Haddon Street (Road), Kent Street (Road), Surrey Place (Road), Dumfries Place (Walk), Tryon Place (Road), Edgerton Road (Place), Hovenden Road (Place), Chelsea Street (Road), Barrington Street (Road), Cedarcroft Road (Place), and Wareham Place (Road). This photograph shows Wicklow Place in 1950. (Courtesy of Q Gardens Gallery.)

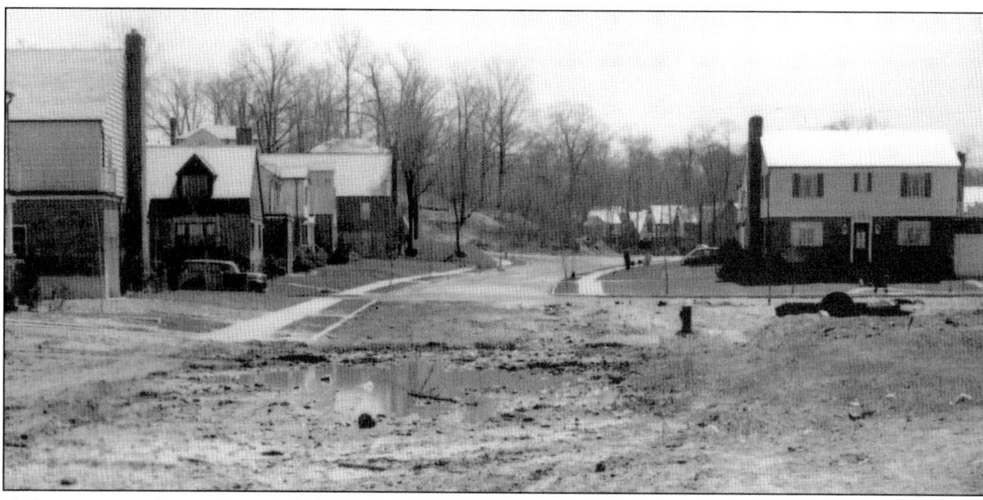

Others streets have changed their names completely, such as Eightieth Road (Roxbury Road), Eightieth Drive (Huntley Drive), Grand Central Parkway (Doncaster Boulevard), Utopia Parkway (Black Stump Road and Fresh Meadows Road), Eton Street (Exeter Road), Wexford Terrace (one section from Avon Road to Chelsea Street was called Woodside Avenue), 188th Street (Holliswood Avenue), Eighty-seventh Road (Cornwall Place), Eighty-seventh Drive (once part of Wexford Terrace), Kendrick Place (Kendrick Road and Pembroke Road), Aspen Place (Hampton Place), Kingston Place (Adel Road and Kingston Road), Highland Avenue (Gilman Avenue and Putney Road), Edgerton Boulevard (South of Hillside Avenue called Homer Lee Avenue today 178th Street) and Ava Place (Derby Place). This 1950 photograph of Chevy Chase Street looks south from Union Turnpike. (Courtesy of Q Gardens Gallery.)

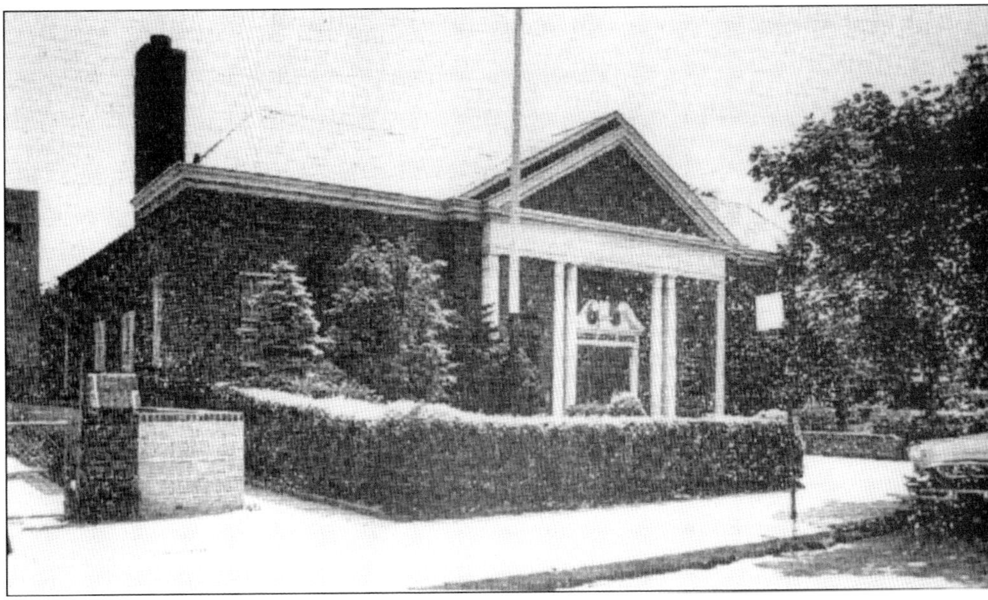

Widely known as the only Afghan-Jewish synagogue in America, Anshei Shalom was founded in 1978 and is a close-knit community. The members of the congregation, which is Orthodox, have roots in Russia, Syria, Lebanon, Yemen, Iraq, and Morocco.

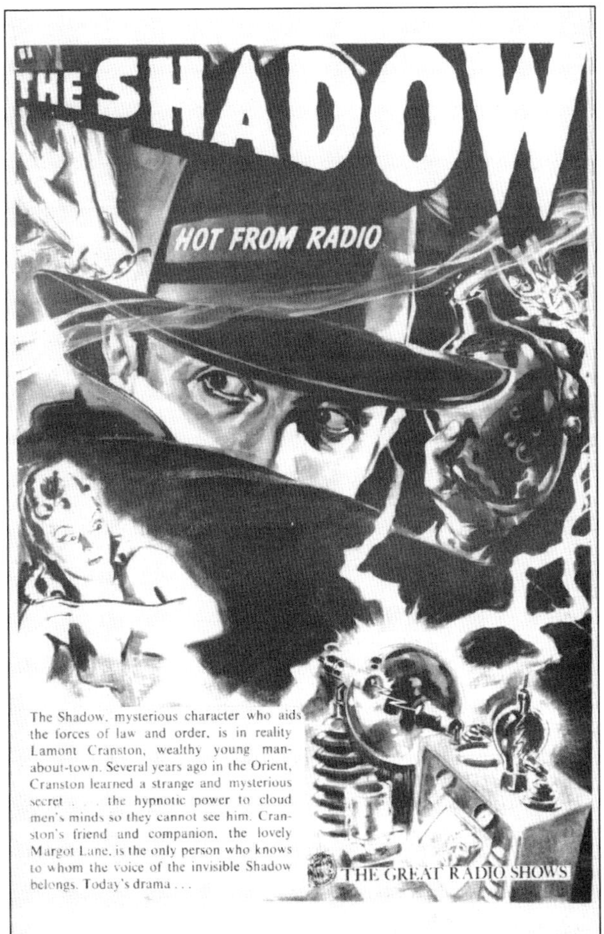

Theodore Mallie (1924–1999) was a radio and television announcer working at WOR-Mutual Radio in New York in the 1940s, announcing for programs such as *John Steele, Adventurer* and *I Love a Mystery*. He is better known as the final announcer for *The Shadow* during its last two seasons (1953–1954). In television, Mallie handled promos and program introductions, most notably for the long-running *Million Dollar Movie* and horror-movie series *Fright Night*.

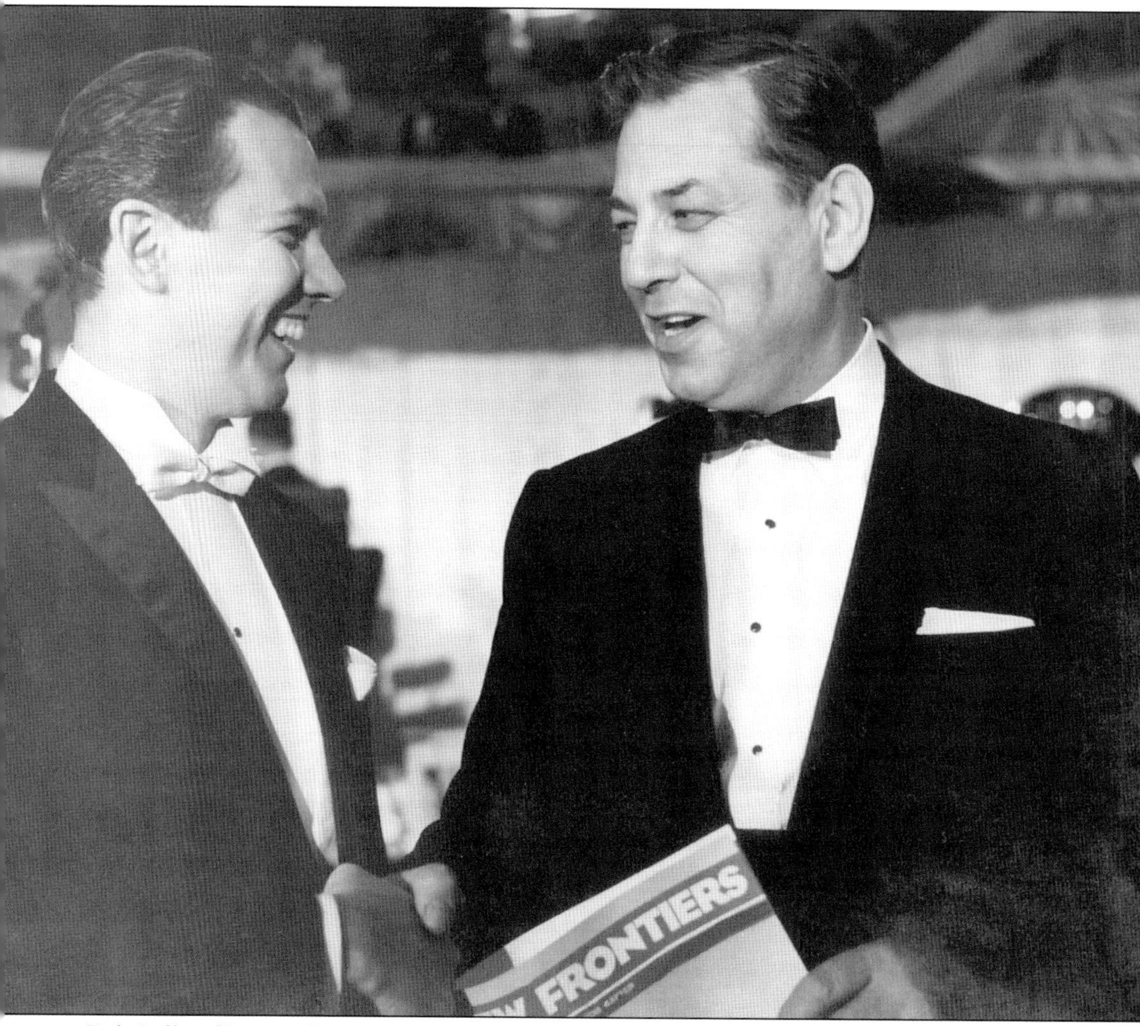

Bob Saffer of Jamaica Estates was a songwriter who wrote the campaign songs for presidents John F. Kennedy and Lyndon Johnson. He is shown here attending the President Kennedy inauguration with Bill Harrington, who sang Saffer's campaign song "New Frontier" at the inauguration. Saffer is holding a copy of the song autographed by President Kennedy. He composed songs sung by Nat King Cole, Gene Autry, Frankie Lymon, and other renowned artists, but he was most proud of "Stand Up for the Flag of America," written at the time of the hostage crisis in Iran in 1979. The lyrics of this song were featured in the *New York Times* and other newspapers throughout the country and are recited every year at Memorial Day ceremonies at the Jamaica Estates Gatehouse. The song calls upon all Americans to "stand up for the flag of America . . . that stands for you and me." (Courtesy of Susan Zigman.)

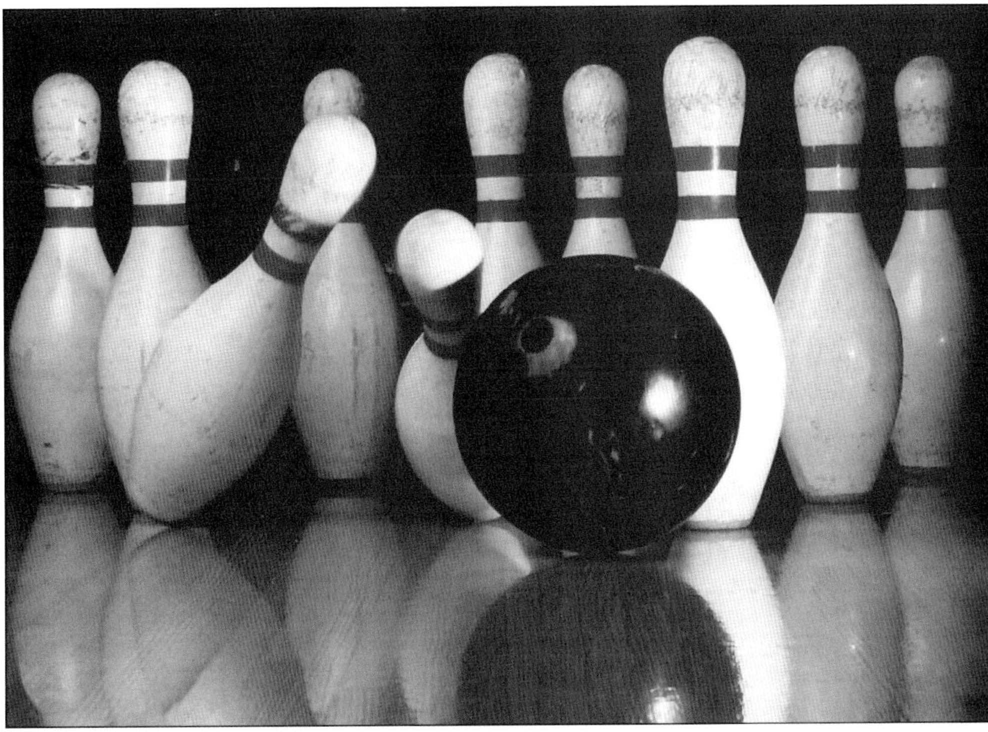

"Utopia Lanes, a Mom and Pop Alley, bowls its 10th frame. The basement alley at 188–08 Union Turnpike in Jamaica Estates is a snapshot of simpler times. There are no electronic scoreboards, no newfangled cash registers and no draft beer. And there never will be. After 44 years as the neighborhood meeting and gossip center, the doors closed this weekend," reported the *New York Times* on June 29, 1997.

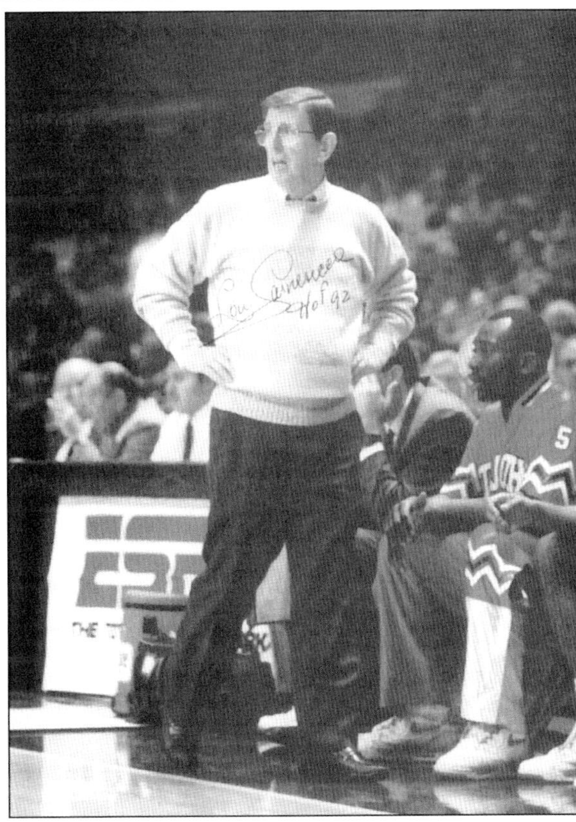

"I grew up in East Harlem. I never thought I'd have a house in Jamaica Estates," reported the *New York Times* on May 16, 1998. Luigi P. Carnesecca, born 1925 in New York City, is a former basketball coach at St. John's University. He coached the Redmen's basketball program to 526 wins and 200 losses over 24 seasons (1965–1970, 1973–1992). He was selected as the National Coach of the Year in 1983 and 1985 by the U.S. Basketball Writers Association.

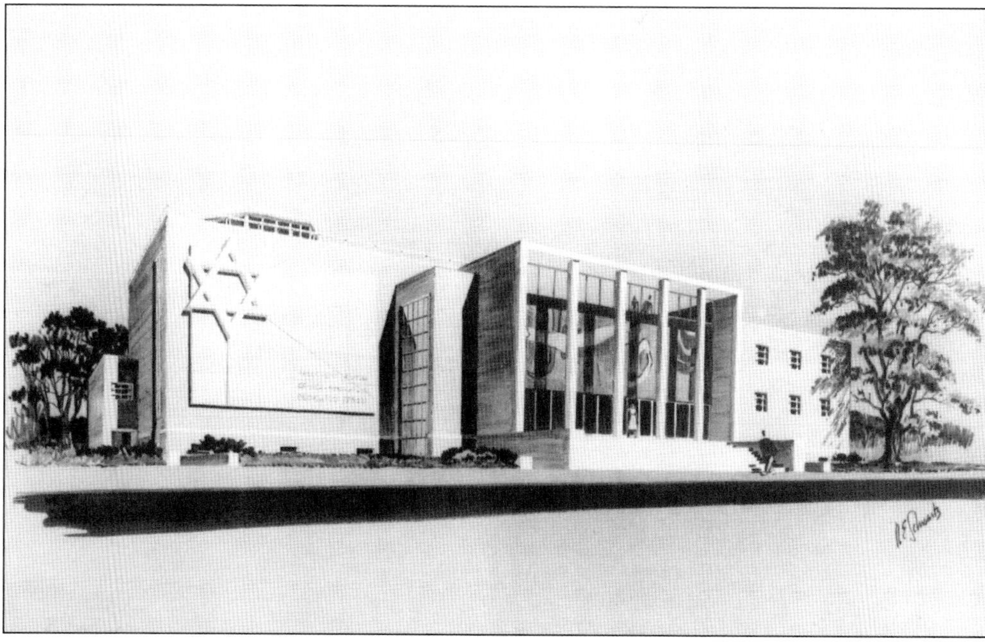

Founded in 1939, the first building of the Hillcrest Jewish Center was dedicated in 1942 on Kent Street, off Union Turnpike. It housed the Sanctuary, Hebrew School, and all the activities. When the congregation outgrew the building, they erected a new structure on the Union Turnpike side. This architectural drawing of the new building above was done by Klein and Glaberson.

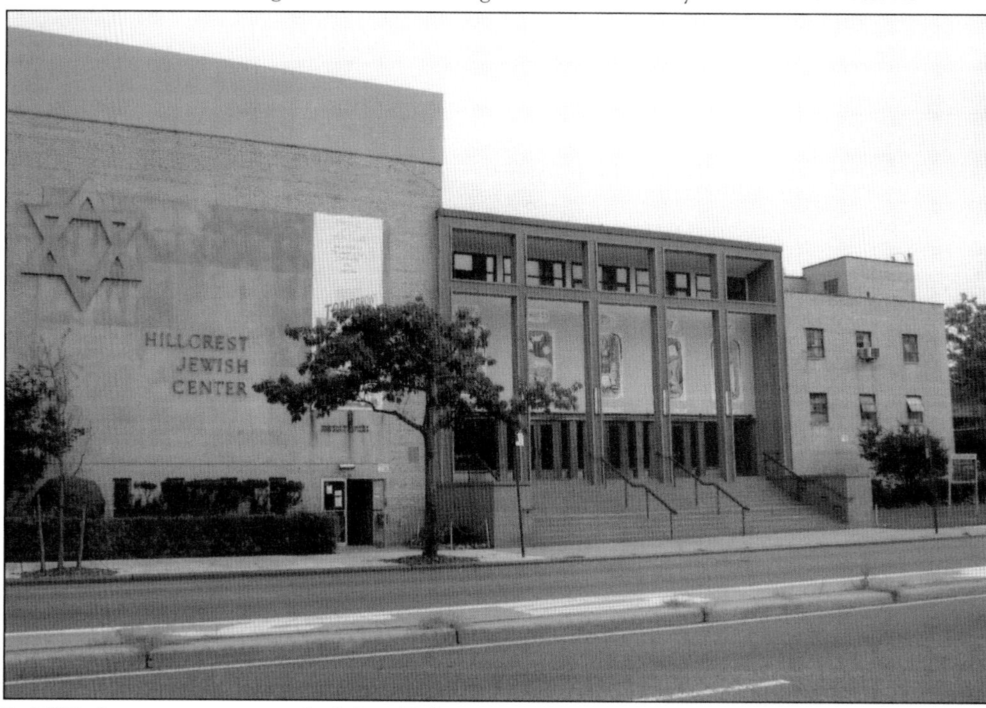

In 2009, the congregation marked their 70th anniversary. Housed here are a religious school, youth and family life center, physical fitness center, men's club, sisterhood organization, the Mowshowitz Library, day camp, and Hadassah.

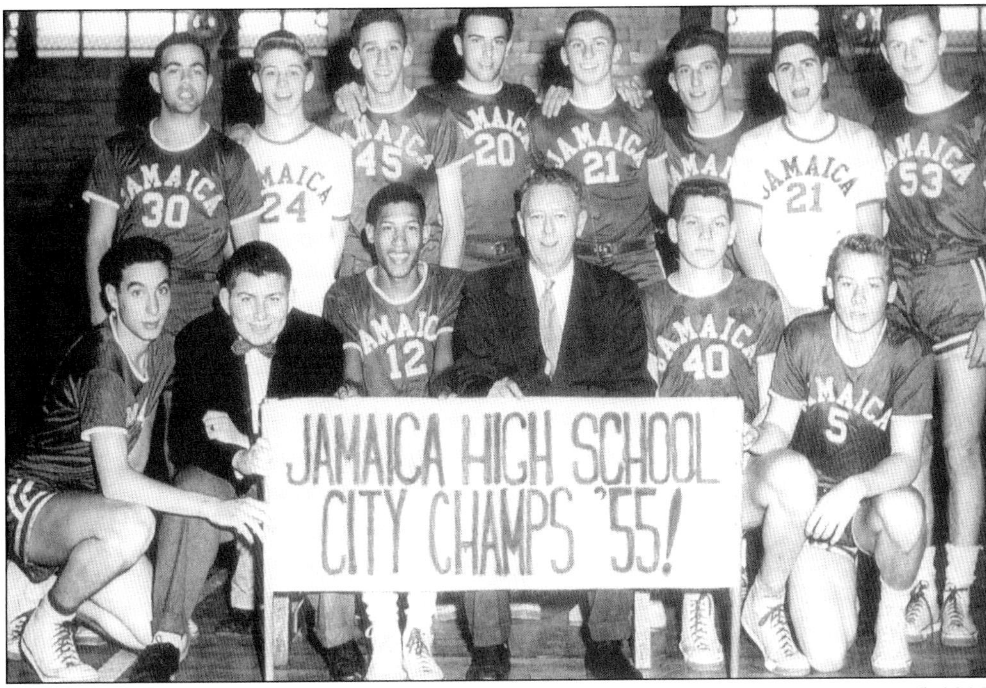

"Alan Seiden died at his home in Jamaica Estates," reported the *New York Times* on May 5, 2008. A member of the St. John's University Athletic Hall of Fame and New York City Basketball Hall of Fame and All-American in 1959, he captained the St. John Redmen to the National Invitational Tournament championship. He also won the Haggerty Award, given to the outstanding player. Seiden is wearing white jersey with No. 21 in this 1955 photograph of the Jamaica High School team.

On July 24, 2008, the Jamaica Estates community celebrated the centennial and restoration of the gatehouse, led by Councilman James F. Gennaro, Parks Commissioner Dorothy Lewandowski, and the Jamaica Estates Association. The Aquinas Honor Society students gave a brief presentation on their historical research. A ribbon cutting followed. Pictured are, from left to right, Michael Bookbinder, Commissioner Lewandowski, Councilman Gennaro, Martha Taylor, Edward Morrill, and Fr. Jed Sumampong, C.P.

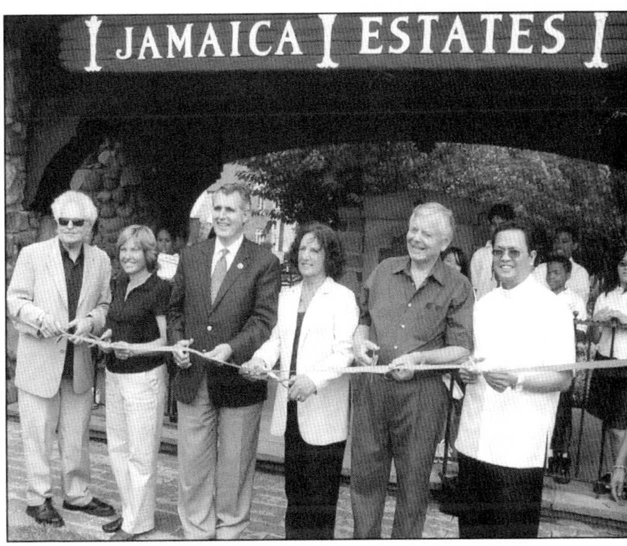

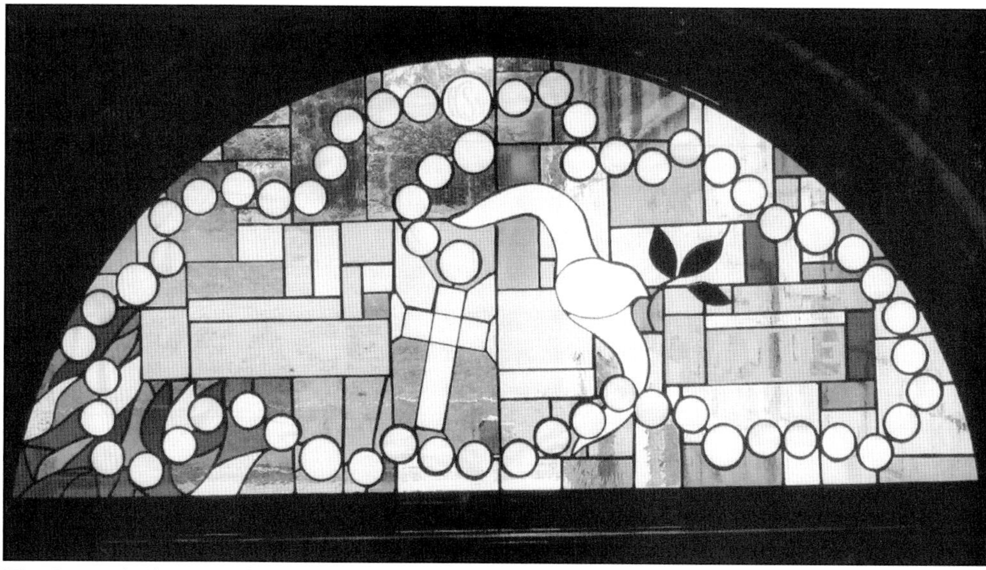

The Stained Glass Window of Peace and Hope project was created by the students of the Aquinas Honor Society and became a 9-11 Memorial. Funding was provided by the Alive in Hope Foundation with artist Ernesto Mendoza guiding them. The flames to the left represent negative virtues with the peace dove representing hope. The leaves of the olive branch were formed from steel from the Twin Towers. It was dedicated at Jamaica Estates in 2008.

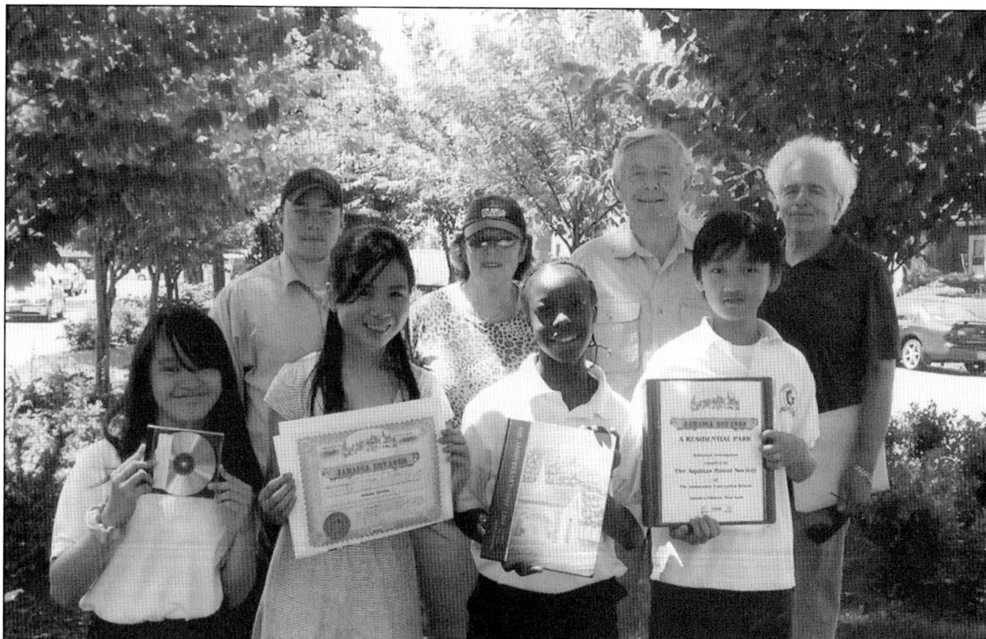

The Aquinas Honor Society takes an active community role. During Open House New York 2008, they gave tours to the public. Securing a $2,000 grant through Sen. Frank Padavan, a historical plaque they have written will be placed on the Midland Malls in 2010. Pictured are some of the students with, from left to right, (second row) Park and Recreation manager Gabriel Echevarria and Phyllis Rosenthal, Edward Morrill, and Michael Bookbinder of the Jamaica Estates Association, meeting to discuss their goals.

Five

The Guardians
Civic Responsibility

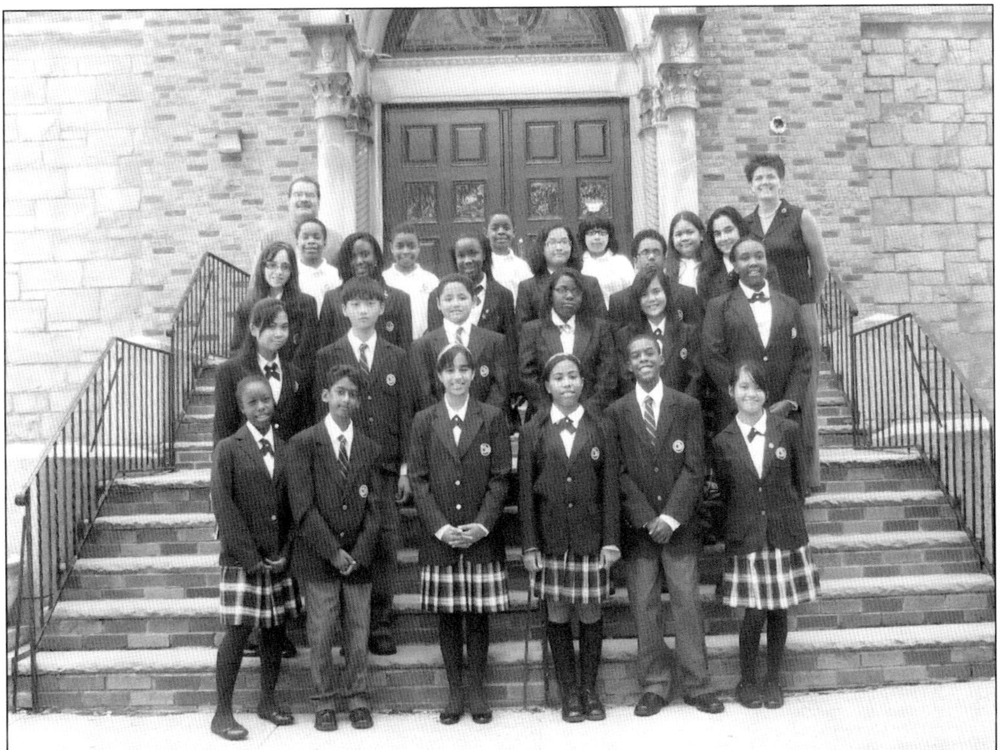

The authors pose with their teacher Carl Ballenas and school principal Dorothea Y. Breen. To quote St. Thomas Aquinas, "Grant me, O Lord my God, a mind to know you, a heart to seek you, wisdom to find you, conduct pleasing to you, faithful perseverance in waiting for you, and hope of finally embracing you."

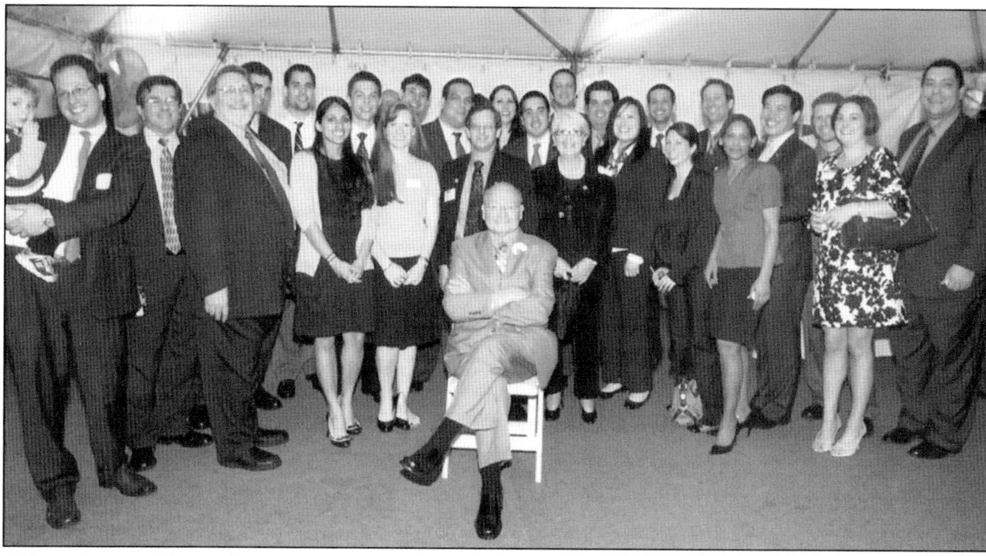

A longtime resident of Jamaica Estates, Gary Ackerman represents the community in the United States Congress. "Jamaica Estates is one of the jewels of New York City. Its outstanding beauty, neighborhood character and exceptional people make it a wonderful place to live and raise a family." Pictured is Congressman Ackerman with present and past members of his staff from both his Queens and Washington, D.C., offices.

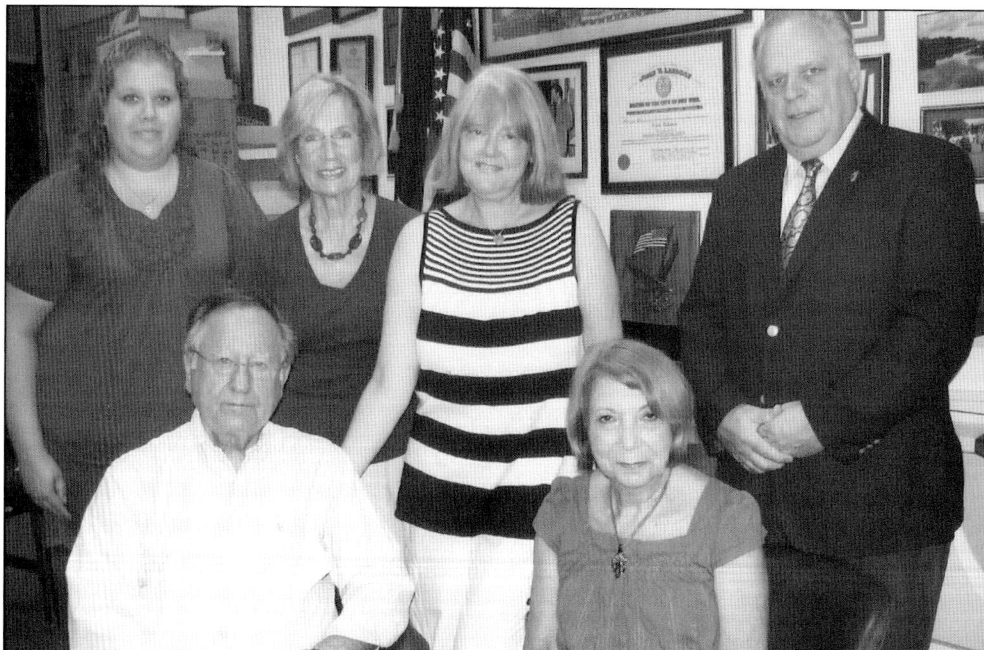

A proud resident of Jamaica Estates, Frank Padavan has represented it and the surrounding communities since 1973. Senator Padavan raised his family here and has long been committed to preserving the beauty and character of the community. "Congratulations to Mr. Ballenas and his students on this wonderful project." Pictured are, from left to right, (first row) Senator Padavan and district manager Angela Fristachi; (second row) legislative aide Erica Goldstein, secretary Virginia Salow, legislative aide Barbara Tabita, and counsel Joseph Dubowski.

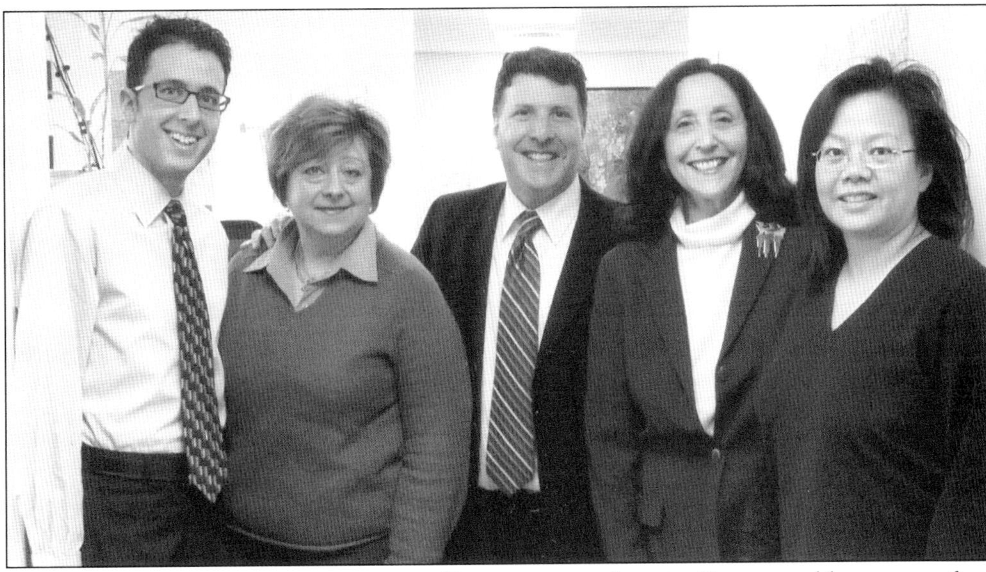

Assembly member Mark S. Weprin says, "I grew up near Jamaica Estates and have many fond memories. Since its founding, it continues to be a beautiful part of New York City, a wonderful place to live, have a family, and retire with peace of mind. I commend Carl Ballenas and his students for their excellent work." Pictured are, from left to right, district manager Ari Gershman, scheduler Arlene A. Bealin, assembly member Weprin, chief of staff Ruth L. Wimpfheimer, and community liaison Irene C. Cheung.

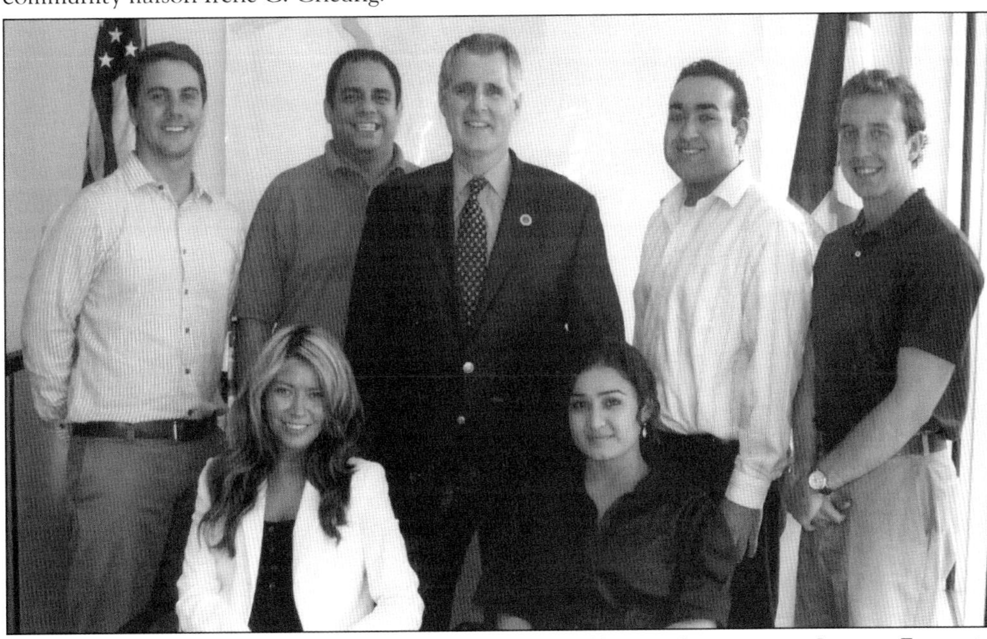

Councilman James F. Gennaro remembers, "I'm proud and honored to represent Jamaica Estates in the council and also to be a long-time resident. My best regards to Carl Ballenas and the Aquinas students in creating this book." Pictured from left to right are (first row) Janna Davis, community relations, and Meena Noori, community liaison; (second row) Brad Groznik, communications; Costa Constantinides, legislative affairs; Councilman Gennaro; David Troise, district manager; and William Murray, legislative aide.

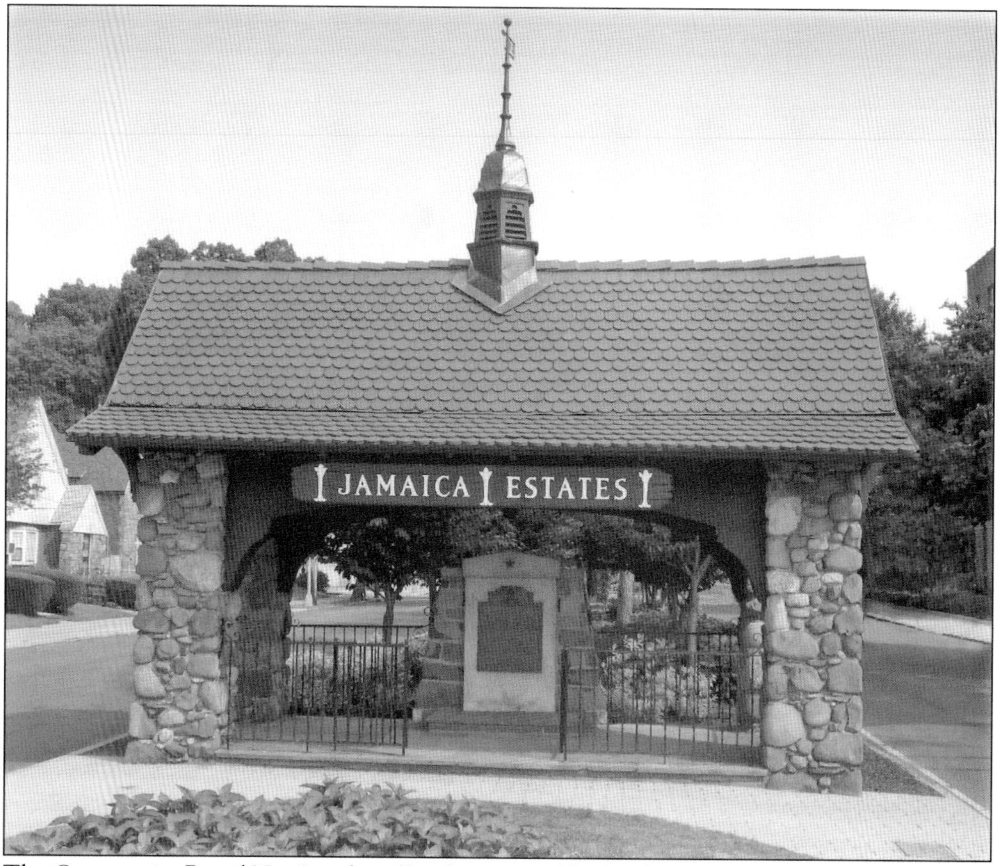

The Community Board No. 8 is the official municipal body whose primary mission is to advise elected officials and government agencies on matters affecting the social welfare of the district. Board members are neighbors—people who live, work, own a business, or have some other significant interest in the community district. This is a recent photograph of the 100-year-old Jamaica Estates Gatehouse. (Courtesy of Edward Morrill.)

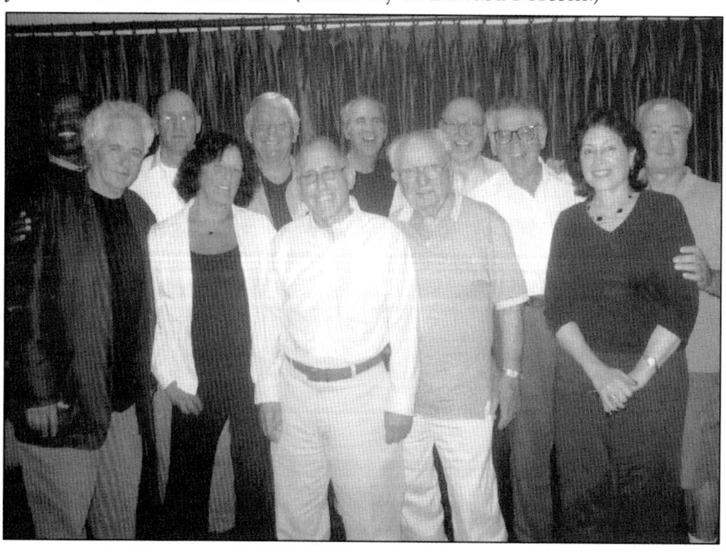

The Jamaica Estates Association was founded in 1929 and is still going strong. Pictured are, from left to right, (first row) Michael Bookbinder, Martha Taylor, Ralph Straus, Ari Sier, Howard Rosenthal, and Susan Zigman; (second row) Ron Pettaway, Edward Torielli, Edward Morrill, Mark Lefkof, Alan Antonelli, and David Zolondek.

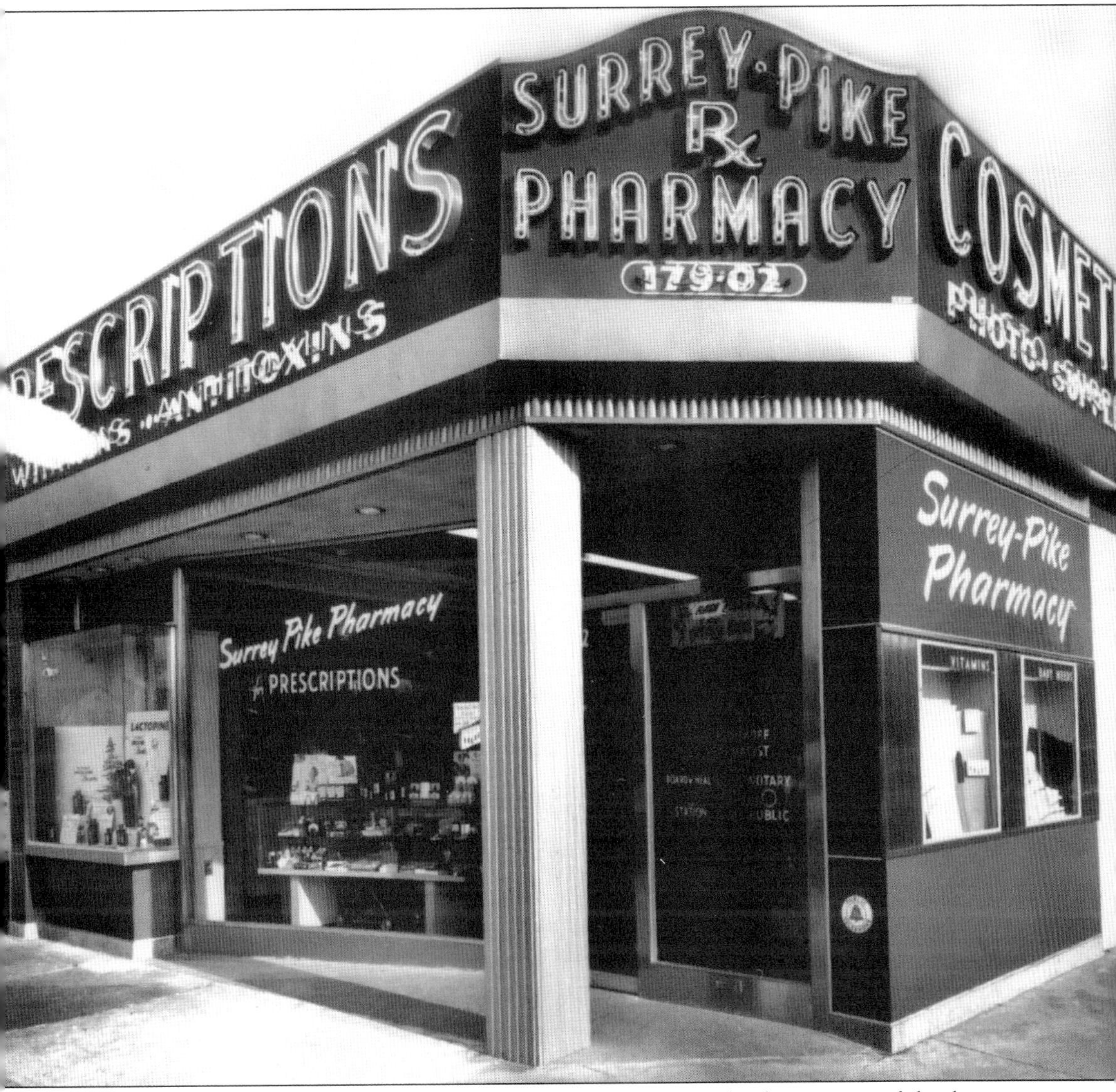

Surrey Pike served the community for years, and residents have fond memories of this business once located at the intersection of Surrey Place and Union Turnpike. Since the development of Jamaica Estates, many businesses and organizations have been an integral part of the community, such as banks, doctors, dentists, lawyers, mom-and-pop stores, delicatessens, clothing stores, pharmacies, carpet stores, jewelry stores, hardware stores, bookstores, fruit and vegetable stores, restaurants of all kinds, dance and karate studios, movie theater, bowling lane, ice cream parlors, stationary, post office, library, and so forth. It also has had public and private schools, including nurseries, elementary, high school, and university and many religious organizations that have provided solace and comfort. There are also police precincts and the fire stations that protect and serve. Last but not least are the citizens who call Jamaica Estates home, who have created a vital, diverse, and harmonious community. All are guardians of Jamaica Estates. (Courtesy of Q Gardens Gallery.)